Detachment

Manchester University Press

Detachment

Essays on the limits of relational thinking

**Edited by Matei Candea, Joanna Cook,
Catherine Trundle and Thomas Yarrow**

Manchester University Press

Copyright © Manchester University Press 2015

While copyright in the volume as a whole is vested in Manchester University Press, copyright in individual chapters belongs to their respective authors, and no chapter may be reproduced wholly or in part without the express permission in writing of both author and publisher.

Published by Manchester University Press
Altrincham Street, Manchester M1 7JA, UK
www.manchesteruniversitypress.co.uk

British Library Cataloguing-in-Publication Data is available

ISBN 978 0 7190 9685 3 hardback
ISBN 978 1 5261 3386 1 paperback

First published by Manchester University Press in hardback 2015

This edition first published 2019

The publisher has no responsibility for the persistence or accuracy of URLs for any external or third-party internet websites referred to in this book, and does not guarantee that any content on such websites is, or will remain, accurate or appropriate.

Typeset by Servis Filmsetting Ltd, Stockport, Cheshire

Contents

List of contributors   *page* vii
Acknowledgements   xii

Introduction: reconsidering detachment   1
Matei Candea, Joanna Cook, Catherine Trundle and *Thomas Yarrow*

Part I Professionalism and expertise

1. Some merits and difficulties of detachment   35
   Maryon McDonald
2. Virtuous detachments in engineering practice – on the ethics of (not) making a difference   58
   Hannah Knox and *Penny Harvey*
3. Artisanal affection: detachment in human–animal relations within intensive pig production in Britain   79
   Kim Crowder
4. Professionalism and expertise: comment   102
   Veena Das

Part II Ritual and religion

5. Engaged disbelief: communities of detachment in Christianity and in the anthropology of Christianity   115
   Joel Robbins

6	Detachment and ethical regard *James Laidlaw*	130
7	Detachment, difference and separation: Lévi Strauss at the wedding feast *Caroline Humphrey*	147
8	Ritual and religion: comment *Michael Carrithers*	168

Part III Detaching and situating knowledge

9	The capacity for re-description *Alberto Corsín Jiménez*	179
10	Test sites: attachments and detachments in community-based ecotourism *Casper Bruun Jensen* and *Brit Ross Winthereik*	197
11	Detachment and engagement in mindfulness-based cognitive therapy *Joanna Cook*	219
12	The discourse of ignorance and the ethics of detachment among Mongolian Tibetan Buddhists in Inner Mongolia, China *Jonathan Mair*	236
13	Detaching and situating knowledge: comment *Marilyn Strathern*	256

Index   265

Contributors

Casper Bruun Jensen is an honorary lecturer at the School of Management, Leicester University. He is the author of *Ontologies for Developing Things* (Sense, 2010) and *Monitoring Movements in Development Aid* (with Brit Ross Winthereik) (MIT, 2013) and the editor of *Deleuzian Intersections: Science, Technology, Anthropology* with Kjetil Rödje (Berghahn, 2009). His present work focuses on environmental infrastructures in South-east Asia.

Matei Candea is a social anthropologist at the University of Cambridge. He is the author of *Corsican Fragments: Difference, Knowledge and Fieldwork* (Indiana University Press, 2010) and the editor of *The Social after Gabriel Tarde* (Routledge, 2010). Since then, he has published a number of articles on interspecies relations in scientific research, with a particular focus on meerkats.

Michael Carrithers has done fieldwork with Buddhist forest monks in Sri Lanka and naked Jain ascetics and the Digambar Jain community in western India. More recently he has worked on German practices and rhetoric concerning various German histories. He is the author of a biography of the Buddha and of an accessible theoretical monograph on the nature of anthropology, *Why Humans Have Cultures* (Oxford University Press, 1992). He has also written more generally on sociality, rhetoric culture and the epistemology of anthropology and related social sciences. He is professor of Anthropology at Durham University.

Joanna Cook is a lecturer in Medical Anthropology at University College London. Her earlier work explored Buddhist meditation as a monastic practice in Thailand. Her current research examines the introduction of meditation techniques into therapeutic practice in the UK focusing on questions of ethics, well-being and the dialogue between religion and therapy. Recent publications include *Meditation in Modern Buddhism: Renunciation and Change in Thai Monastic Life* (Cambridge University Press, 2010) and *Power: Southeast Asian Perspectives* (Routledge, 2012) edited with L. Chua, N. Long and L. Wilson.

Alberto Corsín Jiménez is senior scientist in Social Anthropology at the Spanish National Research Council in Madrid. He has an interest in the organisation of ethnography and anthropological knowledge as descriptive and theoretical forms. In his latest book, *A Trompe L'oeil Anthropology for a Common World* (Berghahn, 2013), description is placed at perpendicular angles vis-à-vis emerging forms of global public knowledge. He is also the editor of *Culture and Well-being: Anthropological Approaches to Freedom and Political Ethics* (Pluto, 2008), *The Anthropology of Organisations* (Ashgate, 2007) and *Prototyping Cultures: Art, Science and Politics in Beta* (Special issue of the *Journal of Cultural Economy*, 2015). His current work examines the rise of an urban commons movement and the development of open-source urban hardware projects by architects, artists and engineers.

Kim Crowder is an anthropologist, visual practitioner and writer, whose research interests focus on rural lives and human–animal interactions in the twenty-first century. She is a visiting research fellow in Anthropology at Goldsmiths, University of London. She has taught anthropology at Goldsmiths, and critical studies at Norwich University of the Arts. Her AHRC-funded Visual Anthropology PhD project (Goldsmiths, 2012) 'Making Meat: People Property and Pigs in East Anglia' documented intimacies and distances between the stockmen, pigs and technologies involved in contemporary industrial pig production.

Veena Das is the Krieger-Eisenhower Professor in the Department of Anthropology at Johns Hopkins University. Her most recent books are *Life and Words: Violence and the Descent into the Ordinary* (University of California Press, 2007), *Affliction: Health, Disease, Poverty* (Fordham University Press, 2015), and a co-edited book, *The Ground Between: Anthropologists Engage Philosophy* (Duke University Press, 2014). Das's research interests include topics of social suffering, violence, aesthetics and ethics, and politics of the urban poor. She is a fellow of the American Academy of Arts and Sciences and a fellow of the Academy of Scientists from Developing Countries. She is a recipient of the Simon Guggenheim Fellowship, and has been awarded honorary doctorates from the University of Chicago (2000) and the University of Edinburgh (2014). She has also received the Anders Retzius Gold Medal (1995) and the Nessim Habif prize (2014).

Penny Harvey is Professor of Social Anthropology at the University of Manchester. She has worked ethnographically in Peru, Spain and the UK and published widely on information and communications technologies, on engineering practice and technical expertise. She is currently conducting research on infrastructural form, material politics and administrative practice drawing on ethnographic work in Peru and in the UK. Recent publications include: *Roads. An Anthropology of Infrastructure and Expertise*, co-authored with Hannah Knox (Cornell University Press, 2015). She also co-edited *Objects and Materials: A Routledge Companion* with colleagues from CRESC (the ESRC Centre for Research on Socio-Cultural Change, 2012).

Caroline Humphrey has worked in the USSR/Russia, Mongolia, Inner Mongolia, Nepal and India. Her research interests include socialist and post-socialist society, religion, ritual, economy, history and the contemporary transformations of cities. Until 2010 she was Sigrid Rausing Professor of Collaborative Anthropology at Cambridge and she is currently Director of Research at the University of Cambridge. Her major publications include: *Karl Marx Collective: Economy, Society and Religion in a Siberian Collective Farm* (Cambridge University Press, 1983); *The Archetypal Actions of Ritual, Illustrated by the Jain Rite of Worship* with James Laidlaw (Clarendon Press, 1994); *Shamans and Elders: Experience, Knowledge and Power among the Daur Mongols* with Urgunge Onon (Clarendon Press, 1996); *The End of Nomadism? Society, the State and the Environment in Inner Asia*, with David Sneath (Duke University Press, NC and White Horse Press, 1999); *The Unmaking of Soviet Life: Everyday Economies After Socialism* (Cornell University Press, 2002); *Urban Life in Post-Soviet Central Asia*, edited by Catherine Alexander, Victor Buchli and Caroline Humphrey (UCL Press, 2007); *A Monastery in Time: the Making of Mongolian Buddhism*, with H. Ujeed (Chicago University Press, 2013); *Frontier Encounters: Knowledge and Practice at the Russian, Chinese and Mongolian Border*, ed. with Franck Billé and Gregory Delaplace (Open Book Publishers, 2013).

Hannah Knox is lecturer in Digital Anthropology and Material Culture at University College London. Her research concerns the anthropological study of processes of technological and social change, with a particular focus on digital technologies, material infrastructures and practices of knowledge-making. She has published in a range of interdisciplinary journals including: *Anthropological Quarterly*, *Economy and Society*, *Current Anthropology* and *Theory, Culture & Society*. Her books include *Objects and Materials: A Routledge Companion* and *Roads: An Anthropology of Infrastructure and Expertise* (Cornell University Press, 2015)

James Laidlaw teaches Social Anthropology at the University of Cambridge, where he is also a Fellow of King's College. His most recent book is *The Subject of Virtue* (Cambridge, 2014). His current fieldwork is on Buddhist ethical self-cultivation in Taiwan.

Jonathan Mair is a social anthropologist with research interests in northern China, where he has studied the revival of Tibetan Buddhism among Mongolians, and in Taiwan, where he has been investigating the ethical teachings and practices of Humanistic Buddhism. He has also written about the cultural and ethical aspects of belief and ignorance, and on the relationship between religion and politics in Buddhism. He is lecturer in Buddhism in the Department of Religions and Theology, University of Manchester, and has held teaching or research posts in the Social Anthropology Department, Manchester University, the Cambridge University Centre for Research in Arts, Social Sciences and Humanities, and St John's College, Cambridge.

Maryon McDonald studied social anthropology at Oxford University, held the post of reader in anthropology at Brunel University, and since 1997 has been Fellow in Social Anthropology at Robinson College, Cambridge. Her main research interests currently focus on anthropologies of science, medical anthropology and the European Union. Relevant recent publications include 'Medical Anthropology and Anthropologies of Science', in U. Kockel, M. Nic Craith and J. Frykman (eds), *Companion to the Anthropology of Europe* (Wiley-Blackwell, 2012), and 'Putting Culture in its Place', in *European Societies* 14(4).

Joel Robbins is Professor of Social Anthropology at the University of Cambridge. He has written extensively on the anthropological study of Christianity, the anthropology of morality and values, and on cultural change. He is the author of *Becoming Sinners: Christianity and Moral Torment in a Papua New Guinea Society* (University of California Press, 2004). He is also co-editor of the journal *Anthropological Theory*.

Marilyn Strathern had the good fortune to receive initial – and indelible – training in Papua New Guinea, which led to work among, other things, on kinship and gender relations. In the UK she subsequently became involved with anthropological approaches to the new reproductive technologies, intellectual property, audit cultures and interdisciplinarity. Now retired from the Cambridge Department of Social Anthropology, she is (honorary) life president of the ASA. Strathern is currently working on issues in the conceptualisation of relations, some of which were sketched out in her 2005 book, *Kinship, Law and the Unexpected: Relatives are Often a Surprise* (Cambridge University Press).

Catherine Trundle is a senior lecturer in Cultural Anthropology at Victoria University of Wellington. Her research centres on the politics of inclusion and exclusion, citizenship and intersubjective ethics. Her book, *Americans in Tuscany: Charity, Compassion and Belonging* (Berghahn, 2014) examines the role of charity practices in migrant communities. Trundle's current research explores military veterans' claims for healthcare and the politics of recognition and responsibility. Trundle's recent publications include *Local Lives: Migration and the Politics of Place* (Ashgate, 2010).

Brit Ross Winthereik is Associate Professor in the Technologies in Practice research group at the IT University of Copenhagen. She received her Ph.D. from Erasmus University Rotterdam in 2004 (anthropology and science and technology studies) and continued working for some years with issues around the implementation of information technology in health care settings. Her interest in standardisation, classification and monitoring and in intersections between anthropology and STS led to joint research with Casper Bruun Jensen (see *Monitoring Movements in Development Aid: Recursive Partnerships and Infrastructures*, MIT Press 2013). As principal investigator of the project *Marine Renewable Energy as Alien: Social Studies of an Emerging Industry* she is now pursuing her interest in experimental ethnography and energy. Brit is one of the co-founders of the Danish Association for Science and Technology Studies (DASTS).

Thomas Yarrow is a senior lecturer in Social Anthropology at Durham University. His research primarily focuses on the production and circulation of expert knowledge. He has explored these interests in relation to ethnographic research on international development, archaeological fieldwork and heritage practice. He is the author of *Development Beyond Politics: Aid, Activism and NGOs in Ghana* (Palgrave Macmillan, 2011), and co-editor of *Differentiating Development: Beyond an anthropology of critique* (Berghahn, 2012) and *Archaeology and Anthropology: Understanding Similarity, Exploring Difference* (Oxbow, 2010).

Acknowledgements

We are grateful to the many participants, discussants and audience members of the 2009 AAA panel 'The End(s) of Engagement', the attendees of a 2010 workshop in Buxton, UK, and the June 2010 conference 'Reconsidering Detachment' in Cambridge. Even though some of the original participants are not represented in this volume, they have been profoundly influential in helping us shape what we have come to think of as 'The Detachment Project'. These include Soumhya Venkatesan, Morten Axel Pedersen, Barbara Bodenhorn, Bob Simpson, Salla Sariola, Evelyn Ruppert, Ann Kelly, Dan Hicks, Adam Reed, Paul du Gay, Eduardo Kohn, Ben Campbell, Jo Sechell, Frédérique Jankowski, Mellisa Demian, Simon Roberts, Allan Abrambson, Gerhard Anders, Antoine Hennion, Stuart Mclean, Rane Willerslev, Gustaaf Houtman, Ven. Chueh Ru Shin, Steven Collins and Ilana Gershon.

The conferences were funded by an ESRC Training and Networking Grant, as well as a grant from the Cambridge University Centre for Research on the Social Sciences and Humanities. We are also grateful to Girton College, Cambridge, for their support in hosting the Reconsidering Detachment conference. The ESRC also funded a detachment collaboratory website, which was designed with considerable technical and aesthetic skill by Georgie Grace. Finally, we would also like to thank Manchester University Press, particularly Tony Mason, for their support, patience and expertise.

Introduction: reconsidering detachment

Matei Candea, Joanna Cook, Catherine Trundle and Thomas Yarrow

This volume urges a reconsideration of the productive potential of disconnection, distance and detachment, as ethical, methodological and philosophical commitments. In so doing, we write against the grain of a strong tendency in contemporary social theory and public life. Engagement has, in a wide range of contexts, become a definitive and unquestionable social good, one that encompasses or abuts with a number of other seductive cultural tropes, such as participation, democracy, voice, equality, diversity and empowerment. Conversely, detachment has come to symbolise a range of social harms: authoritarianism and hierarchy, being out of touch, bureaucratic coldness and unresponsiveness, a lack of empathy, and passivity and inaction. Yet as this book argues, in a wide range of settings detachment is still socially, ethically and politically valued, and the relationship between detachment and engagement is not simple or singular.

The volume developed as a result of an ongoing and collaborative enquiry into detachment by the editors. Beginning with a discussion over a glass of wine on a sunny afternoon in December 2008, we reflected on the diverse ways in which we each separately encountered detachment in our work. In examining the disciplinary relationship between archaeology and anthropology, Yarrow found that it is precisely the disconnection and difference between the ways in which these disciplines produce knowledge that sets up the possibility for productive engagement (Garrow and Yarrow 2010). Following Candea's fieldwork in a research station in the Kalahari desert, where behavioural biologists observe the daily lives of meerkats, he was struck by the peculiar non-interactive relations researchers established with the wild meerkats they studied through what they called 'habituation' (Candea 2010; 2013a). This was no ideological pretence of objective distance, but an embodied practice of detached relationality – a detachment which in turn required volunteers to detach themselves from parts of themselves (Candea 2013a,b).[1]

In her work on *vipassana* meditation, Cook (2010) explored the ways in which Thai monastics engage with specific ascetic introspection techniques in order to cultivate forms of detachment that are consistent with Buddhist teachings. Thai Buddhist monastics work to cultivate experiential insight into the tenets of impermanence, suffering and non-self through meditative discipline. Trundle (2014) found that for the migrant charity givers in Italy she studied, empathy and compassion did not rest simply on processes of connection – on mimicry, transference and imagination, as many scholars has theorised. Rather crucial to their works was a recognition of disconnection, the boundaries that could not be crossed and a failure to appreciate the true nature of recipients' suffering, which created the ethical, structural and affective drive to give. These initial conversations gave rise to a series of interconnected workshops and a conference on the theme of detachment, following our collective sense that similar issues seemed to find resonance in these diverse ethnographic contexts. This volume emerges as the culmination of these conversations and conferences.

Thinking about detachment provides fresh entry points into a range of empirical contexts. But our aim here is more than simply collecting a set of vignettes. We wish to put detachment centre stage as a conceptual problem. Taking detachment seriously does not equate to rejection of relational theories and approaches. Nor does it entail a nostalgic return to older analytics of pure distanced knowledge or solitary disconnected agents. Nor are we calling for a suspension of critical reflection on the potential dangers and limits of tropes and practices of detachment. What we are asking, however, is that detachment be allowed the same ethnographic and conceptual air-time as its opposites. In so doing, the chapters in this volume bring to the foreground the many ways in which detachment and engagement are interwoven; the ways in which they limit, complement and enable each other. A focus on detachment forces us to ask ethnographic questions about the temporality of relations, their intensity, what makes them stick. Is each particular form of detachment a negation, a concealment, an interruption? And conversely, are relations forms that endure and cannot be purposefully unmade, like Umberto Eco's persistent strands of memory (1988)? Are they vectors that pass, energies that must be continually channelled, or are they deciduous pledges whose maintenance requires daily care?

Our aim in this book, in sum, is to bring detachment back to the forefront of theorising in the social sciences and humanities. Our contention is that social theory has tended to naturalise the idea that relations are prior to the entities they connect. Questioning this understanding, we attempt to open up an analytic vocabulary that allows for a more nuanced understanding of the terms in which entities are defined and related. Thus our approach entails an analytic levelling, proposing that neither relations nor entities come first (Candea 2010; Yarrow and Jones 2014). We suggest that this provides a better platform from which to consider the ethnographic senses in which people themselves afford ethical or epistemic priority to practices associated with relating and detaching.

The final section of this introduction returns to these questions through an attempt at a typology of detachments, which also serve as a guide to the chapters in this volume. First, however, we briefly trace the rise and fall of one particular modernist version of detachment, which has borne the brunt of academic and popular critique in recent years. This sets the scene for an attempt to recover detachment as an object of study beyond the resulting dichotomies. In the following section we describe how our own approach builds on, and extends, the work of other scholars, who in different ways contribute to an understanding of detachment as a theoretical and empirical focus of enquiry.

On modernist detachment and its critique

A key argument of this book is that detachment comes in many shapes and sizes. However, one particular version of detachment has loomed over public and academic discourse in what is commonly known as 'the West' since at least the nineteenth century. Alternatively invoked as an unmitigated virtue or as an equally unmitigated sin, the spectre of 'western modernist detachment' has haunted public discourse and social theory and made it hard to think of detachment in any but the most dichotomous and morally charged terms. This section briefly reviews part of the story that leads this particular version of detachment to hold such a prominent place in social theory.

One key strand of the modernist ideal of detachment is epistemological and is frequently traced to the nineteenth century when, in a range of primarily European and American contexts, notions about the desirability of distanced perspectives became increasingly foundational to the pursuit of knowledge. The demarcation of science from other fields of human endeavour, and of scientific practitioners from politicians or the 'common man' was a long-drawn-out process which saw its first significant episodes at least two centuries previously (e.g. Shapin and Schaffer 1985). However, the nineteenth century saw an intensification of this process as well as an increasing leeching out of discourses of scientific detachment into other realms. Daston and Galison (2007) have described how a range of previously distinct ideologies and dispositions were reconfigured as instances of a singular epistemic ideal of objectivity, entailing a particular understanding of the importance of detachment. Where scientific truth was located in relation to an objective bedrock reality, the subjectivity of the researcher became an obstacle to knowledge. Thus detachment became a central regulatory ideal, pertaining to the need for processes and dispositions to enable the management and separation of the individual scientist's subjective emotions, feelings and thoughts from the objective data that was produced. If, in practice, the ideal of objectivity took a range of forms, including ideas about the need for emotional detachment, automatic procedure and methods of quantification, these were configured during the middle of the nineteenth century as instances of a singular over-arching ideal. Such notions of scientific objectivity entailed a commitment to epistemic forms that necessitated distance from the world through specific forms of critical distance from oneself.

During this period, the bifurcation of notions of subjectivity and objectivity related to an increasing bifurcation between science and the arts as concerned with subjectivity and objectivity respectively. If subjectivity was a problem for the scientist in his or her pursuit of the detached knowledge constituted as a 'view from nowhere' (Daston and Galison 2007), it was, for the artist, a source of creativity to be cultivated and celebrated.

The elaboration of a broader modernist/romantic split took in this key distinction, and read it through a range of attendant concerns about the rise of industry and estrangement from nature (Williams 1975), the modernising drive of nationalism and the loss of the soulful, emotional Celt (McDonald 1989), the civilising mission of Empire and the disappearing wisdom of the Other (Rabinow 1975; Said 1978; Stoler 2002). These and other versions of what Latour (1991) termed the Great Divide (between us and them, nature and culture, science and politics, heart and mind, etc.) profoundly marked the intellectual cast of the nineteenth century, and left us with a set of linked dichotomies which persist to this day.

Crucially, however, these dichotomies from which the obviousness of 'modern detachment' seem to emerge so clearly, are an effect of contemporary rhetorics, mediated by simplifying hindsight. A closer historical examination reveals a more complex set of patterns. Thus, for instance, the bifurcation of subjectivity and objectivity did not map straightforwardly on to an opposition between engagement and detachment. Amanda Anderson (2001) notes how, during the same period, changes in literary writing also converged around a set of ideals that celebrated the detached viewpoint. For modernist writers, from the Victorian period onwards, the concern to cultivate detached dispositions, took a range of forms, including the elimination of tendencies to judge and interpret, the suppression of the local and idiosyncratic in favour of the universal, the cultivation of realist forms of representation and an aspiration to a version of literary truth that was grounded in critical distance from the writer's own perspective. Victorian writers debated with competing ideals and virtues when considering what they identified as the power and limits of detachment; debates that were themselves constitutive of the project of modernity. Anderson demonstrates how George Eliot, John Stuart Mill, Charlotte Bronte, Charles Dickens, Matthew Arnold and Oscar Wilde all, in different ways, grapple with morally weighted understandings of detachment. Theirs was a distinctly modern preoccupation with the ambivalences and virtues of practices of detachment – the extent to which such practices might result in forms of distortion and insensitivity, or, alternatively, lead to desirable forms of cultivation and virtue. As an aspiration and ideal Victorian novelists played off various forms of detachment against one another, casting some as progressive and liberating, while presenting others as dangerous and corrupting. Even for romantic critics such as Ruskin and Morris, faith in detachment understood as critical distance from one's own perspective, sustained criticism of the debilitating and alienating effects of modern rationality, particularly in the guise of modern industrial production.

In literature as in science, then, modernist ideals of detachment arose in relation to a range of empirically very different practices, sustained as apparent instances of the same thing. Crucially, in relation to both scientific and literary practice, such ideals were subject to debate and critique which generally took a narrow rather than fundamental form: the scientist was critical of their own or others' ability to sustain in practice their own detachment from the world they observed, but did not question the ideal of detachment per se. Indeed, the narrow critique (that this or that person was not sufficiently objective, or not in this instance) arose from and upheld a broader ideal (the epistemic importance of keeping subject and object distinct).

Thus modernist ideals of detachment were, from the outset precariously achieved, internally contradictory and contested. However, contemporary (nineteenth-century) critiques of this over-arching orientation participated in the elaboration of a master contrast between modernist detachment and romantic engagement, which has solidified with hindsight.

Crucially for our purposes, the rise of the social sciences was fundamental in the solidification of this association between modernity and detachment. In particular, nineteenth-century sociology and anthropology, themselves in the process of detaching from cognate disciplines as proper stand-alone scientific fields (Durkheim 1964 [1895]), contributed to the shoring up of such distinctions by their obsession with pinning down the essence of 'modernity'. Thus evolutionary anthropologists traced, with Morgan, the progressive disengagement of the modern nuclear family from the web of primitive kinship, 'by means of which [Man] raised himself from a state of promiscuous intercourse to final civilisation' (Morgan 1870, 1877; Kuper 2005), while Engels' re-reading of this same narrative as one leading to the rise of private property and the state (Engels 1983 [1884]) fed into Marx's philosophical-historical documentation and lamentation of the multifaceted phenomenon of alienation.

As the nineteenth century gave way to the twentieth, sociologists seeking to grasp the phenomenon of modernity circled around detachment with increasing inevitability: from the rise of modern *gesellschaft* as against traditional *gemeinschaft* (Tönnies 1957), through the curse of modern *anomie* (Durkheim 1997), Simmel's (1976) account of the adoption of a blasé attitude developed as a psychological defence mechanism against the sensual bombardments of modernity and metropolitan life, to Weber's influential characterisations of modern bureaucracy and disenchantment (1978). The association between modernity and detachment became a trope ripe for continual reinvention and re-elaboration. Foucault's work on self-production and the asceticism of modernity is one late instance: 'To be modern is not to accept oneself as one is in the flux of the passing moments; it is to take oneself as object of a complex and difficult elaboration' (Foucault 1979: 166). Bruno Latour's 'We have never been modern' (1991), with its concern for the pairing of 'purification' and 'translation' is another – to which we will return.

Detachment dissolved

Just as we are a long way from drawing all the conclusions from the phrase 'God is dead', we are very far from understanding every implication of the phrase 'The pure observer is dead'. (Sloterdjik 2012: 17)

In sum, the nineteenth and early twentieth centuries saw the increasing formalisation of 'modernist detachment', as an object of both celebration and critique –as both a highly valued ideal (for some) and as a condition of reality with which one had to contend.

The novelty of the late twentieth century turn against detachment was not, then, the fact of its critique of modernist detachment as an ideal – late twentieth century critics could draw (and often did) on a long tradition of romantic and other rejections of ideals of detachment. Rather, the novelty was the single-minded focus on documenting the inexistence and impossibility of modernist detachment. We find ourselves writing today in a conceptual atmosphere in which detachment is not so much critiqued as dissolved. This is an atmosphere in which it might seem, for instance, that 'There is *no way to imagine* a pure nature unmediated by politics' (Choy 2011: 11, emphasis added). This type of restriction of the postmodern imagination is the phenomenon we are attempting to pinpoint in this section.

If attempts to characterise 'the literature' are always problematically violent to its complexity (Mol 2002a), then an attempt to characterise something as broad and shifting as 'the current intellectual landscape in and beyond academia' is all the more so. Clearly, what follows is a partial run through an incredibly complex field. Admittedly far from exhaustive, it is motivated by an effort to illustrate and define the ways in which detachment has been systematically – though far from completely – eclipsed as an empirical and conceptual focus. In the next section we examine a number of authors who, writing against the grain, have been calling attention to detachment in different ways. But let us first try to sketch out what this 'grain' feels like.

A key trope of contemporary social theory, which has now passed into dogma, is that purported detachment can and ought to be revealed as really relational, engaged and entangled. This could be explained through a concatenation of theoretical and political developments: the post-colonial drive to highlight the connection between modern knowledge and colonial power; the post-structural effort to deconstruct notions of textual autonomy and logocentric truth; the work of feminists and queer theorists to reintroduce corporeal, gendered bodies as a locus of thought. In all of these cases the challenge to detachment emerged less in the form of a request to value engagement, and more in an authoritative demonstration that detachment is illusory. This related to an ethical call to recognise the fallacy of detachment as a matter of both fact and principle.

It would be unfair to suggest that this intellectual development was merely a matter of conceptual faddism. The suspicion of detachment had a number of serious and legitimate grounds. A number of events throughout the twentieth century had strenuously chipped away at the promise of a new age of scientific and technological progress, efficiency and development grounded in detached, 'rational' and 'objective' knowledge production. Two world wars demonstrated the destructive potential of new technological systems of killing. The First World War and the new weaponry utilised saw over 5,000 combat deaths a day, an almost tenfold increase on the previous major European war, the Napoleonic Wars (Clodfelter 2002). The bureaucratically efficient means by which Jews and other minorities were exterminated in Nazi gas chambers revealed the difficulty in separating 'rational' scientific modes of human classification, chemistry, and the detached, dehumanising division of labour that came to manage the killing of bodies in Nazi-occupied Europe. Moreover, the codes of human ethics that emerged within bioscience in the wake of the Nuremburg 'Doctors' Trial' signalled a shifting morality of knowledge production, in which the detached pursuit of 'pure' scientific knowledge could no longer be divorced from the human consequences, costs or benefits, and experiences of those experimentally involved or socially implicated (Pellegrino 1997).

Correspondingly, the nuclear arms race, which saw the emergence of an entirely new spectre of global-wide destruction, dawned in August 1945 with the bombing of Hiroshima and Nagasaki. In the bomb's cold-war wake, prominent scientists such as Einstein and Oppenheimer began to publicly question whether ongoing progress in nuclear physics was of benefit to humanity, suggesting that social decisions, ethical considerations, and political realities could, and indeed should, undergird scientific advancement in the future (Schweber 2008). This marked the beginning of a shifting relationship between science and its publics, one that has become increasingly based on the principles of 'engagement', with many scientists now attempting to educate, consult with, inform and listen to public groups and 'stakeholders' (Porter et al. 2013).

In the second half of the twentieth century, the increasing concern with, and visibility of, science's alignment to capitalism and industry gave a new language in which to express doubts about the detached nature of scientific discovery and truth. Industrial scientists had assured publics in many countries that products such as tobacco, lead and thalidomide were safe years after doubts began to arise about their human safety (Rosner 2013; Trundle, Singh and Broer 2014). The chemiconuclear disasters of Chernobyl, Three Mile Island, Love Canal, Bhopal (and, more recently, Fukushima) all further served to undermine the trustworthiness of the industrial-regulatory-science nexus to impartially protect human health (Levine 1982; Walsh 1988; Das 1996; Petryna 2002). In such a context, social movements emerged in the 1970s and 1980s seeking a more democratically engaged, partnership-based mode of involvement between publics, citizen groups, and those who

Introduction: reconsidering detachment

governed them, and demanding to be actively involved in decisions regarding health investment, treatment and testing (Kroll-Smith, Brown and Gunter 2000). Some groups, such as Deaf community advocates, gay rights groups, and mental health support groups, contested the very forms of disease categorisation and the medicalisation of disorder proposed by medical experts, declaring science to be inherently bound up with projects of cultural normalisation (Conrad 2007). Meanwhile, environmentalism and ecology argued for more engaged scientific, social, political, economic and technological realms that could account for the ecological effects of human ways of life. 'Ecology's critique of science and technology ... suggests that ethical neutrality with respect to the results of scientific enterprise is not justified. The ecological position ... challenges the idea that any form of human knowledge can be separated from its consequences' (Aronowitz 1988: 21).

As noted, the polysemy of detachment had enabled it to stand as an ideal for a diverse and even contradictory range of modernist projects. Unsurprisingly, the same polysemy also enabled detachment to stand as a problematic Other for a similarly broad range of late-twentieth century endeavours. Thus the social movements mentioned were in complex and partial communication with critiques of detachment coming from radically different sources. New religious and spiritual movements offered followers new avenues for direct engagement, whether it was with God, society, politics, justice or personal empowerment (Guitierrez 1988; Heelas 1992; Pfeiffer, Gimbel-Sherr and Augusto 2008; Mair in this volume, Chapter 12).

In sum, the twentieth century was marked by the multiplication of historical contexts in which a range of troubling ideologies and practices were found lying beneath claims to epistemic distance and detachment. It is against this background and interwoven with it, that pointed critiques across a broad spectrum of theories and contexts have sought to reveal the illusory nature of the very idea of detachment, suggesting the de facto impossibility of sustaining disconnection from one's own subjectivity and self-interest. Thus, radical feminist thinkers pointed out that the methods of objectivity and detachment driving systems of power, politics, bureaucracy, scientific knowledge and capitalist developments were obscuring a culturally and historically constituted patriarchy that in fact gave such systems their legitimacy. Building on this critique to propose a feminist method of knowledge production, Donna Haraway argued for a mode of thought that 'does not pretend to disengagement: to be from everywhere and so nowhere, to be free from interpretation, from being represented, to [be] fully self contained or fully formalisable. Rational knowledge is a process of on-going critical interpretation between fields of interpreters and decoders. Rational knowledge is a power-sensitive conversation' (Haraway 1988: 590).

From this perspective the political implications of modernist claims to detachment have been spelt out from a range of theoretical and disciplinary perspectives and in relation to diverse substantive contexts. The technical detachment of development agencies has been revealed as an 'anti-politics machine' (Ferguson 1994), constituting 'the third world' as an object of intervention the Europeans claim to know precisely in their distance from it (Esteva 1992; Hobart 1993; Crush 1995). Deconstructive approaches likewise sought to question detached claims to historical truth, and the universalising objectivised visions of 'heritage', foregrounding the inherent relativity of all interpretation, and hence the 'illusory' nature of elite claims to know the past (Lowenthal 1985; Smith 2006). Challenging the seeming self-evidence of human exceptionalism, post-humanist scholars uncovered the practical and conceptual technologies which allow clear distinctions to be made (and to be taken for granted) between humans and other animals – chief among them the contention that humans have no 'objective' access to animal minds (Haraway 1997; Crist 1999; Despret 2004; Milton 2005; see Candea 2013a).

Recent celebratory orientations to the concept of 'engagement', likewise invest the term with a broader explanatory value and in part draw their force from the versions of modernist detachment 'engagement' is imagined to negate. For example, the sociologist and philosopher Richard Sennett suggests that, 'The craftsman represents the special human condition of being engaged' (Sennett 2009: 20). Elaborating how craft practice engenders an ongoing dialogue between people and materials, he suggests that these expose the limits of Cartesian distinctions between mind and world, thinking and doing. Likewise, when Ingold (2000) discusses skilled practice as a process that indissolubly engages people, materials, tools and environments, the wider theoretical significance of the insight lies in its negation of modernist forms of detachment, including between mind and body, organism and world. While such Cartesian understandings start 'from the postulate of an original detachment of the intelligent subject, who has then to construct (or reconstruct) the world in his or her mind, prior to bodily engagement with it' (Ingold 2000: 417) his own discussion works as a reversal of this logic: 'postulating an original condition of engagement, of being in the world, we suppose that the practitioner has then to *detach* himself from the current of his activity in order to reflect upon it' (2000: 417).

In social scientific methodology itself, the detachment between observer and observed came strongly under attack, from those who sought to make explicit the political implications of this methodological and theoretical framing, and to foreground the relativity of academics' own claims to know (Said 1978; Fabian 1983; Clifford and Marcus 1986). A tactic of 'epistemological collapse' relying on experimental writing which revoked the distance between theory and ethnography, informant and anthropologist, was one of the immediate responses to this crisis (Munasinghe 2008: 179). But as Munasinghe notes, the crisis of representation primarily resulted in an entanglement between 'data' and 'theory' *within* academic discourse (2008: 179). A far more potent challenge came with the realisation that social scientific concepts (such as nation, society or culture) circulated and did important work in the world that social scientists were seeking to describe (Munasinghe 2008: 174). Detachment increasingly seemed not simply unpalatable, but impossible. As Annelise Riles astutely observes:

> a once productive distance ethnographers maintained, implicitly or explicitly, purposefully or not, between ourselves and our objects of our study, between the things studied (the data) and the frames we used to study them (the analysis), between theorizing and describing, has now definitively collapsed. (Riles 2006: 3)

Interwoven in complex ways with these conceptual and historical developments in the second half of the twentieth century was a rising language of 'accountability'. Such a language demanded a more 'engaged' approach from organisations, businesses and government, an approach which ideally could meet the needs of 'clients', 'customers', 'citizens' and 'consumers' in ways that previously detached modes of bureaucratic or economic action had failed to deliver (du Gay 2000). Blending the language of neoliberal capitalism, New Management and democratic ideals, new norms of 'responsiveness' emerged within public sectors, policy spheres and economic life (Strathern 2000; Shore 2008). These new approaches demanded of organisations regular inspections, target-setting, a focus on outcomes, new systems of audit and the increased recognition and role of 'users' in organisational action. In Britain, for example, Tony Blair (prime minister from 1997 to 2007) sought to legislatively encourage more direct citizen participation in service provisions in the early 2000s (Taylor and Kelly 2006).

In parallel, technological developments in media and communication have served to foster what is commonly deemed more participatory, engaged modes, by which information and knowledge can circulate, be shared and be constructed, and a more participatory mode of virtual democratic life (e.g. Shirky 2009). Collaborative knowledge building tools such as Wikipedia, the emergence of comments sections on news sites through which readers engage and add their opinions and experiences, crowdfunding websites, web protest campaigns and internet groups formed around common interests or perspectives, have all decentred previously seemingly detached authorities of knowledge, power and production. Such an approach to knowledge is also visible within the sphere of education in which there is now a push away from longstanding methods of knowledge transmission towards new modes of 'active learning', engaged teaching methods and learning outside the 'disconnected' classroom and within 'real life', such as the growth of internships and work-based or community service learning methods (Beck and Maida 2013). Sociologist Frank Furedi suggests that as relativistic understandings of truth have increasingly undermined the authority of higher education academics take refuge in attempts to appear 'relevant', 'accessible' and 'in touch' with popular opinion (Furedi 2004). In sum, technological shifts at the end of the twentieth century both underwrote the seeming obviousness of metaphors of connectivity, and enabled new practices of connection.

Correspondingly, the 'cultural turn' has coincided with the valorisation of connection, relationship and engagement as analytic frameworks for thinking about ethics and knowledge production in the humanities and social sciences. Marilyn Strathern (2014) has recently commented on an intensification of interest in relations in social anthropology, suggesting that this, in part, responds to the collapse of analytic faith in the systems and structures once thought to contain them ('culture', 'society' and the like). No longer as specific, concrete instances of these social, cultural or economic processes, relations appear as prime movers of sociality in their own right. She notes that, at least in this abstract form, 'the concept of relation often seems to carry a positive value. By and large, it is a good thing to have found them!' (Strathern 2014).

In sum, we are arguing that a profound but largely imperceptible shift took place in broad swathes of popular and academic discourse in the latter half of the twentieth century. While an earlier sense of a loaded alternative between engagement and detachment persisted as rhetorics, the moral universe this harked back to in nineteenth- and twentieth-century Europe and America had quietly given way to a more radical sense that relationship and engagement, for better or worse, are all there is. Ethical and intellectual dilemmas were increasingly posed not so much about relations, but within them. Detachment, it seemed, was increasingly if not exclusively conceivable only as a quality encompassed by and hence secondary to the logic of relations.

Reconsidering detachment

As noted at the opening of the previous section, the whirlwind tour above is not offered as a final diagnostic. Rather it is an impressionistic illustration of our sense that we find ourselves writing in a conceptual moment which is overdetermined by the priority of the relational over the non-relational on simultaneously epistemic, ethical and ontological planes. In proposing this diagnosis, we are unambiguously *not* dismissing legitimate concerns about the politics and ethics of detachment in particular contexts; nor are we calling for the 'ruination' (Navaro-Yashin 2009) of the many and varied theoretical approaches touched on above. We are simply mapping the increasing restriction of the conceptual and ethnographic space allowed for the study of detachment as an actual or potential phenomenon.

There are signs, however, that we may be experiencing a more widespread dissatisfaction with this relationalist narrowing of the frame. Thus, in recent years, other versions of the above narrative have emerged, painted on different temporal and disciplinary canvases. See, for instance, Meillassoux's critique of 'correlationism' in philosophy since Kant (Meillassoux 2008), Sloterdijk's investigation into the conceptual 'murder' of the detached subject of knowledge (2012 – see Robbins, this volume, Chapter 5), or Albert Piette's concerned letter to anthropologists 'Against Relationalism' (2014; on Piette's earlier work on 'the minor mode' which prefigures some of these concerns, see Humphrey, this volume, Chapter 7). Each of these, rather like our own account, takes the form of a sweeping review, by nature leaving some things out, collapsing crucial distinctions, but articulating a central sense that something has been lost.

While these diagnoses have appeared largely in parallel to our own, there are a number of authors whose work fed more directly into our initial elaboration of this project. As in the previous section, we cannot possibly list here – let alone give a satisfactory account of – all the various works which have in various ways acted as a catalyst for this project.[2] We will have to strategically narrow our sights to two key approaches, which are particularly clearly represented in the chapters that follow. The first was the turn to ethics, both in anthropology (e.g. Laidlaw 2002, 2013; Lambek 2010; Faubion 2011), and in other disciplines (Anderson 2001; Daston and Galison 2007). The influence here was simultaneously ethnographic, methodological and theoretical. It is not simply that anthropologists and historians interested in ethics and self-formation had, as a matter of course, studied people who aimed at certain forms of detachment (from the world or from themselves).

Just as important was the fact that in the process, these anthropologists and historians of ethics had begun to call more or less explicitly for a moratorium on a particular kind of critical reflex: the kind which reduces people's own accounts of what they were doing, to a kind of false-consciousness to (see, for instance, Laidlaw 2002, on the limits of anthropological accounts of 'agency'; Daston and Galison 2007, on the need to suspend critique in order to take seriously objectivity as an ethical goal).

Amanda Anderson (2001), writing in a similar vein, has warned against the scholarly pitfall theorising detachment as an 'either/or'. Practices in cultivated distance that claim a pure or completed objectivity are, she argues, evidence of a frustrated idealism, the counter-argument to which is that no such absolute detachment, whether it be in objectivity, separation or distance, is ever truly achievable. In her own words, such 'critics show themselves unable to imagine critical distance as a temporary vantage, unstable achievement, or regulative ideal: it's all or nothing' (Anderson 2001: 32). Her critique of both scholarly trends is that they miss the ways in which detachment may be important for people as a practice or as an intention. This interest in ethics, which runs strongly through a number of the contributions to this volume, is one way of getting at the crucial distinction between detachment as ideology and detachment as perfectible – and thus ethnographically accessible – practice.

The second conceptual tradition to which we are strongly indebted has its roots in the anthropology of kinship – a field which through its many incarnations and reconfigurations, has always been centrally concerned with the documentation of connections and disconnections. One instance can be found in Rupert Stasch's exquisitely detailed ethnography of the Korowai, which, informed by the classic sociology of Simmel as much as by the recent musings on alterity of anthropologists such as Viveiros De Castro (2003), brings to the foreground the otherness which lies at the heart of kinship and social relations for the Korowai (Stasch 2009). But the line of analysis which most directly informed our own work was the distinctive recombination of thinking about kinship and knowledge associated with the work of Marilyn Strathern.

Strathern's work is often portrayed – perhaps not unfairly – as belonging squarely to the relational turn of the late twentieth century, which we have sketched in the previous section; it is to her work after all, that anthropology owes one of the most far-reaching articulations of the relationality of persons, for instance (1988). However, Strathern's work simultaneously and recursively brought 'the relation' itself into ethnographic focus as a particular artefact of Euro-American knowledge-making (1992, 1995, 1996). Making the relation visible in this way, bringing it into the foreground, necessarily raises the question of what the background might be. It is thus not coincidental that Strathern is one of the anthropologists who has most thematised the effects of division, cuts, breaks and negative strategies – from the anthropological tactics of comparison, contextualisation and 'bifurcation' (1987, 2004) through to indigenous forms such as Melanesian dividuality (1988) or Euro-American concerns with cutting endless networks through claims of ownership (Strathern 1996). In this way, arguably, Strathern's work already prefigures the moment which some have recently sought to characterise as 'post-relational' (Pedersen 2013). Strathernian relations are, in a manner of speaking, connections that cut themselves. Across multiple contexts and arguments, the point of her analysis was not to celebrate relativity and connection, but to open up a conceptual space in which connections and disconnections could be traced, according to the logic of different ethnographic circumstances.

In this connection, it is worth reading Strathern alongside, and in contrast to, another theorist who looms large over our thinking and over many of the chapters in this book, namely Bruno Latour. Self-consciously seeking to supersede the post-modern critique outlined in the previous section, Bruno Latour's influential 'We have never been modern' (1991) put connections and disconnections on an even keel – almost. Latour argued that modernist attempts to detach, cut, disentangle and 'purify' (nature from culture, humans from non-humans, Them from Us, science from politics, and so on), were only possible because of the increasing accumulation of 'translations' between these different realms, making hybrids, quasi-objects and networks proliferate: that is the strength of what Latour terms the 'Modern Constitution'. In so far as it resists the temptation to reveal practices of engagement and translation as the real underpinning, and of detachment and purification as mere illusion or false consciousness (1991: 40), but rather treats both moves as empirically real, Latour's symmetric anthropology nearly manages to put the two on an even footing. Indeed, a number of the contributors to this volume draw inspiration from his analyses in this respect. However, in the end, we would argue (*pace* for instance Jensen and Winthereik, this volume, Chapter 10) that the Latourian argument implies an analytic asymmetry in its orientation to practices of relating and of separating. While Latour puts relating and separating on the same analytical plane, this is itself an act of *relation*. Purification and translation are both real moves, yes, but the cardinal sin of the moderns was to keep the two moves *separate*, whereas the duty of the 'amodern' analyst is to *relate* them.

> If we understand modernity in terms of the official Constitution that has to make a total distinction between humans and nonhumans on the one hand and between purification and mediation on the other, then no anthropology of the modern world is possible. But if we *link together* in one single picture the work of purification and the work of mediation *that gives it meaning*, we discover, retrospectively that we have never been modern. (Latour 1991: 91, emphasis added)

Both Latour and Strathern's work inhabit a space on the edge of the relational: both point to the ways in which disconnection, cuts and distinctions, accompany, undergird, permit or arise from relations and connections. Unlike Latour, however, whose own language and method is itself thoroughly relational (and the rhetorical indebtedness of Actor-Network Theory to the language of accountability is telling – cf. Latour 2005), Strathern cleaved heuristically to the classic anthropological form of the contrastive comparison, the erection of radical distinctions between Them and Us (see Candea 2011; Tsing 2010). While Latour ultimately trumped his recognition of disconnections through a relational method,[3] Strathern's work (1996) can be seen as establishing a real and effective symmetry between the two: every cut is revealed as also a relation, every relation is also a disengagement from something else.

These two broad sources of theoretical insight – the anthropology of ethics and Strathern's work on the relation – were diversely influential on the four of us, and on the contributors to this volume. They are, it must be said, uneasy companions and point, often implicitly rather than explicitly, to a very different range and type of disconnections, detachments and cuts. We return to some of the tensions between them, which inhabit a number of the chapters in this volume, in the next section. What both have in common with each other and with our project, however, is the more general anthropological concern with the primacy of the ethnographic. This similarity of commitment (take your ethnography seriously), and multiplicity of substantive meanings and implications of 'detachment', influenced the form of our initial call to arms: 'take detachment seriously as an ethnographic object (whatever it might turn out to be)!'

Given how indebted the relational turn has been to the rejection and mistrust of the relatively ill-defined, or at least shifting, target of 'modernist detachment', this open-ended strategy has proved to be extremely productive. Paying close ethnographic attention to specific instances of detachment (both nominally 'modernist' and 'non-modernist') necessarily explodes the monolithic image of the 'failed ideal' of modernist detachment. Ethnography does this both by highlighting the situated and multiple nature of the ideal, and by locating this alongside other ways of living and valuing detachment.

What is detachment? A typology

There are some limits to this purely ethnographic strategy, however. Shortly after the conference from which most of the chapters in this volume are drawn, one of the audience members, philosopher Hallvard Lillehammer, forwarded a somewhat tongue-in cheek list he had compiled of sixty different ways in which detachment had been invoked by participants. The friendly rebuke embedded in this Borgesian catalogue was clear: detachment as we were using it, could be anything and everything. Stolidly, one of us replied that where the philosopher saw a failure to define one's key analytical category, the anthropologist saw the result of a successful campaign to turn detachment into an ethnographic category. Focusing attention on detachment in this sense will quite naturally result in the multiplication of instances, and in the concomitant stretching and reconfiguring of the categorical starting point.

1. Detachment as objectivity
2. Detachment as impartiality
3. Detachment as explanatory reductionism
4. Detachment as disinterestedness
5. Detachment as lack of prejudice
6. Detachment as 'blinding' (in 'blind trials')
7. Detachment as technology-mindedness
8. Detachment as high-mindedness (remoteness from everyday life)
9. Detachment as refusal to be co-opted
10. Detachment as ethos of bureaucratic office/personality
11. Detachment as removal of parts from a whole where other parts stay in place
12. Detachment as interest created by 'external' incentives (e.g. research funding)
13. Detachment as not caring
14. Detachment as bracketing an issue or analysis to avoid openness to criticism
15. Detachment as the closing off of/turning away from something in pursuit of an end
16. Detachment as a pathology/disorder (e.g. social phobia)
17. Detachment as a bulwark against moral zealotry and managerial enthusiasm
18. Detachment as inter- patience/disengaged participation (the integrated, but non-interfering observer)
19. Detachment as forgetting
20. Detachment as non-differentiation
21. Detachment as industrial mechanisation
22. Detachment as distancing
23. Detachment as autonomy/freedom
24. Detachment as cognition/judgement (as opposed to affect)
25. Detachment as invisibility/absence
26. Detachment as untouchability
27. Detachment as excess of scale for being intuitively grasped
28. Detachment as rationality
29. Detachment as division/separation (e.g. of soul from body)
30. Detachment as exclusion/expulsion
31. Detachment as disgust/repugnance
32. Detachment as removal from public view
33. Detachment as mediation

34. Detachment as separation (e.g. of property)
35. Detachment as discipline/order/security
36. Detachment as abstraction (e.g. of concepts)
37. Detachment as a sign of the sacred
38. Detachment as disbelief
39. Detachment as observation
40. Detachment as death
41. Detachment as safe distance (e.g. from spirits)
42. Detachment as the untying of a knot
43. Detachment as sacrifice/giving up something
44. Detachment as using a substitute rather than the real thing
45. Detachment as balancing
46. Detachment as oppression
47. Detachment as liberation through confession
48. Detachment as irony
49. Detachment as spiritual renunciation
50. Detachment as anti-spiritual renunciation (e.g. cutting off from religious practices)
51. Detachment as meditation/prayer
52. Detachment as equanimity
53. Detachment as living without property ('the carefree life')
54. Detachment as freedom from strain/having a balanced mind
55. Detachment as seeing without acting
56. Detachment as fasting to death
57. 'External' detachment: NOT [A is related to B]
58. 'Internal' detachment: A is [NOT related to B]
59. Stronger, third, reading: A is related to [NOT B]
60. Detachment as mutual accommodation/cooperation

(Lillehammer, Pers. Comm.)

A popular anthropological tradition would urge us to stop there, to rest content with the act of documenting the empirical multiplicity and ubiquity of detachment. But our aim is also, more profoundly, to highlight the ways in which, as conceptual abstractions, the foundational status of the terms sociality, relationality and engagement naturalises a relational view of the world that then acts to render detachment as a specific and secondary quality.

In that context, leaving 'detachment' as a general placeholder that could mean anything and everything creates a kind of analytical collapse. At this level of abstraction it is rather easy to conclude that detachment itself is 'just another relation'. The smoothness of this seemingly obvious conclusion flattens crucial ethnographic differences and also masks the fact that in the process, relations have once again been naturalised as the 'real' ground of reality. To make conceptual space for detachment, to give it analytical purchase, requires that we descend from this level of abstraction to something like a typology of kinds of detachment.

Any such typology necessarily entails a simplification of the ethnographic realities it describes. But typology is much like other kinds of detachment: it would be absurd to reject it completely just because it cannot be perfect. In response to Lillehammer's provocation, we espouse

Introduction: reconsidering detachment

typology in this section, not as a revelation of a fixed underlying order, or as a place to rest, but as an ongoing perfectible practice.

Drawing on the classic structuralist technique of the table of crossed binaries (see table 1), we could begin by highlighting two fundamental distinctions cut across invocations of detachment in the chapters that follow. The first is the distinction between completed detachment (detachment as a state) and ongoing detachment (detachment as a process or activity). The second is the distinction between accounts which are in the first person (detachment from the actor's point of view) and those given from a third-party perspective (detachment between any two entities described 'from the outside').

The distinction between state and process is fairly straightforward. In some cases detachment is something which is being done. We see this as a cutting or a drawing away, as when organs are detached from a body, as in Maryon McDonald's chapter (Chapter 1) on surgeons and anatomy classes, or the separation between producers and their product, as in Hannah Knox and Penny Harvey's chapter (Chapter 2) on engineers in Peru. It is also visible in the disconnections drawn between humans and the animals they tend, as exemplified in Kim Crowder's chapter (Chapter 3) on British pig farmers, or in the reflective distance created between persons and their own thoughts, illustrated in Joanna Cook's chapter (Chapter 11) on mindfulness therapy in Britain.

In other cases detachment is a state in which a thing or person finds itself as the outcome of such a process: a state of being unattached to some other thing or person, as in the detachment of the person from the office within new systems of university audit culture, as Corsin-Jimenez describes in Chapter 9, which seeks conceptual purchase from juxtaposing varied forms of interface and effect, from Baroque aesthetics, to digital software and modern university life. Or, as in Chapter 10 where Casper Jensen and Brit Winthereik's examine an international development project in Vietnam aimed at building a long house and micro-enterprises, in which the local 'community', the project and the aid workers find themselves detached from each other in various ways.

One of the questions which runs through a number of these chapter is precisely what the relation, if any, between state and process might be: is a stable state ever achievable (and if so for how long?), or is detachment necessarily an ongoing (and thus ever-incomplete) process? If the latter, is detachment as a stable state then to be understood as a fiction of which the process is the real counterpart, or is it an ideal which enables and is constitutive of the process?[4]

This last question brings us straight to the second distinction, which cuts across the one above, between first-person and third-party descriptions. Speaking of detachment as a process or a state commits us to saying very little about the entities involved. Both states and processes of detachment can be predicated to any entity on any scale, and they can happen both within and between entities. In these pages we find detached (state) or detaching (process) knowledges (Corsín-Jiménez), roads (Knox and Harvey), communities, fieldsites and houses (Jensen and Winthereik), body parts (McDonald), beliefs and relationships (Robbins), as well as, of course, human persons. These various descriptions of detachments (and relations) within and between entities we are referring to as third-party descriptions. In so far as none of the chapters focus solely on the author's own detachment from their material (although a number of the chapters do touch on this theme), all of them include 'third-party' accounts of detachment in this sense.

So what is meant by first-person detachment? A number of our contributors are concerned with investigating detachment in a specific sense which, as we noted above, owes much to the anthropology of ethics, namely as a subject of reflexive commitment or ongoing conscious practice by human persons. Cheryl Mattingly has recently noted the specificity of a 'first-person' approach in the anthropology of ethics, as against post-structural accounts of self-formation in which the self is simply an effect of broader relational forces (2012). We similarly find it useful to mark out the specificity of the contributors' invocations of what we would term a 'first-person' detachment. Detachment, in this first-person sense, is not simply a state of non-connection that any entity might be in, but a stance or a perspective on one's own action. This is clearest perhaps in Caroline Humphrey's chapter on Mongolian weddings (Chapter 7), in which wedding leaders maintain a stance of 'active detachment' from their own subject position, and who can oscillate back and forth between the bride and groom groups' vantage points through rituals and songs. Correspondingly, Joel Robbins, in Chapter 5, reflects on how a Christian ethos of detachment might offer anthropologists studying Christianity a technique through which to overcome distance and recognise shared commitments with their participants.

Whether or not a detached *stance* is considered to be possible or only desired or hoped for, it is clearly the 'first-person' equivalent of what we have described above as a *state*. By contrast, the first-person equivalent of detachment as *process* is that staple of the anthropology of ethics: self-conscious perfectible practice, or to put it more simply and with a nod to Foucault, an *ascetic*. In sum, we could map these two crossed binaries as in Table 1.

Added to these distinctions, two of our contributors, James Laidlaw and Jonathan Mair, draw their own typology of detachment, both

Table 1 *Steps towards a typology of detachment*

	Third-party	First-person
Completed	Detachment as state	Detachment as stance
Ongoing	Detachment as Process	Detachment as Ascetic

inspired in slightly different ways by the work of Jon Elster. In relation to North Indian Jainism and Inner Mongolian Buddhism respectively, they draw a distinction between internal and external detachment, modelled on Elster's Hegelian distinction between internal and external negation. Internal and external here does not refer to perspective as in the distinction between third-party and first person, but rather to the logical relation between terms. In Laidlaw's rendition, external detachment is the thinly specified negation of any kind of relation between two terms – 'Not (A is related to B)', whereas internal detachment marks the more thickly specified state of being in a non-relation – 'A is not-related to B'. If the former merely indexes an absence of relation, specifying only the terms which are not supposed to be related, in the latter case, the substance of what it means to be 'not-related' matters: detachment becomes fleshed out as a particular kind of attitude or stance, and gains particular ethical substance and positive content. To this, Laidlaw adds a third, more radical possibility of 'intransitive' detachment, where no term B is specified – A is simply not related, even to A.

This distinction cuts across our four-part scheme to interesting effect. Thus, with our earlier distinctions in mind, it is notable that the ethnographic instance of this radical detachment in Laidlaw's text is presented as the intended outcome of a *process* (of fasting to death). In other words, as a *state* (let alone as a *stance*), as Laidlaw makes clear, intransitive detachment would be unsustainable by living beings – as an object of *ascesis*, however, it becomes fully understandable.

In Laidlaw's work these three types of detachment are all in what we have termed the first-person mode (as stance or ascetic): they are distinctions drawn between the different ethical content of different kinds of non-relations between persons, and they come with specific interactional and affective valences which Laidlaw describes in vibrant detail. However, one might map this distinction on third-party detachments which require less specific ethical content. It is hard to imagine, by contrast, what 'intransitive' detachment as a state would look like 'ethnographically' – this requires rather a metaphysical postulate.

This work of typologising reveals what a cursory read might perhaps obscure: the often profoundly different logics at stake in the following discussions of detachment. The third-party/first-person distinction points to an important fork in the road, which we also mentioned above. Writing of detachment as a stance or as an ascetic relies implicitly or explicitly on the distinctiveness of an account focused on human persons with an ability to take a perspective, and with characteristics such as intentionality and reflexivity – what one might call, loosely, a humanist approach. By contrast, third-party accounts of detachment as a state or process allows an agnostic account which, while it can easily recoup the humanist account above, can also significantly challenge its underpinnings. For instance, a number of our contributors (Jensen and Winthereik, Corsin-Jimenez, Knox and Harvey) write in communication with analytical traditions such as Actor-Network Theory, or the anthropology of partible personhood, which aim precisely to craft a language of analysis which troubles the humanist distinction between persons and things. More profoundly, both of these traditions, in different ways, seek to evade the very distinction between internal and external relations, challenging accounts of a world made up of stable entities which *then* relate to one another. This does not sit neatly with accounts of detachment for which the primacy and distinctiveness of the human subject is a prerequisite.

Some of the most exciting work in this collection, however, lies precisely at the crossroads between these four ideal types: detachment as process, state, stance and as ascetic, such as when personal aspirations to detachment are worked through practices of material cutting and separation (McDonald, Crowder this volume, Chapters 1 and 3; see also Candea 2010; Yarrow and Jones 2014), or when ascesis requires the operation of detachments and cuts within the person, such as a distance from one's own thoughts and emotional reactions (as in Cook, Chapter 11), or when third-party-accounts in an actor-network theory vein become in turn the medium for the analysts' own reflection on detachment (Jensen and Winthereik, Chapter 10).

Another important fork in the road concerns what now emerge as a number of potential interpretations of this volume's central call to reconsider detachment as a real phenomenon to be taken seriously, by opposition to detachment as an often illusory or ideological 'stable state' – the classic focus of critiques of objectivity, as we have noted above. There are two potential arguments entwined here and it matters which alternative one chooses. To argue that entities are never fully detached (state) but are detaching (process) is not always the same as arguing that persons are not detached in any ultimate sense (state), but that they sincerely wish, hope or commit to being so (stance). In some cases (scientific objectivity seems a case in point) a detached stance is an impossible, or at least fleeting and always partial achievement, however

Introduction: reconsidering detachment

continuous one's ascesis. In others it is a fairly unproblematic structural position that one occupies without seemingly much need for ascesis at all (Humphrey). Sometimes, the first-person *ascesis* of detachment might rely on processes which 'from the outside' are profoundly relational (Cook 2008). Or conversely, as with classic discussions of romantic attitudes to the countryside among an increasingly urbanised population (Williams 1975), a profoundly engaged stance might be premised precisely on being in an increasingly detached state.

In sum, this very tentative typological exercise begins to outline the answer to the two challenges we started from in this section. First, the challenge that detachment means anything and everything. Without letting go of the generative multiplicity of ethnographic contexts and situations, we have identified some points of tension and key questions around which accounts of detachment coalesce, and a number of regularities in the way detachment is invoked in the chapters that follow. As for the second, and more serious challenge, that detachment is just another kind of relation? Once there are *kinds* of detachment and *kinds* of relation,[5] the statement begins to call for specification and loses its neat reductive structure. This simultaneously opens up new lines of empirical enquiry and requires and facilitates new conceptual experiments.

Organisation of the book

This book is organised into three parts: 'professionalism and expertise', 'ritual and religion', and 'detaching and situating knowledge'. These are, of course, not the only areas of contemporary life in which practices of detachment are ethnographically present and analytically interesting. Collectively, however, they cover a wide range of practices of detachment, and offer us a window into key areas of human action in which detachment is particularly good to think with, both for the interlocutors of these studies and for the anthropologists who study them.

Part I on professionalism and expertise focuses on three different types of experts – pig farmers, road engineers, and medical students and transplant surgeons – in order to examine how detachment operates to both enable and curtail action, relationality, ethics and the production of knowledge. The road engineers in Peru to whom Hannah Knox and Penny Harvey introduce us utilise varied modes of detachment – with local people, with natural materials, with politics and with the project – in order to enact the role of a responsible and responsive expert. The pig farmers described by Kim Crowder use a praxis of detachment in order to foster and cut relations and affective connections with animals who must be vitally sustained and cared for, and then killed and commodified. Meanwhile, Maryon McDonald introduces us to the world of medical students who dissect bodies, and surgeons who transplant organs. Here detachment is both a fleshy task of cutting and recomposing bodies, and an uneasy ethical and emotional stance that requires careful negotiation, cultivation and sometimes negation. As Veena Das points out in her commentary for this section, the fragility of death, vulnerability, sacrifice and 'the finitude of human existence' are ever-present here, challenging assumptions that detachment is simply a stance of cold disinterest.

Part II takes us to the realms of ritual and religion. Here Joel Robbins juxtaposes two interrelated dilemmas, one epistemological and one ethnographic, that locate an ethos of detachment within Christianity. Just as an anthropologist studying Christianity must deal with the question of his or her own dis/belief and its impact on 'being in the field', the Urapmin of Papua New Guinea, in converting to charismatic Christianity, must detach from, but also manage, relations with natural spirits. James Laidlaw shifts our ethnographic focus to Shvetambar Jainism in north India, demonstrating how, through annual rituals, alms-giving and fasting practices, diverse types of detachment are achieved based on internal or external modes of negation. In Mongolian Buriads wedding rituals Caroline Humphrey argues that detachment should not be equated with separation (a connection broken), but in this case implies a strategic and cultivated 'third "place", a distancing from any ... situated perspectives'. Michael Carrithers offers a commentary of the three chapters that reflects on the detached stance of the writers as scholars, and then reflects these insights back to the ethnographic world of Buriads, Jains and Pentecostals.

In Part III we turn to practices of knowledge. Alberto Corsín Jiménez takes a seventeenth-century painting by Velázquez, an artist who pioneered a new mode of re-description relying upon forms of suspension, displacement and detachment. Corsín Jiménez then juxtaposes these insights on to an analysis of modern forms of audit, bureaucracy and digital life in order to locate Baroque modes of displacements or enhancements. Casper Bruun Jensen and Brit Ross Winthereik reflect upon an ecotourism development project in Vietnam, asking what an actor-network theory approach to detachment might reveal. They show how detachment and engagement are entangled, that 'they transform over time and emerge in new constellations'. Joanna Cook ethnographically charts the practices associated with Mindfulness-based Cognitive Therapy in Britain. Here detachment emerges as a double figure: both a troubling mental affliction associated with the ills of modern life, and simultaneously as a solution to the above, cultivated as an internal ethos designed to foster healthy modes of engagements with life and the self. In a similar vein, Jon Mair demonstrates how Inner Mongolian Buddhists utilise discourses of humility and ignorance that actively encourage an 'effortful pursuit of an ethic of detachment'. In her commentary, Marilyn Strathern uses two vantage points to gain purchase on this section; Melanesian kinship forms reveal that detachment does not mean separation from social life, while relations in the British colonial Empire cultivated necessary modes of aloofness. Both vantages, Strathern argues, point to the ways in which we might think about the diverse subject positions that stem from the detachments we see in these four chapters, and the types of knowledge about how one must act in relation to self and others.

The chapters of this book situate detachment in diverse actions, ideological positions, modes of relationality and subjective projects. Collectively, they demonstrate the shifting terrains of detachment, its dynamic relationships to modes of engagement, and the ways in which, for many groups and actors, detachment operates as a valued and productive type of knowledge or action.

Notes

1 Although setting up this detached relationship actually took some fairly hands-on intervention (Candea 2013a) and indeed allowed a range of other experimental manipulations to take place (Candea 2013b).
2 Some of these include Simpson (1997), Shryock (1997), Mol (2002b), Reed (2003), Kohn (2007), Gershon (2010) and Jackson (2012).
3 Latour's most recent work on modes of existence (Latour 2013), with its metaphysics of gaps and micro-transcendences, is closer to a genuinely symmetrical account.
4 It might be worth noting in this context, that the very term 'detachment' contains a relationalist bias of its own, in so far as it implies the outcome of a process. The implication then is that *de*tachment – if it is ever achieved – is what comes after the relation. Detachment in this sense is inherently a 'post-relational' term (Pedersen 2013) rather than a non-relational or radically anti-relational one. Consider by contrast the radical anti-relationalism of a philosopher such as Quentin Meillassoux (2008), for whom what is at stake is not just the possibility of getting out of, breaking or cutting relations a posteriori, but the possibility of imagining a reality *before* relations.
5 For an excellent account of 'kinds' of relations, see Strathern (2011).

References

Anderson, Amanda, 2001, *The Powers of Distance: Cosmopolitanism and the Cultivation of Detachment*. Princeton: Princeton University Press.

Aronowitz, Stanley, 1988, *Science as Power: Discourse and Ideology in Modern Society*. Minneapolis: University of Minnesota Press.

Beck, Sam and Carl Maida, 2013, Introduction: Towards Engaged Anthropology. In Sam Beck and Carl Maida, eds, *Towards Engaged Anthropology*. New York and Oxford: Berghahn Books, pp. 15–35.

Candea, Matei, 2010, 'I fell in Love with Carlos the Meerkat': Engagement and Detachment in Human–Animal Relations. *American Ethnologist* 37: 241–258.

Candea, Matei, 2011, Endo/Exo. *Common Knowledge* 17: 146–150.

Candea, Matei, 2013a, Suspending Belief: Epoché in Animal Behavior Science. *American Anthropologist* 115(3): 423–436.

Candea, Matei, 2013b, Habituating Meerkats and Redescribing Animal Behaviour Science. *Theory, Culture and Society* 30(7–8): 105–128.

Choy, T. K., 2011, *Ecologies of Comparison: An Ethnography of Endangerment in Hong Kong*. Durham NC: Duke University Press.

Clifford, J. and Marcus, G., eds, 1986, *Writing Culture: The Poetics and Politics of Ethnography*. Berkeley: University of California Press.

Clodfelter, Michael, 2002, *Warfare and Armed Conflicts: A Statistical Reference to Casualty and Other Figures, 1500–2000*, 2nd edn. Jefferson, NC: McFarland & Company.

Conrad, Peter, 2007, *The Medicalization of Society: On the Transformation of Human Conditions into Medical Disorders*. Baltimore, MD: Johns Hopkins University Press.

Cook, Joanna, 2008, Alms, Money and Reciprocity: Buddhist Nuns as Mediators of Generalized Exchange in Thailand. *Anthropology in Action*, Special Edition: Gift Exchange in Modern Society 15(3): 8–21.

Cook, Joanna, 2010 *Meditation in Modern Buddhism: Renunciation and Change in Thai Monastic Life*. Cambridge: Cambridge University Press.

Crist, E., 1999 *Images of Animals: Anthropomorphism and Animal Mind*. Philadelphia, PA: Temple University Press.

Crush, J., 1995, *Power of Development*. London and New York, Routledge.

Das, Veena, 1996, *Critical Events: An Anthropological Perspective on Contemporary India*. Oxford: Oxford University Press.

Daston, L. and Galison, P., 2007, *Objectivity*. Brooklyn, NY: Zone Books.

Despret Vinciane, 2004, The Body We Care For: Figures of Anthropo-zoo-genesis. *Body & Society* 10(2–3): 111–134.

Du Gay, Paul, 2000, *In Praise of Bureaucracy. Weber – Organisation – Ethics*. London: Sage Publishing.

Durkheim, Emile, 1964, *The Rules of Sociological Method*. New York: Free Press.

Durkheim, Emile, 1997[1893], *The Division of Labour in Society* (trans. W. D. Halls). New York: Free Press.

Eco, U., 1988, An Ars Oblivionaris? Forget it. *PMLA* 103: 254–261.
Engels, Friedrich, 1983[1884], *The Origin of the Family, Private Property, and the State*. London: Pathfinder Press.
Esteva, G., 1992, Development. In W. Sachs, *The Development Dictionary: A Guide to Knowledge as Power*. London: Zed Books.
Fabian, J., 1983, *Time and the Other, How Anthropology Makes its Object*. New York: Columbia University Press.
Faubion, J. D., 2011, *An Anthropology of Ethics*. Cambridge and New York: Cambridge University Press.
Ferguson, James, 1994, *The Anti-Politics Machine: 'Development', Depoliticisation, and Bureaucratic Power in Lesotho*. Minneapolis and London: University of Minnesota Press.
Foucault, Michel, 1979, What is Enlightenment? In Paul Rabinow and William M. Sullivan, eds, *Interpretive Social Science: A Second Look*. Berkeley: University of California Press, pp. 157–175.
Furedi, Frank, 2004, *Where Have all the Intellectuals Gone*. London and New York: Continuum.
Garrow, D. and Yarrow, Thomas, 2010 *Archaeology and Anthropology: Understanding Similarity, Exploring Difference*. Oxford: Oxbow.
Gershon, I., 2010, *The Breakup 2.0: Disconnecting Over New Media*. Ithaca, New York: Cornell University Press.
Guitierrez, Gustavo, 1988, *A Theology of Liberation: History, Politics, and Salvation*. Maryknoll NY: Orbis Books.
Haraway, Donna, 1988, Situated Knowledge: The Science Question in Feminism and the Privilege of Partial Perspective. *Feminist Studies* 14(3): 575–599.
Haraway, D. J., 1997, *Modest-Witness@Second-Millennium.FemaleMan-Meets-OncoMouse: Feminism and Technoscience*. New York, Routledge.
Heelas, Paul, 1992, The Sacralisation of the Self and New Age Capitalism. In N. Abercrombie and A Warde, eds, *Social Change and Contemporary Britain*. Cambridge: Polity Press, pp. 139–166.
Hobart, M., 1993, *An Anthropological Critique of Development: The Growth of Ignorance*. London and New York: Routledge.
Ingold, Tim, 2000, *The Perception of the Environment: Essays in Livelihood, Dwelling and Skill*. London: Routledge.
Jackson, Michael, 2012, *Between One and One Another*. Berkeley and Los Angeles: University of California Press.
Kohn, Eduardo, 2007, How Dogs Dream: Amazonian Natures and the Politics of Trans-species Engagement. *American Ethnologist* 34(1): 3–24.
Kohn, Eduardo, 2013, *How Forests Think: Toward an Anthropology Beyond the Human*. Berkeley: University of California Press.
Kroll-Smith, Steve, Brown Phil, and Gunter, Valerie J., 2000, Introduction: Environments and Disease in a Postnatural World. In Steve Kroll-Smith, Phil Brown and Valerie J. Gunter, eds, *Illness and the Environment: A Reader in Contested Medicine*. New York: New York University Press, pp. 1–8.

Kuper, Adam, 2005, *The Reinvention of Primitive Society: Transformations of a Myth*. London: Routledge.
Laidlaw, James, 2002, For an Anthropology of Ethics and Freedom (The Malinowski Memorial Lecture, 2001). *Journal of the Royal Anthropological Institute* 8(2): 311–332.
Laidlaw, James, 2014, *The Subject of Virtue: An Anthropology of Ethics and Freedom*. New York: Cambridge University Press.
Lambek, Michael, 2010, *Ordinary Ethics: Anthropology, Language, and Action*. New York: Fordham University Press.
Latour, Bruno, 1991, *We Have Never Been Modern*. Cambridge: Harvard University Press.
Latour, Bruno, 2004, Why Has Critique Run Out of Steam? From Matters of Fact to Matters of Concern. *Critical Inquiry* 30(2): 225–248.
Latour, Bruno, 2005, *Reassembling the Social: An Introduction to Actor Network Theory*. Oxford: Oxford University Press.
Latour, Bruno, 2013, *An Inquiry into Modes of Existence: An Anthropology of the Moderns*. Cambridge, MA: Harvard University Press.
Levine, A. G., 1982, *Love Canal: Science, Politics, and People*. Lexington, MA: Lexington Books.
Lowenthal, D., 1985, *The Past is a Foreign Country*. Cambridge: Cambridge University Press.
Mattingly, Cheryl, 2012, Two Virtue Ethics and the Anthropology of Morality. *Anthropological Theory* 12(2): 161–184.
McDonald, Maryon, 1989, *'We are not French!': Language, Culture, and Identity in Brittany*. London: Routledge.
Meillassoux, Quentin, 2008, *After Finitude: An Essay on the Necessity of Contingency* (trans. Ray Brassier). New York: Continuum.
Milton, K., 2005. Anthropomorphism or Egomorphism? The Perception of Non-human Persons by Human Ones. *Animals in Person: Cultural Perspectives on Human-Animal Intimacy*. J. Knight. Oxford: Berg.
Mol, Annemarie, 2002a, *The Body Multiple: Ontology in Medical Practice*, Durham NC and London: Duke University Press.
Mol, Annemarie, 2002b, Cutting Surgeons, Walking Patients: Some Complexities Involved in Comparing. In J. Law and A. Mol, eds, *Complexities: Social Studies of Knowledge Practices*. Durham: Duke University Press, pp. 218–257.
Morgan, Lewis Henry, 1870, *Systems of Consanguinity and Affinity of the Human Family, Smithsonian Contributions to Knowledge*, vol xvii, art. 2. Washington: Smithsonian Institution.
Morgan, Lewis Henry, 1877, *Ancient Society*. New York: H. Holt and Company.
Munasinghe, V., 2008, Rescuing Theory from the Nation. In N. Halstead, E. Hirsch and J. Okely, *Knowing How to Know: Fieldwork and the Ethnographic Present*. New York: Berghahn Books.
Navaro-Yashin, Y., 2009, Affective Spaces, Melancholic Objects: Ruination

and the Production of Anthropological Knowledge, *Journal of the Royal Anthropological Institute* 15(1): 1–18.

Pedersen, Morten, 2012, Proposing the Motion. *Critique of Anthropology* 32(1):59–65.

Pedersen, Morten, 2013, The Fetish of Connectivity. In G. Evans, E. Silva and N. Thoburn, eds, *Objects and Materials. A Routledge Companion*. London: Routledge, pp. 197–207.

Pellegrino, E., 1997, The Nazi Doctors and Nuremberg: Some Moral Lessons Revisited. *Annals of Internal Medicine* 127(4): 307–308.

Petryna, Adriana, 2002, *Life Exposed: Biological Citizens after Chernobyl*. Princeton, NJ: Princeton University Press.

Piette, A., 2014, *Contre le Relationisme: Lettre aux anthropologues*. Paris: Le Bord de l'Eau.

Pfeiffer, James, Kenneth Gimbel-Sherr and Orvalho Augusto, 2008, The Holy Spirit in the Household: Pentecostalism, Gender, and Neoliberalism in Mozambique. *American Anthropology* 109(4): 688–700.

Porter, James, Williams, Clare, Wainwright, Steven, and Cribb, Alan, 2013, On Being a (Modern) Scientist: Risks of Public Engagement in the UK Interspecies Embryo Debate. *New Genetics and Society* 31(4): 408–423.

Rabinow, Paul, 1975, *Symbolic Domination: Cultural Form and Historical Change in Morocco*, University of Chicago Press.

Reed, A. D. E., 2003, *Papua New Guinea's Last Place: Experiences of Constraint in a Postcolonial Prison*. New York: Berghahn Books.

Riles, Annelise, 2006, Introduction: In Annelise Riles, ed., *Response in Documents: Artifacts of Modern Knowledge*. Ann Arbor: University of Michigan Press, pp. 1–38.

Rosner, David, 2013, *Lead Wars: The Politics of Science and the Fate of America's Children*. Berkeley: University of California Press.

Said, Edward, 1978, *Orientalism*. New York: Vintage Books.

Schweber, Silvan S., 2008, *Einstein and Oppenheimer: The Meaning of Genius*. Cambridge, MA: Harvard University Press.

Sennett, Richard, 2009, *The Craftsman*. St Ives: Penguin.

Shapin, S. and Schaffer, S., 1985, *Leviathan and the Air-pump: Hobbes, Boyle, and the Experimental Life: Including a Translation of Thomas Hobbes, Dialogus physicus de natura aeris by Simon Schaffer*. Princeton, NJ: Princeton University Press.

Shirky, Clay, 2009, *Here Comes Everybody: The Power of Organizing Without Organizations*. New York and London: Penguin Books.

Shore, Cris, 2008, Audit Culture and Illiberal Governance: Universities and the Politics of Accountability. *Anthropological Theory* 8(3): 278–298.

Shryock, A., 1997, *Nationalism and the Genealogical Imagination: Oral History and Textual Authority in Tribal Jordan*. Berkeley: University of California Press.

Simmel, Georg, 1976[1904], *The Metropolis and Mental Life in the Sociology of Georg Simmel*. New York: Free Press.

Simpson, B., 1997, On Gifts, Payments and Disputes: Divorce and Changing Family Structures in Contemporary Britain. *Journal of the Royal Anthropological Institute* 3(4): 731–745.

Sloterdijk, Peter, 2012 *The Art of Philosophy: Wisdom as a Practice*. New York: Columbia University Press.

Smith, L., 2006 *The Uses of Heritage*. London and New York, Routledge.

Stasch, Rupert, 2003, *Society of Others: Kinship and Mourning in a West Papuan Place*. Berkeley: University of California Press.

Stoler, Ann L., 2002, *Carnal Knowledge and Imperial Power: Race and the Intimate in Colonial Rule*. Berkeley: University of California Press.

Strathern, Marilyn, 1987, Out of Context: The Persuasive Fictions of Anthropology. *Current Anthropology* 28(3): 251–281.

Strathern, Marilyn, 1988, *The Gender of the Gift: Problems with Women and Problems with Society in Melanesia*. Berkeley: University of California Press.

Strathern, Marilyn, 1992, *After Nature: English Kinship in the Late Twentieth Century*. Cambridge: Cambridge University Press.

Strathern, Marilyn, 1995, *The Relation: Issues in Complexity and Scale*. Chicago: Prickly Pear Press.

Strathern, Marilyn, 1996, Cutting the Network. *The Journal of the Royal Anthropological Institute* 2(3): 517–535.

Strathern, Marilyn, 2000, Introduction: New Accountabilities. In Marilyn Strathern, ed., *Audit Cultures: Anthropological Studies in Accountability, Ethics and the Academy*. New York and London: Routledge, pp. 1–18.

Strathern, Marilyn, 2004, *Partial Connections*. Walnut Creek: AltaMira Press

Strathern, Marilyn, 2011, Binary License. *Common Knowledge* 17(1): 87–103.

Strathern, Marilyn, 2014, Reading Relations Backwards, *Journal of the Royal Anthropological Institute* 20(1): 3–19.

Taylor, Ian and Kelly, Josie, 2006, Professionals, Discretion and Public Sector Reform in the UK: Re-visiting Lipsky. *International Journal of Public Sector Management* 19(7): 629–642.

Tönnies, Ferdinand, 1957[1887], *Community and Society* (trans. Charles Price Loomis). East Lansing: Michigan State University Press.

Trundle, Catherine, 2014, *American in Tuscany: Charity, Compassion and Belonging*. Oxford and New York: Berghahn Books.

Trundle Catherine, Singh Ilina, and Broer, Christian, 2014, Fighting to be Heard: Contested Diagnoses. In Annemarie Jutel and Kevin Dew, eds, *Social Issues in Diagnosis: An Introduction for Students and Clinicians*. Baltimore, MD: Johns Hopkins University Press, pp. 165–182.

Tsing, A., 2010, Worlding the Matsutake Diaspora, or, Can Actor-Network-Theory Experiment with Holism? In T. Otto and N. Bubandt, *Experiments in Holism: Theory and Practice in Contemporary Anthropology*. Oxford: Wiley-Blackwell.

Viveiros de Castro, Eduardo, 2003, *And*. Manchester Papers in Social Anthropology 7. Manchester: Manchester University Press.

Walsh, E., 1988, *Democracy in the Shadows: Citizen Mobilization in the Wake of the Accident at Three Mile Island*. New York: Greenwood.
Weber, Max, 1978[1922], *Economy and Society: An Outline of Interpretive Sociology*. Berkeley: University of California Press.
Williams, Raymond, 1975[1973], *The Country and the City*. Oxford University Press.
Yarrow, Thomas and Jones, S., 2014, 'Stone is Stone': Engagement and Detachment in the Craft of Conservation Masonry. *Journal of the Royal Anthropological Institute* 20(2): 256–275.

Part I
Professionalism and expertise

1

Some merits and difficulties of detachment

Maryon McDonald

Introduction

This chapter is about the world of organ transplantation in the UK. A central point discussed here is one that may not be willingly discussed by everyone in their everyday life but it is one that professionals dealing with transplantation have to face on a daily basis. For transplantation to take place, a very difficult redefinition has to be effected in the body before them, from person to organs. The scenario is this: a person who has become a 'patient' may die and they may have wished to be an organ donor. The functional life of the organs then takes over from the functional life of the patient or person. This can sound blunt or straightforward but the moral materiality of this redefinitional process is one that cannot be effected by the untrained or faint-hearted.

We might say that there are clearly ontological shifts here of some import. They demand a form of professional engagement that we might recognise as detachment. This chapter is about clinical detachment and especially surgery, in which detachment is deemed to be evident within medicine. More particularly, we are going to be looking at some of the work of eradicating the social – at some of the activities that do the work of turning the person, an inherently social body (Lambert and McDonald 2009), into what can appear to be 'spare parts' (Fox and Swazey 1992). We will pay special attention to the field of anatomy, which is especially important in the training of surgeons, and has been important in making transplantation thinkable and practicable.

Social connection

While we will be paying attention here to fields that can seem to demand the eradication of the social, they also both rely on, and reproduce, social connection. Organ transplantation relies on the 'donation' of organs. At transplant conferences, presentations by medical professionals often begin with slides of graphs showing a disparity between the numbers of organs retrieved and of organs needed.[1] Exhortations to donation rely on notions of 'organ shortage'. Fewer fatal motor accidents in Europe, the wearing of motorcycle helmets, more Intensive Care Units (ICUs) and improved ICU technology (meaning greater medical effectiveness in the treatment of brain injuries) – plus an ageing population generally – have been among the many factors cited as having restricted the number of available organs. At the same time, demand has increased. An ageing population, increasing and better diagnoses of diseases such as end-stage kidney disease and liver disease, and the growing success of transplant technologies, have all resulted in more patients expecting or being eligible for treatment through transplantation. Fewer organs and more potential recipients were the concerns behind the UK Organ Donation taskforce report of 2008 (UKDT 2008). One ambitious aim that resulted was to increase the number or organs donated by 50 per cent within five years. Through greater advertising and, importantly, infrastructural changes within hospitals – including more nurses trained as transplant coordinators – this aim was achieved. There has been no room for complacency, however, and donation remains a paramount concern.

The donation of bodies, and later of body tissue and organs, seems to have begun in the nineteenth century through the actions of men such as Jeremy Bentham who bequeathed his body 'to Mankind' partly to help extricate anatomical dissection from its associations with punishment, the bodies of executed criminals and body-snatching. The bequeathing of their bodies by well-known men directly to science and medical science gained in momentum as the sciences took disciplinary shape and were seen to offer benefits. The language of the 'gift' occasionally made its appearance in, or through, these bequeathals but it was through the development of blood transfusions, then a new understanding of blood types, and the demands of two world wars, that the 'gift' and 'donation' became explicit and paramount in framing corporeal transactions of this kind. The Second World War both re-created and reinforced imaginary relationships of reciprocity, seen now as society congruent with the British nation in peril and need.[2] In this period, both gift and giver were redefined, with an increasing physical separation between 'donors' and 'recipients' reframed through the connections of both gift and nation. To this national society, the post-war welfare state gave further impetus and practical form – and it was within this framework that organ, and then other tissue, donation was launched. The association of gift and welfare has been emphasised most famously by Titmuss (1997)[3] but donation was already important (Whitfield 2013). From donation of whole bodies to blood and then on to organs and other tissue, a rhetoric of the 'gift' has suggested and confirmed social connection.

In the now heavily marketised world of the USA and the UK, it has remained an individual decision whether to 'opt-in' to the relations of donation (a situation upheld by the 2008 Task Force report in the UK), but in other European countries where nation or society have been given greater force, or where the 'individual' is less idealised than in the UK, then consent to donation might be presumed, unless a person chooses to 'opt out'.[4] Two further dualities are currently important in any donation of bodies or body parts: the distinction between person and thing, as well as that between gift and market. The first has been important since the abolition of slavery and the second can seem like an everyday experience – but both are distinctions that we have to work at. We buy gifts in a one-off market transaction and then the gifts will be used to established or renew social connection. Selling organs is rigorously excluded in European legislation.

The tendency towards an imagined collective in organ donation can seem to run counter to the tendency in social science in recent years to stop taking collective notions such as 'society', or indeed a domain of the social, for granted. Some of this latter theorising was born of worlds in the USA and UK in which 'society' cannot easily be found, and we might note that these are also worlds of voluntary 'opt-in' organ donation, requiring explicit consent. In France, whence some of the prominent theorists (e.g. Latour 2005) also emanate, the loss of an imagined Durkheimian cohesion and of the *lien social* have been a preoccupation over the last decade or more, with politicians critical of the liberalisation of the economy and a perceived growth of individualism. However, a strong *lien social* in organ 'donation', with consent presumed rather than required to be explicit, had already been operative in France since the earlier era of the 1970s. As notions of society, nation and the like have seemed to fade empirically in the UK, then some new modes of encouragement – such as not allowing waiting recipients to die – have been noticeable in the recruitment of organ donors in particular but donation is still the frame within which other lives are enhanced or saved.

In some form, organ donation and its rhetoric of the gift make it clear that transplantation relies on ideals of social connection, whether explicitly opted into or not. Within the hospital, however, some of the empirical practices of donation and transplantation currently rely on forms of social disconnection. What is meant here is not the social disconnection of the socially excluded – but forms of disconnection that range from anonymity in the objectified organ, for example, to aspirations by transplant professionals to a 'distanced' view that might have some strong historical resonance with ideals running from disinterestedness to cosmopolitanism (see Dear 1992; Anderson 2001). In the world of transplants, once we move away from the metaphoric of donation, the social and the personal can seem, ethnographically, to drain away.

We will turn first to anatomy. It is an anatomical body that affords organs within a dense tissue that has to be sorted out into relational parts in a world of structure and function. In scholarly historiographies of medicine, the development of the competing discipline of physiology in the eighteenth and nineteenth centuries is seen to have encouraged the import of function into the structures of anatomy, and this, together with lessons learnt from the removal of body parts through surgery, helped to develop a 'medico-surgery' (or 'surgicalised physiology') through which organ removal could later become organ replacement.[5] The learning of anatomy is particularly important in the training of the surgeons on whom transplantation relies. The details given in the following paragraphs are heavily condensed from some of the fieldwork I have undertaken in the domain of medical education and organ transplantation in the UK. The material in this chapter is taken from fieldwork carried out, first, in the anatomy classes of medical students, which implicate social bodies and disconnected cadavers;[6] and second, in the operating theatres of transplant surgeons in which organs are retrieved. This chapter takes the reader into these two sites in that order. These two arenas – that of anatomy classes and that of retrieval operating theatres – have been chosen, in part, for the congruence they offer. They might also suggest some of the merits and the difficulties that the accomplishment of professional detachment can imply.

Acquiring the body of a surgeon

The human body

In the medical curriculum, bodies have proliferated. Learning gross anatomy is still important even if it has been increasingly jostled by cellular and sub-cellular bodies. Anatomical bodies have themselves changed historically. This last point is evident in the anatomical atlases consulted by medical students. Late eighteenth- or early nineteenth-century images of bloodied, dead persons – posed decorously but with their bodies cut open and internal anatomical structures exposed – have progressively given way to depersonalised images, often reduced to diagrams.[7] Diagrams need no shadows, suggesting a view from nowhere. Progressively, such images became representations of nobody in particular. They have been important in the invention of – and have been required to represent – 'the human body'.

These later images were the outcome of various forms of 'objectivity' that developed during the nineteenth century, themselves part of the many strategies of impersonality and impartiality that followed on the universalist ambitions of the what we like still to call 'the Enlightenment'. Knowledge became divided into subjective and objective, and science and the arts developed distinct identities. Important in the practice of objectivity was an epistemic virtue of self-discipline and restraint (Daston and Galison 2007). For some, this was akin to the ideal of a factory machine. At the least, it involved discipline through which aspirations to dispassion, civility and disinterestedness from earlier periods were re-shaped. The idea was to quieten the observer so that nature could get on to the page. Ideally, a self-denying, interchangeable observer could offer direct representations of nature, of 'the body' as it is. For this purpose, the personal and artistic, and later the social and cultural, had ideally to be excluded.

Within the learning environment of an anatomy class, anatomical bodies are themselves multiple now. Some of them – for example, atlases or X-rays – are flat, two-dimensional and mobile. Many bodies are brought together within one space – within centimetres of each other. In any one class, we might see atlases, diagrams, manuals, posters, radiology (including X-rays, CT scans and MRIs), cadavers for dissection, skeletons, prosections, black or whiteboards, colleagues and teachers. Each of these media, these bodies, whether two- or three-dimensional and whether human or otherwise, could be said to condense its own trajectory of cognition. Atlases show the strong influence of cartography and of geology, which helped to supply the three-dimensional visual language of anatomy in the nineteenth century and have since provided a structural language to other areas of medicine too (Rudwick 1976; Varela 2001; Daston and Galison 2007). Anatomy often seems to be a world of topography – of sections, planes and landmarks – with these last terms common in the classes in both orientation and the naming of inherently relational parts. The result is an important three-dimensional topographical map that will ideally enable the students as medical professionals empirically to engage with a body and its parts, and to locate lesions.

In a modern dissection room in the UK, students do their own dissection, a practice described as having originated in Paris but already carried out in London in the eighteenth century (Cunningham 2010: 135ff). The order of anatomical dissection once followed roughly that of putrefaction, then drew attention to 'systems' (given impetus by the work of men such as Harvey as well as by the French Revolution), but returned to regions of the body again by the late nineteenth century under the influence of a surgery that had gained new confidence with the development of anaesthetics (Tobias 1992; Sawchuk 2012). This consolidation of surgery and anatomy brought landmarks to the fore, a standardised orientating body-language was instituted in the early twentieth century, and an orderly sequential manner for travelling into a body demarcated through a series of planes and landmarks became common convention in anatomy, pathology and surgery (Sawchuk 2012: 146). Systems or parts of them are still shown to be interconnected within regions, following three-dimensional innervations and perfusion 'routes', for example, seeing where nerves, veins and arteries 'run', or what they 'serve'.

Modern anatomy also uses sliced cadaveric cross-sections that seem to respect neither region nor system – but are influenced by MRIs and CTs, and the slices of the Visible Human Project (Waldby 2000; Prentice 2005). In the dissection room where I worked most often, the teachers met before classes and decided on inclusion and exclusion, what to 'see' and not to see, for the dissection to follow – and they would remind each other to 'keep it simple'(cf. Lynch 1985). In the classes, the students move from one medium to another – atlas, manual, skeleton, teacher, a drawing on the board, a diagram in a textbook, a colleague and the cadaver. It is not a case of a simple reality in all this – 'the human body' – of which students as subjects make a representation in their heads. The circumstances are more complicated. The students themselves acquire the medical body of an anatomist or surgeon – and they do so relationally both with other students and in an environment in which the boundary of 'cognition' or cognitive agency is not simply in the head but around the room and beyond. It is there not only in their own bodies, but in other persons, instruments, images and other artefacts, the cadavers included.

Cadavers, where present, loom large. These are persons discreetly transformed into important anatomical working objects of structures and functions. This transformation has many aspects. Standardisation of a kind occurs, and not just through publications. If we take the case of a cadaver and an atlas or manual: first, there is a selection of the body (avoiding gross pathology and obesity, for example, or the very young). The body then becomes, in this context, 'a cadaver' and the cadaver is dissected to approximate to the manual or atlas: drawings are made from dissections or prosections and these in turn guide dissection.[8] The process can move from diagrams to dissection to diagrams. It is a process of 'sculpting', as some technicians and teachers describe it (cf.

Hirschauer 1991 and below, on surgery). Such circularity is not uncommon in the production of working objects.

Within these classes, the cadaver holds authority as a referent. The cadaver is still seen to be necessary to confer authority on what are otherwise seen as 'representations'. This seems to be so within any one dissection room as well as between institutions, with medical students coming from elsewhere to take vacation courses in those institutions that still have cadaveric material. It seems to be so even if the cadaveric referent gets 'corrected' in turn by what a 'living body would look like'. What is sometimes known as 'living anatomy' or 'surface anatomy', using peers or models in classes, often goes on side by side with or after dissection classes. This is felt to be important and increasingly so. In the dissection room, time has been stopped. A cadaver involves an isolation and holding still of an object for inspection, from which students then depart in 'variations', in dynamics – in cellular and in living bodies – but to which they may well return. The medical images to which they will increasingly have recourse present similar issues (Cohn 2010; Edwards et al. 2010).

Consent and containment

'Get off!'
The students acquire new bodies in these classes in a dynamic way. It is a sensuous and progressive enterprise, producing at once a sensory medium and a sensitive world. The cadavers here are part and parcel of what it is to have a body, a particular body. Students are learning to be affected.

Sight and touch are especially important. Particular eyes are acquired; in an occulocentric world, they learn to see. Seeing 'what there is' always requires a practised vision but vision is never solely vision. The students look at a picture of the femoral triangle (an anatomical region of the upper inner thigh). They dissect and examine the relevant part of the cadaver. They recite a mnemonic many times, tapping three fingers in the air: 'V.A.N … vein, artery nerve.' It is important to know these distinctions. They feel the distinctions in the cadaver. Diagrams, manuals, atlases are consulted. The students reproduce the images, with the important distinctions drawn in their own colouring atlas, or actively coloured in by them in the manuals provided. The primary value of the colours is in their distinction. They do not 'represent' what is real but shape what is real. The students return to the cadaver: 'What are we looking at?' they ask each other. They consult the diagram again, then their own coloured notebooks and the atlases; then others' notes and pictures. They look at other dissections, other cadavers on neighbouring trolley-tables in the dissection room, then back to their own dissection and again at their own images, arrayed around the table now, and held up by colleagues to help.

The students may well, in their own terms, be matching up 'representations' with a reality here. However, the anthropologist might want to say that they are reconciling different objects – an image, an atlas picture or model with another image, model or cadaver – with both images and cadaver already 'landmarked' by the very same processes of 'representation'.

About six students, dressed in white coats and wearing gloves, are grouped around each cadaver, with each cadaver on a trolley-table. Students take it in turns in their group to dissect. One student cuts carefully with a scalpel, then pulls and tears with her fingers in what is known as 'blunt dissection'. They are through the skin, and then tackle the fascia and fat. One holds an atlas, another is asked to hold her hair back 'so I can see'. 'Show me my manual.' 'Where are my notes?' 'No, the coloured picture.' 'What has he drawn on the board over there?' Discussion with colleagues helps in the adjudication of 'what there is'. All the media are reconciled, some with more difficulty than others, through discussion and landmarks. The fingers are in the air and one of the ever-present mnemonics rings out again: 'V.A.N.'

Students are simultaneously seeing, touching and verbally defining, going back and forth. In the haptics of difference, they feel the distinctions in the cadaver and talk about them. The artery is large and springs back. The nerve is thinner. A male student practices meanwhile the triangle of 'V.A.N.' in both sing-song and fingers on a female colleague. She pulls away: 'Get off me!' This is a living person, a self in a body, a 'me'. Gendered and sexual bodies are not easily divested. But there is something else at work here. 'You should ask,' she says. 'OK – may I?' he responds. 'No,' comes the swift reply. In that touch is a definitional or ontological resolution of persons and of person and object. Important boundaries are effected in this way and the person is reconstituted in such micro-articulations as an individuated embodied self, autonomous with a will and choice.

We know from careful historical scholarship[9] that this body-self came into being historically over a long period in which – with considerable help from early anatomy – divisibility and indivisibility emerged together alongside, and then at the expense of, previously common ideas and practices of permeability. From roughly the sixteenth and seventeenth centuries onwards, the bounded and individuated body took shape in so many tiny instances of everyday life in articulation with the changing circumstances of religious reformation (and Protestant interiority), land enclosure, new conventions of landscape painting (separating person and the world), new architectures of privacy, machines and reflection on them, the publications of theologians and philosophers and new forms of knowledge, new institutions of work and education, ideas of improvement and progress, and new policings of body boundaries making leakage and spillage in both life and death abhorrent. And so on. There was no switch in all this from ideas of permeable bodies to a boundedness of bodies because it was discovered that they were not permeable; rather, there was an increasing idealisation and regulation of new comportments and bodily control that began to speak of an autonomous 'self' within the individuated boundaries of the skin.

This autonomous, bounded body-self is part of what students may already have acquired in relational everyday instances of their lives – but which they have to learn here in a new way. It is not a natural given: 'Get off!' This is a boundary formally marked in the medical arena by 'informed consent', the foundation of modern bioethical governance. The bodies that have been donated to form the working objects of anatomy will have had the consent of the individual donor carefully documented and stored in backrooms.

Long gone are the days when to study an element of God's creation or of some 'natural' world meant tasting or smelling it (see Roberts 1995; Daston and Galison 2007). The sensory regime of modern anatomical learning may not require smell and taste as part of its corporeal technology of learning but it does involve learning that there are at least five senses plus proprioception – and the experience of the dissection room tends to get resolved in turn into this sensory regime. Smell figures strongly. Indeed, the boundary of the sequestered world where dissection takes place is commonly marked by a pungent smell. It is often described by students as 'formaldehyde', although teachers insisted to me that there was very little formaldehyde in the preservation fluid used in the cadavers (and it was mixed with chemicals such as glycerine, liquid phenol and methylated spirits). Not being able to bear the smell was one reason given by students who felt they could not face dissection. That smell marked the boundary between the dissection room and a social world outside, and between bodies and cadavers.

'Get a grip!'
The transformation of donated body from the world outside to cadaver within is not simple. Once a body has been donated and accepted, it then has to be transformed into an anatomical model. The separation of the

self, the person, from the body is very difficult here as in other areas of life and death (e.g. Kaufman 2000; McDonald 2011). A person may be re-evoked – but the anatomical objectification is important. The process is not the disfigurement of a body as some might see it but is the creation of a body, of a particular anatomical body or cadaver.

Many aspects of the initial transformation process for anatomy, the transformation of person to cadaver, are deliberately occluded. They have been so since the nineteenth century but have become even more so in the UK with the post-Alder Hey Human Tissue Acts of 2004 and 2006. This occlusion is built into the architecture of the university buildings up and down the country where dissection takes place. There are discrete entrances where bodies can be brought, often hidden entrances where vans or lorries can be backed in.

The preservation process is then effected largely by technicians in back rooms. It is important work and is hidden from the eyes of the students and from most of the teachers. The buildings housing Dissection Rooms have high or opaque windows, if any at all. This social sequestration of anatomical dissection was, some scholars have argued, part of the salvation of anatomy in the eighteenth and nineteenth centuries, rescuing it from associations with execution, taking it out of the realm of not only public spectacle but also of public and punitary dissections (Chaplin 2007).

The preservation arrests the process of death in preventing putrefaction; it fixes a moment in which the timing and registration of death have already colluded. Further practices then emphasise the sequestration process at work. Bodies that are inherently social become cadavers here and are anonymised: anonymity severs relations. The outside social world is kept at bay. Cloths are sometimes placed over faces, or students or teachers cover up parts not being dissected.

When students first encounter the cadavers they have to dissect – when they encounter them with the bodies the students have themselves acquired up to that point – it is not uncommon for some to faint, feel sick, or in some instances to give up medicine altogether. Common excuses emerge from those so affected: they have recognised the dead man; they are menstruating or they have simply drunk too much the night before and need to sit on the floor, cling to the trolley, leave the room to be sick. There are difficult boundaries to cross, boundaries at once conceptual and practical, and very particular technologies of self are required. New bodies have to be acquired. 'When you start the dissection, it's science,' said one teacher. 'Just bear that in mind and it becomes easier.' 'Be objective', 'Distance yourself.' Students commonly warned each other to do this and described their own epistemological proprieties in these terms. 'You have to distance yourself.'

We see at work here a particular heritage of largely eighteenth- and nineteenth-century creations of the self in Europe – a period when knowledge became parsed in terms of objectivity and subjectivity. Objectivity and subjectivity constituted a duality of 'perspectives' on a world (or 'nature') deemed to exist independently. They were often congruent with other dualities of the time – male and female, reason and emotions, and so on. The subject of largely eighteenth- and nineteenth-century creation has to learn discipline, to learn or re-learn that they are a body-self composed internally of reason and emotions, a self that has to hold itself in check by acts of 'will' manifest in comportment.[10] If they do not hold it in check, the self or subjectivity will dominate the objectivity of the representation or activity, getting in the way. This is the force here of 'get a grip!' The self, as in the nineteenth century, often appears now in dissection classes as the site of emotions, of the person and partiality. Students fear they will cry, will faint, will get silly or simply not be able to learn. 'Just detach yourself from it' one student warned another who was finding the process difficult. 'Distance yourself …' 'You've just got to get a grip!'

I have suggested that in the nineteenth century, anatomical representations (for so they were often seen to be) such as atlases – similarly went through the transformations of different objectivities in which the self was felt to be dangerous intrusion. I have described the images that resulted. New ontologies were wrought by a clear-eyed and disciplined scientific vision (Daston and Galison 2007). This was and is a moral position – sobriety and self-discipline for the common good. Often what was once a prized, 'hands off' objectivity is now deemed to be a matter of embodied clinical judgement. But the clinician's body that is capable of such judgement has to be acquired and it takes discipline.

Transformations of the epistemological virtue that claimed objectivity in the representations of bodies in the nineteenth century can now seem to present themselves in practical conceptions of the capacity to get through, and learn from, dissection. 'Distancing yourself' is part of the technology of learning and it is also part of what is learnt. A demeanour of seriousness and equanimity results much of the time and is felt to be important. It is a demeanour gradually attained as the imbrications and articulations of cadavers, students and surrounding colleagues and technologies become routine. This is an epistemological propriety with which respect for the dead can, and does, collude. But it is not appropriate to cry in the dissection room. 'Get a grip'.

Both horror and amusement are common in these circumstances.

There is some deliberate teasing of those unable to 'get a grip' and there are jokes and pranks which it is feared that a new bioethical governance of medical and dissection room comportment, with respect and human dignity emphasised, will exclude. We live in a world quite accustomed to ontological multiplicities but the instability of the cadaver is important and can be worrying. The person re-emerges at various points: when a tattoo is noticed, or nail varnish or a catheter or pacemaker, or the colour of the lungs (suggesting smoking) or when blood is seen – 'yuk' – or when it is announced that the arms have gone or other parts have been removed for prosections: 'Oh my God ... gruesome ... I can't take this.' Such claims – or a 'yuk' – increasingly elicit a 'don't be silly' or 'get a grip' from colleagues. This is ideally a world of reason not emotions, of sobriety not silliness. Often a 'yuk', or a similar concern, is heard when the person seems to re-emerge in the cadaver during the dissection classes. When violated, that individuated body-self properly bounded by its skin elicits exclamations of 'gruesome'. Both horror and laughter can result when the reflexive selves of the students bring the outside world into the dissection room in this way. Humour is generated when students notionally reflect on their activity and the cadaveric objects as if it were all viewed by an outsider, by someone who has not acquired the bodies they are themselves acquiring: 'If my mother could see me now ...' Or, in a deliberately mundane accent when washing hands at the basins afterwards: 'How time flies when you're cutting up dead bodies!' Both the humour and the chivvying to 'get a grip' are engagements that play on the ontological instability of the cadaver, but they also, through the team around it, support the detachment acquired – a necessary detachment lived as a calmness and equanimity in the face of death, nakedness, leaking and spillages, and a scalpel into the skin, bowels on the surface, or an arm missing and organs exposed.

A social body again

The cadavers are deliberately moved back to bodies – to social bodies – again at the end of the year. Memorial, thanksgiving services are generally held everywhere at the end of the course annually or biannually once the dissection is over. Donation and the gift are emphasised in speeches and poems from students, who express gratitude and respect for the donor and the help they have given. This becomes a world of social connection again, but it is one that has moved from Bentham's pioneering donation through a newer national rhetoric of 'society' and post-Second World War welfare and on to a bioethical governance of which the object now is the *will* of donors (with their willing choice monitored in documentation) and for which, in these services, thanks are given.[11] These are services attended by both students and teachers, constituted as grateful recipients. Over the preceding year, everything from each individual cadaver – all the bits, all the fascia and fat, et cetera – had gone into single, individuated receptacles under the tables throughout the dissection process. Now every part goes back together into individuated coffins. The coffins may be lined up in the services and sometimes relatives of the deceased also attend. In such services, the social person is reinstantiated – a subject again at the centre of relations.

Organ retrieval

We move now to the rather different scene of an operating theatre in which organs are removed by trained surgeons from organ donors.

In an operating theatre, we are already in a world protected not only from germs but from the wider social world. Within the hospital, operating theatres are often difficult to find. Within the theatre, staff, instruments and patients each have their own circuits of hygiene, moving in and out by different routes, eliminating the 'dirt' of everyday socialities. At the centre is a zone of sterility. Street clothes are changed for gowns and masks, surgeons get 'scrubbed up', and the person who has become a patient in hospital routines now disappears on a trolley – an operating table here – under green drapes. In place of the person, a scientific object appears to be constructed – a space in which the anatomy is 'sculpted' (as Hirschauer 1991 has pointed out), ideally to replicate the textbook.

If the patient is a live donor, as may well be the case with kidneys or a liver lobe, for example, the process will have begun the day before, when the surgeon begins the conversion of the person into an anatomical body with diagrammatic sweeps of a pen on patient flesh. These required marks can have regulatory force – ensuring the right body part or side is marked – but surgeons may talk of them as 'thinking lines', giving the time and space to think in advance about 'the structures underneath'. In theatre, there is talk of dissection, landmarks, planes. The body is strongly cartographic in both anatomical representation and in its replication in the operating theatre. Different bodies from CTs, MRIs and patient records have to be reconciled with each other and further reconciled with the mass of human tissue on the operating table. The senior surgeon may point out landmarks, and staff consult and re-consult images and notes. Surgeons have got be able to 'see': they have to cut to see and have to see to cut. It is vital here to sculpt carefully. A senior surgeon may offer guidance or self-commentary, chatter and jokes can intrude, but a silent concentration, encouraged by hushed whispers, will often dominate long moments of tension. This is not the more traditional surgery of extirpation – cutting out a diseased body part. In this surgery, anatomical dissection and resection seek out an organ that is not 'waste' but a therapeutic tool. Precision is, therefore, doubly vital, for both donor and future recipient. This tool, once the operation has begun, will cease to be talked of as the kidney of the patient on the operating table. It gradually becomes not Mrs Smith's kidney – but 'the kidney'. Progressively, social and surgical resection are one. We are then momentarily in a world of organs, in a different ontological order.

Following an operation, requests from an observer for clarification from the attending surgeons are often responded to with swift and helpful diagrams. The organs removed do not always look like the images. A lump of yellow fat removed and placed on a back table in one operation prompted a 'what's that?' exclamation from another surgeon. From within this fat, a kidney had to be surgically sculpted, with vein-artery-ureter concern.

This world of organs is largely a mechanistic one. Organs have historically had a long emblematic life, once linking the corporeal to the spiritual. Important changes occurred in the nineteenth century especially. From organs as the instruments of the soul, demonstrating an external or extra-somatic source of life, a new perception gained shape – of life residing in the depth and interiority of the body, in the very organisation of the body's constituent parts. This body and its parts were already largely mechanical in their workings, and particularly the major organs. By the late nineteenth century, disease had been located within the patient and the organs presented circumscribed objects for surgical intervention. From being the last abode of vitalism, the kidney had become a part of the machine and, by the 1930s, had clear and important functions of filtration. Technologies from imaging to staining have given a kidney of glomerular filtration, and then measurable levels of creatinine. A 'good kidney', in situ, will leave low creatinine levels. While external machines are currently in development to test this before transplantation, it is the clinical judgement of the surgeon – through sight and touch – that still offers the main resources for judging whether a good kidney has been retrieved. It is the kidney that became the historical prototype of organ replacement (Schlich 2010).

Most organs, kidneys included, are supplied through 'cadaveric donation'. This means that the relevant organ or organs are removed after the death of the patient who wished to be a donor. Consent will have been tracked through documentation. Generally, if the individual himself or herself has not given explicit consent, then kin are asked – or the closest relations through whom the notional 'individual' has been constituted. Once the retrieval operation is scheduled, we are very much in a world of the 'anatomy lesson': this was a description that nurses and transplant coordinators often volunteered of a surgical operation that is otherwise subsumed under 'organ retrieval'.

Retrieval from cadaveric donation is acknowledged to be a difficult operation to face – and it is one which, in some hospitals, nurses are allowed to opt out of attending if they wish. Part – but only part – of the difficulty is presented by the fact that the patient on the operating table is dead: there will be no recovery. Throughout the procedure we are watching life-and-death practices of ontological definition. We can take the example here of a patient – a would-be donor – who has died from cardio-respiratory failure. The person fades away but the organs are alive and must remain so. A minimum of a stipulated five-minute wait after asystole passes – and we are then in the world of organs.[12] There can be a great deal of noise and a sense of speed and nervousness but equanimity must reign and careful dissection is paramount. Surgeons may call out anatomical landmarks and procedures as they dissect. But the choreography is not quite that of the live donor operation. Staff sometimes bump into one another, each pursuing their own task – a specific organ or perfusion, another bag or label. Directions may be given, anatomical structures cross-checked between colleagues. 'What have we got here?' Some body parts are hurriedly moved aside or resected. A receptacle is available for collection if necessary. There is a great deal of blood. The spilling of blood is not material here. Only the organs must remain perfused and this will have been done as a priority through the insertion of cannulas. Some staff (and the anthropologist) can feel tested for their capacity to switch – and to switch fast – from social to anatomical body, tested for their detachment. I am offered a chair to sit down if I wish, and told stories of those who have fainted. 'Anatomy lesson' it is. But it is one effected on the very recently dead and under serious time pressures: we are in the time of the organs, which is noted carefully before despatch.[13]

It needs to be stressed here that such an operation is very far from any careless disfigurement of a person but is a necessarily careful effort to get good organs and thereby save lives.[14] A few surgeons have appeared to worry that a non-medical observer (one, in our terms, who has not acquired a surgical body) might misunderstand, and have later stressed their place in a world of social connection, albeit anonymous: they are trying to ensure that the donor's wishes are fulfilled and that a recipient life will be duly enhanced or saved. In the meantime, back in the operating theatre, a variety of other caring practices continue. Once the organs are out and on their way to recipient(s), any fears by donor relatives of disfigurement (a fear sometimes voiced to coordinators) are carefully assuaged in advance as surgical sutures are effected and then nursing staff carry out the 'last offices'. The deceased person then re-emerges on the operating table, gently washed and clothed in a shroud. This is again a time of the social and a time of emotions. Nurses work together, one of them a transplant coordinator, and they notice personal aspects – the hair of the deceased, for example, which they may touchingly comb or smooth. They are shifting back into a world in which the family may want to see the person again, a subject once more at the centre of relations.

Occasionally, there can be noticeable differences between an operating theatre nurse and the transplant coordinator if, when doing the last offices together, a nurse places a cloth over the face of the deceased. It is the transplant coordinator who has to move between this very difficult 'anatomy lesson' and the family of the deceased, and who is the more concerned to move the deceased smartly from anatomical object to person again. She may then tactfully remove the face cloth. In the meantime, the retrieval surgeon will usually sit at one side of the operating theatre checking and filling in paperwork that medically tracks the organ. It is not uncommon for a clasped hand of the deceased to be opened by nurses in the washing process – and then family mementoes, so recently placed into the hand of the dying person by someone close to them, may be revealed. Nurses take care to replace them, to keep these with the deceased. 'Isn't it sad?' comments one nurse to the surgeon. 'I don't want to know, I don't want to know!' comes the sharp reply from a disinterested surgical focus that is deliberately elsewhere. As surgical hands wave in the air at once dismissively and protectively in company with this comment, a stereotypical world – in which surgical detachment is traduced as social pathology and uncaring arrogance – is confirmed in the instantaneous condemnation of nursing whispers: 'Oh, isn't he awful?'

Conclusion: a social accomplishment

Since the cultivation of various recensions of detachment in Europe might be seen historically to have carried with it all the promises of modernity (Anderson 2001: 4) then it is perhaps inevitable that a world that has passed through critical dissent from modernity will find that detachment eliding with other objects of due criticism. The clinical detachment we have seen, however, is an important social accomplishment and there is a danger of throwing the baby out with the bathwater.

Strong relations of mutual support, and jokes, occur among all staff – including between surgeons – in the operating theatres. As in the anatomy classes, this mutual support is important, enabling the ideal surgical comportment of disciplined detachment during surgical practice. This comportment has to be worked at but is still congruent in some important ways with the ideal of masculinity as it developed with national education and military service from the nineteenth century onwards particularly. It is ideally self-restrained, unemotional and has a pantheon of heroic exemplars. This has no doubt made it difficult for women to enter the profession. From the 1960s onwards, various feminisms and populisms and protests against a variously patriarchal or high-tech medicine and science alike have helped to put any such medical comportment in question. It has been partly for these reasons that the teaching of anatomy through cadaveric dissection has also been through periods of recent controversy.[15]

Other medical specialists still variously tease, fear or resent surgeons, and medical students have worried about whether it is a specialty to enter or not (Cherrington 2008). A gowned and masked surgeon with a precision-sharp scalpel can certainly seem to be the scarier end of detachment. It is no doubt possible, and empirically confirmed, for any individual surgeon to slide in their own behaviour from clinical detachment to machismo or arrogance, whether perceived by others or self-assumed, and senior surgeons have openly expressed worries to me that those unable to make social relations easily may be attracted to a socially sequestered speciality, as surgery can appear to be much of the time. The achievement and practice of detachment in this milieu could be said to involve profoundly relational and associative work, and the detachment required is not meant to be, and is increasingly not allowed to be, any easy and inherent social disconnection. Where surgeons practise in interdisciplinary teams, as transplant specialists have to do, it is noticeable that the same medical staff who may seem relentlessly to tease or condemn surgeons – and describe them as awful – may also praise their kindness to patients and the care and commitment they show. Increasingly, changes in medical education and in the demands placed on surgical practitioners have meant that any serious difficulties in switching from 'the anatomy lesson' to caring communication with a patient ill in bed might be recognised, by all, as itself pathological. It is also precisely through the social connection of these specialists, both historically (Maulitz 1987, 1993) and today, in the meetings and assemblages of scientific medicine and academia more generally, that a world of apparently universal 'organs' and both their retrieval and transplant procedures have been effected and perfected. In the UK, some active version of 'ontological choreography'[16] is acquired or practised by everyone in their daily lives. One important difference here is that, in the construction of the spaces of anatomical intervention and surgical practice, this choreography is in many ways one of life and death.

I opened this chapter with the learning of anatomy. It is anatomy that affords organs, and anatomy that is still central to the production of surgeons. We have seen that learning anatomy is not a matter of individuated minds representing a world 'out there' and it is not a world analytically of either subjects or objects anterior to the relations that produce them. Rather, both students and students, and students and teachers, and students and teachers and all the working objects, are all articulated the one with the other – and this continues in the operating theatre when surgery is practised. For the student or practitioner, other bodies intrude but their divestment, or the apparent conversion of a person into an object of examination or intervention, requires self-conscious attention to a subject with a will and choice – consent. An ontology of will, choice and consent has been evident in the very large 'ethical' industry that organ transplantation has spawned around itself. In the 'science and society' couplet as it has appeared in the UK and elsewhere, it is as 'ethics' that the social has most noticeably re-entered, and it is as 'bioethics' that the social body makes one of its reappearances, in reassuringly normative form, in the ambit of medicine. While ethics as a category and practice can seem to sit ethnographically at the edges of medicine in this way, it is also the case that, analytically, processes of ethical self-transformation (Laidlaw 2014) could be said to be at its core.

The use of technologies and objects – and of one another – to extend human capacities is not new, although it has been given some novel formulations in studies of scientific practice.[17] In the case of anatomical and surgical dissection, bodies become very much a part of the technology of learning and are necessarily changed by it. In a perhaps appropriately occulocentric conclusion, we might say that becoming a surgeon involves the acquisition of a surgical body – and this is a distributed process relying on connections between landmarks which are only marks to the knowing eye, and to eyes which are only knowing in the right body.[18] The surgeon's body is one that has learnt to be affected by circumstances that have shaped an ethnographically interesting being: an individual composed of reason and emotions in a context valuing self-containment. The detachment acquired is not the distanced view of cosmopolitanism, even if congruent with it in some ways, nor is it an inherent 'lack' – a lack of sensitivity, emotions or empathy, for example (cf. Hildebrandt 2010) – even if the limits of certain lived dualities might seem to require that. Rather, it is the acquisition of a newly sensitised and sensitive body that has demanded, and continues to demand, its own engagement.

Acknowledgements

I would like to thank all those who tolerated me in their anatomy classes and operating theatres (as part of local clinical audit) and who patiently helped me to understand something of their skills, the efforts required in their acquisition and practice, and some of the problems they face. I am grateful to the Leverhulme Trust for funding the research on which this chapter draws, and to the anonymous reviewers for their comments.

Notes

1. See also www.nhsbt.nhs.uk (accessed 15 May 2014).
2. The experience of war in the twentieth century also created a reciprocity based on bodily sacrifice, and a sense of 'sacrifice' is often salient for organ donor families in the UK (see especially Sque et al. 2006). On the changes war effected in the understandings of debility – male debility in particular – which became another means through which nation, society and welfare were thought and instantiated, see, for example, Bourke 1996. I am grateful to Catherine Trundle for drawing my attention to this work.
3. Titmuss had, of course, been inspired by the work of the socialist-leaning Frenchman, Marcel Mauss, whose *Essai sur le don*, written in the 1920s, had already been translated into English (Mauss 1966[1954]). The work of Mauss has generated much discussion within anthropology and outside it. In the field of organ donation, the sense of debt that the donation of an organ can generate in the recipient, with the Maussian gift seeming to demand repayment, has raised very real and widespread concerns about 'the tyranny of the gift' (Fox and Swazey 1992) and encouraged practices of donor and recipient anonymisation.
4. From 2015, Wales will become the first nation of the UK to try its own 'opt-out' system – to be known, however, as 'deemed consent'.
5. See e.g. Maulitz 1993; Trohler 1993; Cunningham 1997, 2010; Schlich 2010.
6. The outline of the learning of anatomy in this chapter is taken in large part from McDonald 2014, where more details can be found.
7. As examples of a common format, see Gosling, Harris, Whitmore and Willan (2002), or Whitaker and Borley (2000). For sample figures showing these changes, see McDonald (2014).
8. Dissection done by technicians produces 'prosections' – meaning already dissected parts of the cadaver – for classes or tests on specific regions, or on regions that might be considered too complicated or time-consuming for the students themselves to dissect.
9. See Tarlow (2011); Robb and Harris (2013).
10. There were several diseases of the will in nineteenth century – including addiction.
11. On some related aspects of retrieval and donation in the UK, see Titmuss

1997[1970]; Richardson (1987); McDonald (2009); Reubi (2012). For the USA, see Young (1997); Sappol (2002); Goodwin (2006).
12 For some critical issues here, see McDonald (2011) and the references therein.
13 Warm ischaemic time is the most critical; the literature on warm and cold ischaemic times is immense but see the guidelines from the British Transplantation Society (2013).
14 Detachment might be said to be one of the many, not always obvious, practices of 'care' in medicine; on this theme more generally, see Mol (2008).
15 Anatomical study through cadavers, or the time spent on this, has been diminishing in the UK for several reasons – partly pedagogical. Less memorising of parts and more clinical problem solving was advocated in the 1990s, with reforms in medical education also seeking to bring the personal and the social back in (GMC 1993, 1997; BMA 1995). Some of the lived dualities involved (including objectivity/subjectivity, reason/emotions) have appeared to impose their own elisions and constraints to the point that dissection, and the detachment acquired, have been feared to be eclipsing the capacity for 'empathy' in medicine (see Halpern 2001 and Hildebrandt 2010 on the USA). The best-known dissection rooms have continued in the UK, with both dissection of cadavers and living anatomy taught. See Turney (2007) for some of the changes in anatomy teaching in recent times; and Ganguly and Chan (2008) for a more general discussion. Plastic models, digital models (e.g. the Visible Human) and body painting are not uncommon in anatomy classes in the UK; plastinated prosections are also used, in one instance bought directly from Von Hagens. Histology – or the microscopic anatomy of cellular structures – is everywhere taught alongside, but is not part of, gross anatomy. One new medical school in the UK famously declined to have cadaveric material for gross anatomy, whether for dissection or as prosections: see Mclachlan and Regan de Bere (2004).
16 Cf. Cussins (1996).
17 See McDonald (2012) for a summary.
18 Cf. Candea (2008: 209) on 'knowing' a place. I say earlier that this is perhaps an 'appropriately occulocentric conclusion' because a historical dominance of vision in certain parts of the world – including Europe and the USA – is often said to have facilitated a 'distancing' effect; on this, see for example Howes (2004); and other sources noted both there and in McDonald (2012).

References

Anderson, Amanda, 2001, *Powers of Distance: Cosmopolitanism and the Cultivation of Detachment*. Princeton: Princeton University Press.
Bourke, Joanna, 1996, *Dismembering the Male. Men's Bodies, Britain and the Great War*. London: Reaktion Books.
British Medical Association, 1995, *Report of the Working Party on Medical Education*. London: BMA.
British Transplantation Society, 2013, *United Kingdom Guidelines*.

Transplantation from Donors after Deceased Circulatory Death. Available at www.bts.org.uk, posted March 2013 (accessed 15 May 2014).

Candea, Matei, 2008, Fire and Identity as Matters of Concern in Corsica. *Anthropological Theory* 8(2): 201–216.

Chaplin, Simon, 2007, Exemplary Bodies: Public and Private Dissections in Georgian London. Paper presented at Representations of Early Modern Anatomy and the Human Body Workshop, Centre for the History of Disease, Durham University.

Cherrington, Laura, 2008, 'I'm a Surgeon. Respect Me!' *StudentBMJ* 16: 13–15. Available at www.studentbmj.com (accessed 15 May 2014).

Cohn, Simon, 2010, Picturing the Brain Inside, Revealing the Illness Outside. In J. Edwards, P. Harvey, and P. Wade, eds, *Technologized Images, Technologized Bodies*. Oxford and New York: Berghahn, pp. 65–84.

Cunningham, Andrew, 1997, *The Anatomical Renaissance: the Resurrection of the Anatomical projects of the Ancients*. Aldershot: Scolar.

Cunningham, Andrew, 2010 *The Anatomist Anatomis'd. An Experimental Discipline in Enlightenment Europe*. Farnham: Ashgate (The History of Medicine in Context Series).

Cussins, Charis, 1996, Ontological Choreography: Agency through Objectification in Infertility Clinics. *Social Studies of Science* 26(3): 575–610.

Daston, Lorraine and Peter Galison, 2007, *Objectivity*. New York: Zone Books.

Dear, Peter, 1992, From Truth to Disinterestedness in the Seventeenth Century. *Social Studies of Science* 22: 610–631.

Edwards, Jeanette, Harvey, Penelope and Peter Wade, eds, 2010, *Technologized Images, Technologized Bodies*. Oxford and New York: Berghahn.

Fox, Renée and Swazey, Judith, 1992, *Spare Parts: Organ Replacement in American Society*. New York: Oxford University Press.

Ganguly, Pallab K. and Lap K. Chan, 2008, Living Anatomy in the 21st Century: How Far can we Go? *South East Asian Journal of Medical Education* 2(2): 52–57.

General Medical Council (GMC), 1993, *Tomorrow's Doctors*. London: GMC.

General Medical Council (GMC), 1997, *The New Doctors*. London: GMC.

Goodwin, Michele, 2006, *Black Markets: The Supply and Demand of Body Parts*. New York: Cambridge University Press.

Gosling, John A., Harris, Philip, Whitmore, Ian and Willan, Peter L. T., 2002, *Human Anatomy: Color Atlas and Text*. London and New York: Elsevier.

Halpern, Jodi, 2001, *From Detached Concern to Empathy. Humanizing Medical Education*. New York and Oxford: Oxford University Press.

Hildebrandt, Sabine, 2010, Developing Empathy and Clinical Detachment During the Dissection Course in Gross Anatomy. *Anatomical Sciences Education* 3(4): 216.

Hirschauer, Stefan, 1991, The Manufacture of Bodies in Surgery. *Social Studies of Science* 21: 279–319.

Howes, David (ed.), 2004, *The Empire of the Senses*. Oxford: Berg.

Kaufman, Sharon, 2000, In the Shadow of 'Death with Dignity': Medicine and Cultural Quandaries of the Vegetative State. *American Anthropologist* 102(1): 69–83.

Laidlaw, James, 2014, *The Subject of Virtue. An Anthropology of Ethics and Freedom*. Cambridge: Cambridge University Press.

Lambert, Helen and McDonald, Maryon, 2009, Introduction. In H. Lambert and M. McDonald, eds, *Social Bodies*. NY and Oxford: Berghahn, pp. 1–15.

Latour, Bruno, 2005, *Reassembling the Social: An Introduction to Actor-Network Theory*. Oxford and New York: Oxford University Press.

Lynch, Michael, 1985, Discipline and the Material Forms of Images: An Analysis of Scientific Visibility. *Social Studies of Science* 15(1): 37–66.

McDonald, Maryon, 2011, Deceased Organ Donation, Culture and the Objectivity of Death. In W. Weimar, ed., *Organ Transplantation: Ethical, Legal and Psycho-Social Aspects*. Eichengrund: Pabst Science Publishers, pp. 267–273.

McDonald, Maryon, 2012, Medical Anthropology and Anthropological Studies of Science. In U. Kockel, M. Nic Craith and J. Frykman, eds, *Companion to the Anthropology of Europe*. Oxford: Wiley-Blackwell, pp. 459–479.

McDonald, Maryon, 2014, Bodies and Cadavers. In Penny Harvey, Eleanor Conlin Casella, Gillian Evans, Hannah Knox, Christine McLean, Elizabeth B. Silva, Nicholas Thoburn, Kath Woodwards, eds, *Objects and Materials. A Routledge Companion*. London and New York: Routledge, pp. 128–143.

Mclachlan, John C. and Regan De Bere, Samantha, 2004, How We Teach Anatomy Without Cadavers. *The Clinical Teacher* 1(2): 49–52.

Manson, Neil and O'Neill, Onora, 2007, *Rethinking Informed Consent in Bioethics*. Cambridge: Cambridge University Press.

Maulitz, Russell, 1987, *Morbid Appearances: The Anatomy of Pathology in the Early Nineteenth Century*. Cambridge: Cambridge University Press.

Maulitz, Russell, 1993, The Pathological Tradition. In W. Bynum and R. Porter, eds, *Companion Encyclopedia of the History of Medicine*, vol. 1. London: Routledge, pp. 169–191.

Mauss, Marcel, 1966[1954], *The Gift. Forms and Functions of Exchange in Archaic Societies* (translated by Ian Cunnision). London: Cohen and West Ltd.

Mol, Annemarie, 2002, *The Body Multiple. Ontology in Medical Practice*. Durham: Duke University Press.

Mol, Annemarie, 2008 *The Logic of Care*. Abingdon: Routledge.

Prentice, Rachel, 2005, The Anatomy of a Surgical Simulation: The Mutual Articulation of Bodies in and through the Machine. *Social Studies of Science* 35(6): 837–866.

Reubi, David, 2010, The Will to Modernize: A Genealogy of Biomedical Research Ethics in Singapore. *International Political Sociology* 4(2):142–158.

Reubi, David, 2012, The Human Capacity to Reflect and Decide. *Social Studies of Science* 42(3): 348–368.

Richardson, Ruth, 1987, *Death, Dissection, and the Destitute*. London: Routledge & Kegan Paul.

Richardson, Ruth, 2000, A Necessary Inhumanity. *Journal of Medical Ethics: Medical Humanities* 26: 104–106.

Roberts, Lissa, 1995, The Death of the Sensuous Chemist: the 'New' Chemistry and the Transformation of Sensuous Technology. *Studies in the History and Philosophy of Science* 26(4): 503–529.

Robb, John and Harris, Oliver et al., 2013, *The Body in History*. Cambridge: Cambridge University Press.

Rudwick, Martin, 1976, The Emergence of a Visual Language for Geological Science 1760–1840. *History of Science* 14: 149–195.

Sappol, Michael, 2002, *A Traffic in Dead Bodies: Anatomy and Embodied Social Identity in Nineteenth-Century America*. Princeton, NJ: Princeton University Press.

Sawchuk, Kim, 2012, Animating the Anatomical Specimen: Regional Dissection and the Incorporation of Photography in J. C. B. Grant's An Atlas of Anatomy. *Body & Society* 18(1): 120–150.

Schlich, Thomas, 2010, *The Origins of Organ Transplantation*. Rochester, NY: University of Rochester Press

Sque, Magi, Payne, Susan and Macleod Clark, Jill, 2006, Gift of Life or Sacrifice? Key Discourses to Understanding Organ Donor Families' Decision-making. Mortality 11(2): 117–132.

Tarlow, Sarah, 2011, *Ritual, Belief and the Dead in Early Modern Britain and Ireland*. Cambridge: Cambridge University Press.

Tobias, Phillip, 1992, The Contributions of J. C. Boileau Grant to the Teaching of Anatomy. *South African Journal of Medicine* 83: 352–353.

Titmuss, Richard, 1997[1970], *The Gift Relationship: From Blood to Social Policy*, edited by Ann Oakley and John Ashton. London: London School of Economics.

Trohler, Ulrich, 1993, Surgery(Modern). In W. Bynum and R. Porter, eds, *Companion Encyclopedia of the History of Medicine*, vol. 2. London: Routledge, pp. 984–1028.

Turney, Ben, 2007, Anatomy in a Modern Medical Curriculum. *Annals of the Royal College of Surgeons of England* 89(2): 104–107.

UK Donation Taskforce (UKDT), 2008, *Organs for Transplants. A Report from the Organ Donation Taskforce*. London: Department of Health.

Varela, F., 2001, Intimate Distances, in *Journal of Consciousness Studies* 8 (5–7): 259–271.

Waldby, Catherine, 2000, *The Visible Human Project: Informatic Bodies and Posthuman Medicine*. London and New York: Routledge.

Whitaker, R. and Borley, N., 2000, *Instant Anatomy*. Oxford: Blackwell.

Whitfield, Nicholas, 2013, Who is my Stranger? Origins of the Gift in Wartime London, 1939–45. *Journal of the Royal Anthropological Institute* 19 (Supplement S1): S95–S117.

Young, K., 1997, *Presence in the Flesh: The Body in Medicine*. Cambridge, MA: Harvard University Press.

2

Virtuous detachments in engineering practice – on the ethics of (not) making a difference

Hannah Knox and Penny Harvey

Introduction

Enrique Solari Swayne's play, *Collacocha*,[1] first performed in Lima in 1956, tells the apocryphal tale of a Peruvian engineer and his encounter with the forces of nature and society. Echecopar is the charismatic, driven and single-minded head engineer of an Andean mineral mine. More at home underground in the oppressive heat of the mine, than in the cosmopolitan society life of Lima, he is defined by his incapacity for conventional norms of social attachment and his unswerving belief in the structural integrity of the mine that he oversees as he works to transform nature in the name of progress. However, Echecopar's world is literally shaken to its core when disaster befalls the mine and a cave collapses killing 180 workers. The play follows Echecopar's denial of the impending catastrophe that is foretold by the shuddering and shaking of the mountain walls and the exhortations of his colleagues, his response to the disaster as it unfolds and the subsequent transformation that the event brings about in Echecopar's character. Master of all he surveys (Burnett 2000), yet powerless in the face of disaster, working in the name of social transformation yet seemingly indifferent to the social world that surrounds him, Echecopar provides a caricature of the modernist engineer. His attitude to impending disaster exemplifies the detachment that is necessary to make action possible in a world of dangerous uncertainties. And yet as the story unfolds, his character transforms as he struggles to reconcile such detachment with the impulse to engage with the complex and unforeseen social effects of engineering practice.

In this chapter we set out to explore how these dynamics of detachment and responsibility play out in contemporary engineering practice. Since Latour and Woolgar's groundbreaking study of laboratory life (Latour and Woolgar 1979), the epistemological practices of attachment and detachment through which contemporary forms of knowledge are enacted has become a concern of both anthropology and science and technology studies. Anthropologists have a long-standing interest in the relational basis of human beings, exemplified by their very particular commitment to study of kinship, as the study of the ways in which human beings create (open) and limit (close) relational fields (Strathern 1995). As such, anthropologists have often been critical of modern knowledge practices, which are deemed reductive of the inherent complexity and richness of social and material life, and are thus violent in their bureaucratic and administrative effects (e.g. Scott 1998; Kirsch 2014). This critique of modern knowledge making has also been extended to the production of academic knowledge, including established forms of ethnographic research. The descriptive techniques of traditional ethnography that worked to stabilise and delimit relations between people and things, by focusing on local practice and specific situational encounters, were unsettled by approaches that demanded attention to more extended geographical, social and political relations (e.g. Ong and Collier 2004). Crossing over with science and technology studies in their interest in material relations, other anthropologists have been at pains to demonstrate the intrinsic sociality of things, tracing how objects acquire relational biographies as they circulate and become entangled in the complex histories of those who produce and dispose of them (e.g. Appadurai 1986; Thomas 1991). Central to these approaches has been a focus on relational ontologies, that is, an understanding of all entities as multiple and emergent (Brown 2001; Law and Mol 2002; Mol 2002; Harvey et al. 2013).

Despite disagreements between anthropologists and actor network theorists as to how the relation is best construed (as network or meshwork, e.g. Ingold 2011), there is a general agreement between scholars working in these fields, that relational dynamics should be the focus of analytical attention. Bruno Latour, for example, recovers Gabriel Tarde as the ancestral influence for this approach, revisiting the historical conflict between Durkheim and Tarde and suggesting that the latter offers a more productive approach to the relational complexities of material life (Latour 2002, 2005; Candea 2010). Deleuzian approaches have also been very influential in provoking scholars to attend to those heterogeneous assemblages that combine the material, the symbolic, the technical and the political in complex ways (Bruun Jensen and Rödje 2010).

Like the potentiality of a relativist approach, which always finds a way of responding to seemingly indisputable realist problems (Grint and Woolgar 1992), a sensitivity to connection produces a cascading panoply of lines of interconnectedness and complexity. Following these connections produces a rich and multifaceted account of social process, but even the most vociferous adherent to a philosophy of connection finds that they must stop somewhere (Strathern 1996). The description of social realities entails its own practices of detachment, its own choices over what is deemed important or relevant for inclusion. A sensitivity to connection produces the impetus for re-description, but description itself never ensues without acts of detachment as well.

This acceptance that people, places and things are often far more entangled than they might as first seem has consequently prompted critical analysis of those modern knowledge practices that assume particular categorical structures and divisions without acknowledging the role that these analytical devices have in shaping the worlds that they set out to understand and transform (e.g. Lampland and Star 2008; Bowker and Star 1999; Hacking 1999; Lury and Wakeford 2012). Latour (1987, 1993) for example, has explored science as the enactment of particular set of practices and technologies whose capacity for establishing boundaries and divisions lies at the heart of their generative potential. Similarly, Callon (1998) has analysed economics through attention to practices of 'framing' which he has argued renders the world calculable, and in doing so has produced the conditions within which the figure of a rational calculative agency is born. The importance of detachment to modern forms of knowledge production has also been explored imaginatively by scholars of the history of science who have shown in some detail what it takes to isolate (i.e. to fully identify and define) an object of experimental concern or professional attention (Shapin and Schaffer 1985). They have shown us how the value accorded to objectivity, derives at least in part from the skill and effort required to achieve this act of identification, describing the massively complex arrangements of persons, things, ideas and practices involved (Latour and Woolgar 1979; Daston and Galison 2007). Moreover, they have shown us that despite the efforts and the struggles, scientific expertise is not only hard won, but also socially vulnerable and needs a further institutional apparatus to protect the standards and the standing of the skilled practitioner (Latour 1988; Bensaude-Vincent and Stengers 1996).

This chapter moves from the study of science and economics into the sphere of engineering to explore the practices of 'detachment' in which engineers engage in the course of their work. If science and economics provide models of how the world is supposed to work, engineering operationalises these models to bring about concrete transformations for specific social effects. Just as in science, detachment is central to engineering's capacity to deal with complex webs of relationality.

Nonetheless, the circumstances within which these detachments are deployed raise important new insights into the work that detachment does in processes of material transformation. To explore this, we attend to the way in which engineers deploy modern techniques of objectivity in ways that both mirror and yet also exceed the practices of scientists with which these literatures have enabled us to become so familiar. Specifically, we draw attention to the way in which the requirements of detachment that engineers share with scientists are coupled with an equally important need to make a direct social difference. Thus we argue that in place of a primary commitment to the stabilisation of epistemological truths, the road construction engineers with whom we worked deployed practices of detachment as a means of negotiating a contemporary politics of responsibility.

Engineering is founded on an explicit imperative to transform the world through procedures of stabilisation. This is not a latent project of a hoped-for transformation in some as yet undetermined future, but a pragmatic engagement with socio-material transformations in the here and now. Engineering is a pragmatic science. It involves devising technical interventions to bring about concrete and tangible social effects. In this respect it is a practice that both understands and attends to the intrinsic relationality of things (materials and persons) while holding to the possibility of shaping, and containing, this play of relations. In practice, this double-take on the nature of reality requires engineering professionals to confront the problem of how to deal with the unexpected consequences of actions which take place in a world that exceeds the more familiar detachments and stabilisations that made action possible in the first place. The play of expected and unexpected consequences of intervention thus puts the question of responsibility – personal, corporate or social – both at the very heart of engineering and, paradoxically, outside its remit. We take this dilemma as our starting point, and drawing on ethnographic fieldwork carried out with highway engineers in Peru, we focus on the specific work required to make choices about which relations should be left alone and which need to be transformed. In focusing on a variety of practices of detachment, we aim to better understand both how the problematic question of responsibility comes to be posed for experts interested in social transformation, and the possibilities that lie open for its negotiation.

The ethics of (not) making a difference

The engineers whom we describe in this chapter were the employees of a consortium that had been established to build the Interoceanic

Highway in the south of Peru. This was a large construction project which formed a central part of an ethnographic study of Peruvian roads that we conducted between 2005 and 2009. The Interoceanic Highway construction project was a bilateral Peruvian-Brazilian initiative to build a widened and asphalted road across the southern Andean highlands of Peru and through the Amazonian lowlands to the border between Peru and Brazil. The aim of the project was to produce a paved road between the sea-ports on the Pacific coast of Peru and those on the Atlantic coast of Brazil, providing a new means of transporting goods across South America and out to international markets in Europe and Asia. For four years we followed the ratification and construction of this highway, conducting ethnographic research with the engineers, planners, designers, scientists, government officials, local politicians, communities, drivers and travellers who were concerned in one way or another with the appearance of this 700 km stretch of widened highway. We spent time with the engineering consortium: living in the engineering camps, interviewing senior managers and shadowing technicians and engineers in their daily work of analysis, construction and community relations. We also travelled the road, speaking to local residents about their memories and experiences of the construction project, and, building on Penny's prior ethnographic research in this part of Peru, participating in the daily life of communities along the route. Further afield our interest in the road led us to the documents of the World Bank, the loan agreements of Credit Suisse and the environmental concerns of the World Wildlife Fund, among others. We came across historical characters from Poland, Russia and Japan, while the engineers we met linked the construction to French engineering prowess, African road building experiences, American standards and Chinese markets.

Our interest in the Interoceanic Highway project was prompted, in the first instance, by the explicit ambition of politicians and engineers to mobilise a technical and material process as a means of bringing about large-scale social change. The huge effort and expenditure that goes into infrastructure projects is justified by the causal relationship that is promised between the material intervention (construction of a road) and a particular social effect (e.g. economic prosperity consequent on enhanced connectivity). Engineers often spoke to us of the great pride that they took from their involvement in such a project of social transformation, identifying themselves as agents who might be seen as, in part, responsible for social progress and improvement.

However, the contours of this responsibility were far from straightforward, we soon found out, as we began to follow the construction process in more detail. As technologies whose very rationale is the planned connection of distant places, roads also produce all kinds of unplanned linkages. An attention to the road construction process led us to explore the licit and illicit movements of goods such as beer, coca and drugs, the migration of people into and out of the area through which the road was to pass, the extraction of gold and timber, trades infused with both promise and danger, and the histories of slavery and exploration through which this region had originally been revealed as a site of productive potential. It also took us to the construction camps, which were set up for the workers and built to house some 2000 people. We watched how the engineering company established themselves in local towns: how the site of the engineering camp was identified and surveyed, and the earth flattened to accommodate the white prefab cabins that began to appear in lines along the contours of the field. Teams of men in yellow overcoats dug trenches which were filled with concrete, drainage was installed to collect run-off water, systems of garbage disposal were put in place with different coloured bins for different kinds of waste. A checkpoint was built at the entrance to the camp and cars and lorries were allocated their space. Electricity was connected, satellite dishes installed and the basic accoutrements of life were brought in – bedding and televisions, tables and chairs, wardrobes and wash basins. In the nearby town certain restaurants were certified as safe to eat in. The road into town was widened so that lorries could get through, and notices were put up calling people to public meetings.

Once established, the camps attracted many more in search of work and more again who were employed in the layers of sub-contraction that surrounded the activities of the core partners to the consortium. People came from far afield to work in often dangerous circumstances, leaving behind families and provoking fears of crime and disease in their new host populations. On signing a contract of employment some were provided with healthcare, some with accommodation of differing standards, producing new dynamics of social differentiation and hierarchical organisation. Engineers were proud of the generative potential of the roads that they were constructing, but they were also fully aware of the risks, realising that social change was an unpredictable business.

In addition to the unpredictability of the social consequences of road construction, the material process of building a road itself was also generative of extensive knock-on effects which the engineering consortium had to manage on a day-to-day basis. As well as laying asphalt on the land, road construction involves the establishment of quarries and materials dumps to dispose of excess construction materials, and the building of drains, bridges and pavements. The construction process also mobilises many thousands of trucks and heavy machines that require maintenance and fuel that leeches into the environment. It involves the quarrying, transport, processing and disposal of huge quantities of earth, stone and asphalt concrete; it has implications for the water tables and for future land usage.

The question of how to operate responsibly in these fragile and vulnerable local environments is one of the key issues that engineering companies face and one which the engineers took very seriously. One senior engineer told us that the company was like a flock of migrating birds. 'We come and we move on. While we are here we have to fit into local people's ways of living, not interfere or damage their customs in any way. It is our responsibility to make sure that we leave these places as we found them.' He argued that the company's responsibility was to produce a road which they could hand over to the people who had campaigned for it, letting them work out how to use it to their best advantage.

Building a road without undue consequences is generally presented by engineering as a naturalised ideal and the requirement to deal with all kinds of polluting issues is a necessary aberration to this ideal. However, in practice, we found engineers were constantly engaged with the question of how to police the relational effects of their work. When the construction company begins on a project they have to associate themselves with the places that they are intending to move through. They have to lease the land for the camps and expropriate land for construction, they have to locate, excavate and dispose of materials, and contract and provision a local workforce. At the same time they have to manage their connection to the local setting. Their relationship with the changes that they effect has to be carefully negotiated through a series of technical, legal, affective and descriptive practices. While engineering entails the making of new attachments to new places, the overwhelming demands they generate at times threaten to compromise the integrity of the vision of clean, responsible infrastructural transformation that engineers are working to effect. Thus pollution is not a trivial issue but lies at the very heart of the engineering practices we set out to study. It is in this respect that we suggest engineering is a practice that relies on a series of acts of what we call 'virtuous detachment' that engineers perform to extract themselves from the complex web of connections that are required to get the job done. We suggest that a focus on these practices of detachment have the potential to teach us not just about the limitations of modern epistemology but also about how and why engineering knowledge takes the form it does, and what its generative effects might be. In what follows we trace three examples of 'virtuous detachments' in engineering practice: the work of detachment involved in planning a road; the role of detachment in the construction process; and the practices of detachment that are deployed to deal with community relations. In each we explore how detachments in engineering are practices that are oriented to the problem of how to delimit the contours of social, technical and political responsibility (see also McCarthy and Kelty 2010).

Detachments of anticipation

Whilst it is impossible for engineers to predict precisely what kinds of challenges they will face in the course of construction, the anticipation of potential problems is a key aspect of engineering practice, and constitutes our first sphere of 'virtuous detachment'. In order to even begin the process of construction, the thorny issue of how to delimit and define the field of action has to be tackled. When we began our research into the construction of the Interoceanic Highway, a feasibility study was underway which had to provide robust multi-disciplinary evidence that the routes proposed and the technical specification of the road itself, were appropriate for the needs identified in earlier studies. Such evidence had to be compiled across multiple scales and required an analysis of soils, water courses, geological formations, climate and data on the social and economic conditions of the regions through which the road would pass, including settlement patterns, modes of land tenure, existing transportation plans, trading activities, all considered from international, national, regional and local perspectives. The descriptions that were produced in the feasibility study had to manage huge complexity. Even though the study finally amounted to seven hefty volumes, it is of course the case that the data presented was but a fragment of what could have been told about the 700 km stretch of territory over which the road was to be built. The data was selected carefully and presented in a compact and standardised form in order to generate a sense of trust that what was accounted for did indeed encompass the important facts. Ironically, however, while the engineering consortium worked to generate trust through this document, their integrity was being challenged from other quarters.

When we first interviewed the chief engineer of the Interoceanic Highway project, we began by asking, simply, what the company was doing. We were surprised to get a defensive response to what seemed to us a benign question. At the very early stages of the project, prior to the commencement of the building phase, we were looking for possible sites for ethnographic participation and engagement. He, however, was concerned that in asking for an account of the company's activities we were alluding to claims that were raging in the local press which criticised the company for being in a state of paralysis.

In Peru, large infrastructure projects are often assumed to suffer from endemic corruption (see Knox and Harvey, forthcoming). Following a series of scandals concerning the widespread embezzlements of infrastructure funds during the Fujimori government, the press and the public frequently see infrastructure projects as a front for the rich and powerful to make personal gains. Everybody knew, the stories went, that millions of dollars had been invested in this project, and they knew that engineering personnel were in the area but there was little evidence on the ground that anyone was actually working. People in hard hats would sometimes appear in the towns along the proposed route, hold a meeting, take some measurements or samples and then be gone, but where were the heavy machines, where were the jobs, and why was the land not being torn up and re-laid? The people who had campaigned tirelessly for the road to be built were nervous that the lack of action was connected to a change of political will, or worse still that the company was embezzling the funds.

From the perspective of the engineer, however, they were in a very difficult position. Acknowledging people's fears, he argued that the public was misinterpreting a lack of visible construction as a lack of activity. He worried that people fundamentally misunderstood how the construction process works, exasperatedly asking us: 'What do people want? It takes a woman nine months to have a child – you just can't do it in three months! ... It might be possible for 1,000 people to build 1,000 houses in 1,000 days but it is impossible for 1,000 people to build one house in one day!' People wanted to see some tangible activity but in the eyes of this engineer they were far from inactive, involved as they were in the huge amount of definitional work that had to be carried out before construction could begin.

The definitional work of the feasibility study was necessary to produce the initial stabilisations that allow work to commence: the materialisation of legal contracts; the securing of funding sources and the determination of ideal routes for the planned highway. Many of the figures and descriptions produced for such documents are provisional and might never even be used in the actual process of road construction which was to follow. The remarkable production of such a complex future-oriented study of a social and material terrain that itself was in flux, was achieved in conversations with layers of legal and technical regulatory frameworks that delineated the contours of what should and what should not be included in such studies, and what should and should not be measured. Taking place out of public view, engineers designing the project were engaged in a complex process of consulting regulations, norms and standards in order to enable the conversion of 'raw data' into data that would produce a road project that could fulfil its generic social and political ambitions.

This is not to say that the plans that resulted from these calculations were without contestation. The proposed routing that the engineers had developed in the feasibility study was the subject of great conflict among those communities who feared that the road would bypass their villages. Community members in some towns protested by setting up road blocks to publicise their desire that the routings be altered, hoping that in later studies their protestations might be factored into the decision about where the road might go. However, at the feasibility stage, the engineers were not directly involved in debates with communities about routing. They were, nonetheless, aware that decisions about where the road would go would be interpreted politically.

Although these studies were produced through huge amounts of research and analysis, we suggest that what were being produced were not so much the 'facts' of scientists ideally separated from the 'values' of interested parties on the ground (Latour 2004), but were rather 'factish' (Latour 2010) attempts at delineating the parameters and ownership of the relative forms of responsibility that would arise in the construction process. Far from sitting comfortably on one or other side of the facts/values divide, the necessity that engineers face of working within regulatory framings has, we suggest, a doubling effect. In one respect it immerses the civil engineer in a world of politics – for the legal regulations and the technical norms are themselves produced through prior political process – for example, the outcome of decisions taken in Parliament about how to contain the intrinsic multiplicity and indeterminacy of the material and social world. In another respect the regulations act as a buffer between the engineer and the world of politics. Just as the requirement to adhere to regulatory requirement appears to render them inactive in the eyes of those who are not involved in the construction process, it also provides a legitimate response to accusations that delays or routings might be due to a failure of engineers to enact proper or adequate social responsibility.[2]

The political formation of the regulatory frame points us to the ways in which standards are devices that allow engineer to control without personal responsibility, without having to acknowledge their involvement and certainly without having to confront the issue of what gets left out of the picture once the regulations are applied. These are the 'locationless logics' that Timothy Mitchell refers to in his book *The Rule of Experts*, which describes the emergence of the modern economy in Egypt where the human cost of regulatory regimes and the implementation of 'rational procedures' dramatically undermines the narrative of progress and social transformation that the macro-economic evidence seems to support (Mitchell 2002). And so too with the engineers we worked with in Peru. Regulatory standards, norms and numerical standards helped the engineers to keep their distance – and to show that their designs had been arrived at rationally – unswayed by volatile circumstances on the ground such as local protests, floods or landslides. The key designers, based in Brazil, never even visited the site where the road was to be built but made their predictions on the basis of collated data sets provided by those in the field.

And yet, there is a twist here which we found interesting. While all the engineers we met understood the regulatory devices as providing the fundamental grounding of their expertise, these same people were the first to point out that social and material worlds are inherently unstable, that the anticipatory data they produce is therefore provisional and that the standards are not always fixed. This insistent acknowledgement of a volatile uncertain world led us to think about the design process in the terms that Annelise Riles coined in relation to her ethnography of Japanese financial traders – who acted in accordance with the subjunctive philosophy of the 'as if' (Riles 2011). The anticipatory work of defining a field of action, foregrounds practices of detachment whereby engineers use standards and regulations to act as if the world could be controlled, as if the data were stable. In Riles's terms the 'as if' abstractions are useful fictions, accounts that enable political terrain to be negotiated, decisions taken, funders and publics kept informed and on board, but only for so long.

Road construction parts with futures trading because at some point somebody starts to build a road. The work of detachment, which generated data at the anticipatory stage of the construction process, was itself detached from the actual construction of the road, through the chronograms and organisational charts of project management. If the work of anticipation appeared to allow the question of responsibility to be deflected away from the individual engineer, responsibility reappeared once the engineers turned their attention to the construction process itself. Here we find ourselves no longer in a pure realm of future-oriented facts determined by externally agreed standards, but in the muddy materiality of production.

Remarkably, the feasibility study literally disappeared from view once construction began, filed away behind cabinet doors. The final specification stipulated in the feasibility study remained important as it was integral to the contract that the state drew up with the construction company, but as other concerns took over, the subjunctive philosophy of 'as if', was supplemented and replaced by what we call a conditional philosophy of 'as long as' whose primary requirement was the functionality of the end-product – a road that works (Harvey and Knox forthcoming).

Responsive detachments

Six months after we had worried the engineer by asking him what the company was doing, life on the road had transformed into a hive of activity. One site of intense work was the field laboratories where the detailed analytical work of construction takes place. These laboratories offer an interesting contrast to the data gathering directed to the completion of the feasibility study and, as we hope to show, reveal 'virtuous detachments' of a somewhat different order. While still invoking abstraction and still mediated by number, this time these calculations are overtly shaped by the engagement of the engineer and his technical assistants with the materials that they are looking to transform. Here politics is seemingly pushed right out of the picture as a concern with the relations between political actors and finance capital are excluded to allow relations between things to appear. Nonetheless, as we will see, the outcome of these practices of detachment are still somewhat different to the detachments of scientists in their pursuit and production of stable 'facts'.

Laboratory technicians work with soil samples that have been collected from along the length of the projected route. On arrival at the lab they are graded and sorted. The process of classification starts off with an ordering of matter, but it does so with the broader aim of determining not only abstract and continuous details about the soil – its weight, its volume or its particle size, but also the dynamic qualities that the material could potentially manifest. It is these potential qualities which the engineers seek to make visible under experimental conditions. We often heard engineers talking about the battles that they had with their materials as they struggled to build the road: mud that was like an undulating mattress; capricious water spouts which, however hard you tried to tap them would reappear in different places; the recalcitrant webbing that would not unfold and concrete that would not set. The job of the laboratories was to transform this site specific and embodied experiential knowledge of unruly matter into a mathematical description that would make the terms of its unstable qualities knowable and the possibilities for its stabilisation calculable – clearly an exercise in virtuous detachment – but which, unlike the data gathering of the design process is carried out through intense, experimental engagement with the material qualities of things.

Watching a technician carry out the 'plasticity' test on a sample of soil, she explained to us that experimentation was a central part of the process of discovering the qualities of the soil she was working with. She explained that once they have been able to determine, through repeated testing, when the soil sample achieves what they referred to as the 'limite liquido' (liquid limit), the amount of water that has been added to achieve this level is written in a notebook, thus stabilising this piece of knowledge about the mud and allowing the second stage of the test to begin. However, the process of testing does not take place in a relational void. As pointed out earlier, an awareness of the qualities of the materials under analysis precedes their appearance in the lab. Road projects were characterised by engineers in terms of the material challenges that they threw up – earth that was too muddy, a lack of sand, an abundance of rock, the presence of earthquakes. The tests that took place in the laboratories were conducted in relation to an already formed expectation of the qualities of the materials undergoing the test – these were the hypotheses built into the pre-determined measures and procedures of the experimental process. In the field laboratories engineers encouraged the materials to manifest their particular qualities in numerical form. The purpose of the analysis was to identify the suitability of the materials found along the road for use in the construction process, and to assess the stability of the current road surface so that a new surface could be successfully laid on top. The method of analysis incorporated all the histories of experimentation, and like a machine, operated by the engineer, appeared to become the conduit that is capable of transforming matter into number and back into matter. The engineers as operators, on the other hand, are responsible for encouraging the matter to pass through the machine of scientific method in the correct way, a skill which requires an embodied sensitivity to the process (Collins 1985). They find themselves engaged in the act of coaxing the numbers out of the matter, with mathematics and experimental method providing a means of translating a relationship between engineers and the matter that they engage with on a day-to-day basis and that is already knowable in other ways.

The tendency to see scientific practice as a stripping out of certain social relations prevents us from focusing on the productive aspects of such practices of detachment. Far from providing a reduced version of a relationship to the soil, in this case we can see that the experimental relations which stabilised matter into a numerical equivalent were the means through which engineers could become located within a nexus of relations of responsibility. In not only understanding materials, but also mobilising them for future effects, practices of detachment in the laboratories can be seen as provisional acts in a longer process whereby the engineer must take responsibility for future material relations (i.e. the performance of the road once constructed). Operators of a historically emergent method, custodians of data, it is in the laboratories and in their work with materials that engineers delimit the domain for which they can be responsible.

In the laboratories, we find that detachment does not deflect the problem of responsibility but rather defines those practices for which engineers might legitimately be held responsible. In the laboratories engineers take responsibility for the intimate relationship that they are able to develop with materials. Echoes of the etymology of the term 'responsibility' remind us of the communicative origins of the act of being responsible, the requirement to answer or to provide a reply.[3] Connected to everything but unable to respond, engineering would find itself without a language to communicate with matter, or a means of judging the success or failure of its action. Through mathematically informed methodologies of analysis and experimentation however, numerical translations come to provide a language within which engineers can claim a limited domain of 'respons-ability'.[4] The actions of trial and error, in a constant conversation with materials which is mediated by numerical data is the action that produces a material object like a road.

While mathematics enables materials to enter into a form of conversation with humans, it at the same time makes incommunicable other kinds of non-mathematical responses to the engineering process. If engineers have a language through which they can respond to matter, their status as engineers is challenged when they are asked to respond to other claims that are not capable of being translated into numerical form.[5] It is to ways in which the virtuous detachments of engineering are challenged by the slippery social claims of various different groups, and consequently the way in which the domain of the engineer is detached from other fields of action that we turn in the following section.

Incommunicable dilemmas

A road block had been set up by one of the communities living alongside the road. People were upset by the removal of soil from their fields. Their protest was at first seen as a failure to 'let go' of their land in order to allow for the road, which was paradoxical given the strength of their campaign to get the road built. But as discussions ensued it transpired that their main concern was about the soil itself. They wanted it to be relocated for their future use but the company was insisting on taking it away. As we have seen, much of the engineers' work of detaching and reattaching materials takes place in the laboratories. One of their tasks is to identify the sites from which materials can be drawn (quarries, river beds etc.) and sites where excess materials can be dumped. The laboratories assist in determining the compatibility of materials, and consideration is given to the effects on the water table and environmental stability. Soils are potentially toxic if misplaced. The company understood that the community might not want to see the soil carried away, but they only had the resources to test specific reception sites and could not carry out tests for ad hoc relocations. The protest had arisen because the engineers could only respond to soil as either a chemical substance for which they have a responsibility in mathematical analysis, or an economic resource for which they could refer people to the state compensation schemes, deferring responsibility on to another body with another set of standardisations and delimitations. The protesters, however, had other claims that related more specifically to their sense of loss. The soil is a substance that they had cared for, that has its own vitality, and powerful relational connectivity to their community. It was part of them and its loss was painful despite their desire for the road (Harvey 2010).

This problem with the soil recurred in relation to the obligation of the company to return land that they had leased for the construction of the engineering camps, the dumps and the quarries. They are obliged by law to return these sites to the owners in the same state in which they were found. The task is tricky for various reasons – former owners are sometimes keen to strike deals for all kinds of modifications which suit their future ambitions. But there is a more intransigent problem of how to 'repair' the land once it has been substantially transformed. The repair is in effect not a return to a prior state but the substitution of one piece of land for another – the substitute deemed equivalent by reference to a set of legally stipulated standards. Given that the transformational projects of civil engineering also require the engineers to leave places 'as they find them', the repair is in some respects a highly performative conjuring trick. A successful project is one where it appears by the end, that the new road has simply been laid down over the land which the engineer had no intention or right to change. Nature remains unified and unblemished while the technology of social progress is laid down upon it. Yet as we have seen, this sleight of hand is not an inevitable outcome but the result of considerable work, particularly with respect to the company's need and right to designate the relational qualities of the land prior to their interventions.

From the perspective of some landowners the repairs might be legal but the equivalence is clearly partial. People complain, for example, that the layer of topsoil provided is insufficient for agricultural purposes.

Their complaints point to a sense that the company does not attend to their understandings and experience of what makes land viable. Meanwhile, the production of legal equivalence allows the company to defer responsibility to those left to make something of their transformed world. The move effectively produces working limits to the company's remit of responsibility by separating the construction process from the complex and extensive social relations through which land sustains its productive vitality. From the perspective of the engineers the possibility for acting responsibly comes from an act of detachment rather than from following an ill-defined and unlimited engagement.

From these examples we can see that engineering companies are able to limit their engagement with respect to the potential effects of their transformational practice. In the first case the land cannot be returned because there are no resources (or obligations) to ensure the compatibility of existing and newly introduced soils and so the soil is removed to the safety of the previously designated (and tested) dumping ground; in the second case where repairs have to be made the company mobilises its resources with respect to a pre-specified set of relations. In both cases the cuts which they perform are highlighted as the ones that are crucial for the designation of relevant material qualities and capacities in the task of producing a road that is successful 'as long as' its material coherence is not compromised.

We are of course, in familiar neo-liberal terrain where the ethics of corporate responsibility emerge in practice as a regulatory framework that works to limit corporate responsibility to a specific set of relations that corporations themselves produce as relevant. As private corporations take on the work of infrastructural development that used to be the domain of the state, the question of whose interests such corporations are working in become pertinent. Corporate social responsibility (CSR) allows private corporations to demonstrate that they are both serving the interests of shareholders and the public, although, as studies of CSR have demonstrated inherent tensions regarding questions of responsibility remain (see Welker 2009). On the Interoceanic Highway project, CSR was enacted in the form of specific legal negotiations like those described above, and in a number of discrete charitable projects: for example, providing health advice and dental care to local communities. Beyond that the engineering company simply teach local people that the rest is up to them. Once the practice of expert detachment determines the conditions within which responsibility can be claimed, it leaves as a remainder, or externality, all other unforeseen consequences for which they cannot take responsibility. With the practices of detachment having produced the terms within which every action must have a potential cause, all phenomena the potential to be associated with a prior action, the conditions are produced within which someone must ultimately step up to the mantle and take responsibility for the successes and failures of the road as technology of social progress. The message that local populations frequently hear is that it will be their fault if it all goes wrong. However, to stop at this diagnosis would be to see the work of detachment as reaching a premature resolution. In actual fact, what we saw in the process of road building was the repeated unsettling of the forms of detachment which engineers were required to deploy in order to stabilise social and material environments. Working in defence of local populations and the natural environment, both of which are rendered as the passive subjects of state-led projects of material transformation, development organisations and ecological groups work hard to rearticulate a language through which states and corporations might be forced to recognise a more extended sense of responsibility. Frequently, this entails the attempted translation of previously incalculable qualities into numerical form, in an attempt to turn issues such as standards of living, healthcare, pollution and human rights into those that can be evaluated via material or economic calculations.

Responsibility thus appears to be not simply a moral imperative nor a stable position toward which one might aim, but the outcome of acts of contestation which work to draw out the qualities of things in order to make them elicit a response from a variety of different actors. Delimiting and detaching is more than just an epistemological position, or a form of ignorance or blindness to the interconnectedness of everything. In civil engineering it provides the conditions of possibility for action, for keeping some things in their place so that others can move, keeping some things stable so that others can change and for generating a language through which transformation will occur. A world without detachment would be a world without transformation, a world where 'we can no longer pass. We can no longer create. We can no longer live' (Latour 2010: 28). Far from merely celebrating attachment in the face of its other, what the work of engineers teaches us is that detachment is productive and that part of its productivity comes from the challenge it poses to the consolidation of any particular form of change.

Conclusion

In this chapter we have tracked the detachments upon which the modern project of engineering is reproduced. In doing so we have illustrated how the detachments of engineering practice are so much more than simple reductions of complexity that enable the reproduction of conventional contours of power and inequality. Instead, we have demonstrated that detachment in engineering practice is primarily a matter of navigating a complex and uncertain terrain regarding the demarcation of political responsibility. We have described three related moments of what we have thus called 'virtuous detachment' to illustrate that the relationship between practices of detachment and enactments of responsibility is not settled, but an ongoing process of political negotiation. In the mode of detachment, the question of responsibility is both the impetus for engineering, but also its limit condition.

In Swayne's *Collacocha*, the protagonist Echecopar intrigues us for he is the very embodiment of the predicament of the engineer. With no corporation, state, or public upon whom to deflect the question of extended responsibility, we find a character who has internalised all the force of engineering and the possibilities and dangers that it holds for social transformation. Echecopar is passionate about the capacity of engineering to transform Peruvian society and equally devastated at the destruction of the social/natural edifice he inhabits in the form of his mine. The final act of the play invites us to watch as Echecopar tries once again to generate through material intervention, a better future for his country – this time, having learnt that the detachment he exhibited from his fellow workers when he ignored their expertise and their warnings of impending disaster, placed him in a perilous position. The tale of *Collacocha* is not a call for connectedness, but an exhortation to be aware of both the dangers and the potential of detachment in engineering practice.

Inspired by Swayne and his protagonist Echecopar, we have argued that an acknowledgement of the centrality of detachment allows for a reassessment of a theoretical position that privileges the ontological importance of attachment (everything is connected to everything else) and critiques those moments when attachments are curtailed. In contrast, Echecopar and the engineers we worked with have led us to consider the truly radical nature of a proposition that maintains the generative potential of detachment. By providing us with an archetype of the struggles of the modern engineer, Echecopar gives us a means of reinterpreting the particular struggles that infrastructural engineers face in bringing contemporary infrastructure projects into being. These struggles are not simply about the work of stabilising knowledge but are rather ways of negotiating the relationship between personal, corporate and social responsibility that remain at the heart of contemporary projects of material transformation.

Notes

1 Swayne (1955: 319–409).
2 In the production of predictive data, none of the engineers that we worked with saw their role as one of transforming the standards to which they worked. The engineer who acted correctly followed the letter of the law, and we found engineers to be very committed to the ideal of normative standards. However, was also common for engineers to acknowledge that standards are not always strictly adhered to. Indeed, the obligation to find pragmatic solutions to unforeseen events was a necessary skill, albeit a dangerous one that made them vulnerable to the criticisms and rumors of malpractice that construction projects generate. However, such rumours served to reinforce the image of virtuous detachment expected of a professional engineer who is shielded by regulations and standards from individual fallibility, self-interest and personal opinion.
3 'Anglo-Norman responssable, ressponsable, Anglo-Norman and Middle French responsable answerable, entitled to an answer (13th cent. in Anglo-Norman in spec. legal use), answerable, required to answer (14th cent. in Anglo-Norman in spec. legal use), falling under a particular jurisdiction (14th cent.), accountable, standing surety for (15th cent.), that responds, that constitutes a reply (15th cent)' *Oxford English Dictionary*, 2011.
4 Donna Haraway also uses the formulation of respons-ability in her work on human–animal relations. Our use of the term differs from Haraway's usage – whereas Haraway wishes to establish respons-ability as a manifesto for human–animal co-becoming, we use the term to describe the boundary making practices through which engineers demarcate who they can legitimately engage with in a professional capacity, and thus where the contours of their liability lies.
5 See Callon (1998) for an analysis of how economies are similarly constituted through the detachments of economic theory.

References

Appadurai, Arjun, 1986, *The Social Life of Things: Commodities in a Cultural Perspective*. Cambridge: Cambridge University Press.
Bensaude-Vincent, Bernadette and Stengers, Isabelle, 1996, *A History of Chemistry*. Cambridge, MA: Harvard University Press.
Bowker, Geoffrey and Star, Susan Leigh, 1999, *Sorting Things Out. Classification and its Consequences*. Cambridge, MA: MIT Press.
Brown, Bill, 2001, Thing Theory. *Critical Inquiry* 28(1): 1–22.
Bruun Jensen, Casper and Rödje, Kjetil, 2010, *Deleuzian Intersections: Science, Technology, Anthropology*. London: Routledge.
Burnett, Graham, 2000, *Masters of all they Surveyed: Exploration, Geography, and a British El Dorado*. Chicago: University of Chicago Press.
Callon, Michel, 1998, *The Laws of the Markets*. Oxford: Blackwell.
Candea, Matei, ed., 2010, *The Social after Gabriel Tarde: Debates and Assessments*. London: Routledge.

Collins, Harry, 1985, Replicating the TEA Laser. In *Changing Order: Replication and Induction in Scientific Practice*. Chicago: University of Chicago Press, pp. 51–78.

Daston, Lorriane and Galison, Peter, 2007, *Objectivity*. London: Zone Books.

Grint, Keith and Woolgar, Steve, 1992, Computers, Guns and Roses: What's Social about Being Shot. *Science, Technology and Human Values* 17(3): 376–378.

Hacking, Ian, 1999, *The Social Construction of What?* Cambridge, MA: Harvard University Press.

Harvey, Penny, 2010, Cementing Relations: The Materiality of Roads and Public Spaces in Provincial Peru. *Social Analysis* 54(2): 28–46.

Harvey, Penny and Hannah Knox, 2015, *Roads: An Anthropology of Infrastructure and Expertise*. Ithaca: Cornell University Press.

Harvey, Penny, with Eleanor Casella, Gillian Evans, Hannah Knox, Christine McLean, Elizabeth Silva, Nicholas Thoburn and Kath Woodward, 2013, *Objects and Materials: A Routledge Companion*. London: Routledge

Ingold, Timothy, 2011, *Being Alive: Essays on Movement, Knowledge and Description*. London: Routledge.

Kirsch, Stuart, 2014, *Mining Capitalism: The Relationship Between Corporations and their Critics*. Berkeley: University of California Press.

Lampland, Martha and Star, Susan Leigh, 2008, *Standards and Their Stories: How Quantifying, Classifying and Formalizing Practices Shape Everyday Life*. Cornell: Cornell University Press.

Latour, Bruno, 1987, *Science in Action*. Cambridge, MA: Harvard University Press.

Latour, Bruno, 1988, *The Pasteurization of France*. Cambridge, MA: Harvard University Press.

Latour, Bruno, 1993, *We Have Never Been Modern*. Cambridge, MA: Harvard University Press.

Latour, Bruno, 2002, Gabriel Tarde and the End of the Social. In Patrick Joyce, ed., *The Social in Question: New Bearings in History and the Social Sciences*. London: Routledge, pp. 117–132.

Latour, Bruno, 2004, *Politics of Nature: How to Bring the Sciences into Democracy*. Cambridge, MA: London: Harvard University Press.

Latour, Bruno, 2005, *Reassembling the Social: An Introduction to Actor Network Theory*. Oxford: Oxford University Press.

Latour, Bruno, 2010, *On the Modern Cult of the Factish Gods*. Durham: Duke University Press.

Latour, Bruno and Woolgar, Steve, 1979, *Laboratory Life: The Social Construction of Scientific Fact*. London: Sage.

Law, John and Annemarie Mol, 2002, *Complexities: Social Studies of Knowledge Practices*. Durham: Duke University Press.

Lury, Celia and Wakeford, Nina, 2012, *Inventive Methods: The Happening of the Social*. London: Routledge.

McCarthy, Elise and Kelty, Christopher, 2010, Responsibility and Nanotechnology. *Social Studies of Science* 40(3): 405–432.

Mitchell, Timothy, 2002, *Rule of Experts: Egypt, Techno-politics, Modernity.* Berkeley: University of California Press.

Mol, Annemarie, 2002, *The Body Multiple: Ontology in Medical Practice.* Durham, Duke University Press.

Ong, Aihwa and Collier, Steven, 2004, *Global Assemblages: Technology, Politics, and Ethics as Anthropological Problems.* Oxford: Blackwell.

Riles, Annelise, 2011, *Collateral Knowledge: Legal Reasoning in the Global Financial Markets.* Chicago: University of Chicago Press.

Scott, James, 1998, *Seeing Like a State: How Certain Schemes to Improve the Human Condition have Failed.* New Haven: Yale University Press.

Shapin, Steven and Schaffer, Simon, 1985, *Leviathan and the Air Pump. Hobbes, Boyle and the Experimental Life.* Princeton: Princeton University Press.

Strathern, Marilyn, 1995, *The Relation.* Cambridge: Prickly Pear Press.

Strathern, Marilyn, 1996, Cutting the Network. *Journal of the Royal Anthropological Institute* 2(3): 517–535.

Swayne, Enrique Solari, 1955, Collacocha. In J. Hesse Murga, ed., *Teatro Peruano Contemporáneo.* Madrid: Aguilar, pp. 319–409.

Thomas, Nicholas, 1991, *Entangled Objects: Exchange, Material Culture, and Colonialism in the Pacific.* Cambridge, MA: London: Harvard University Press.

Welker, Marina, 2009, 'Corporate Security begins in the Community': Mining, the Corporate Social Responsibility Industry and Environmental Advocacy in Indonesia. *Cultural Anthropology* 24(1): 142–179.

3

Artisanal affection: detachment in human–animal relations within intensive pig production in Britain

Kim Crowder

Introduction: pigs and polarities

'I am completely ruthless!' This was the candid claim made by an experienced senior pigman[1] when I asked him about the underpinning rationale of his daily work on an East Anglian indoor intensive pig unit, which some would classify as a 'factory farm'. The pigman's self-description matters on both sides of the farm gate – relevant to consumers who concern themselves with what else they 'eat' when they ingest pork, and to increasingly image-conscious pig producers themselves. At stake is the degree of putative completeness in the pigman's ruthlessness since it accentuates the space between livestock workers' occupational reputation and consumers' confidence. The comment seems to play into the hands of intensive livestock farming's critics who claim that animals are not known closely as individuals, and consequently cannot be properly cared for. While these criticisms imply a passive human indifference to livestock, a distance between stockmen and animals, the vocabulary of animal welfarist and activist literature is unequivocal, asserting that deliberately inflicted cruelty, neglect, indifference, lack of compassion and inhumane treatment are endemic.[2] The theme of uncaring, routinised objectification and exploitation of livestock in dystopic farms has been an enduring one in animal rights/feminist literature since the 1960s (Harrison 1964; Singer 1976; Adams 1990; Regan 2001).

Current scholarship is beginning to challenge such generalist and indiscriminately pejorative designations and to suggest that relationships between livestock producers and their animals are not as restricted in range as critical accounts suggest – an idea given concrete expression in media coverage of farmers' emotional reactions to the wholesale slaughter of herds during the foot and mouth disease epidemic of 2001.[3]

Contemporaneous reportage of farmers' grief at the loss of their herds contradicted and unsettled the prevalent idea that livestock farmers' relationships with their animals are exclusively money-driven and, by definition, affect-free. In acknowledging that the human–animal relationships pertaining in farming may not be so simplistically characterised as uncaring at best and brutal at worst, sources such as Tovey (2002), Hemsworth (2003), Miele and Bock (2007) and Mayfield et al. (2007) have laid the ground for in-depth exploration of human–livestock interactions. In opening up this troubled territory, such scholarship begins to indicate the existence of hitherto unsuspected complexity within such relationships. Importantly, Wilkie (2010: 38–39) has noted that while welfare and rights groups have exposed problems, they have disregarded instances of good practice. This reportage bias has contributed to negative stereotyping of stockworkers as social misfits or emotional illiterates unsuited to working with animals. Perceived linkages between 'bad people' and 'bad jobs' (Davis 1984) are reinforced in the pig sector by contact with stigmatised 'bad animals'.

Using ethnographic material focusing on pigmen's professional dispassions, I show how a coextensive closeness, or affinity, with pigs becomes apparent at the very site where it is both unanticipated and contested. This chapter utilises data generated during ethnographic fieldwork conducted on British pig farms from 2006 to 2013. Research methodologies embraced participant observation, a situated learning 'apprenticeship' and legitimate peripheral participation (Lave and Wenger 1991; Cassidy 2002; Wacquant 2004).

Sentiment, stigma and invisibility

In deliberately avoiding the kind of reductivist views that reinforce the problem Wilkie identifies, this chapter asks: what forms does detachment take in pig farming: what does it do, and for whom? Where pigmen and their views are normally pushed out to the social periphery, this chapter attempts to make space within current debate for their insights. It sets out to expand knowledge of the means by which these workers mediate the highly conflicting demands of a production system that requires them to exercise unspoken and dispassionate behaviours within little acknowledged, yet often intensely affective relationships with pigs. In this context, detachment is synonymous with a kind of vanishing: while pigmen, a stigmatised, professionally isolated group, fall off the social map, pigs themselves disappear into the disjoining processes of meat production.

Pigmen are well aware of their industry's dubious public reputation and of popular misperceptions relating to intensive pig farming, issues that can make them self-defensive. An experienced pig stockman told me:

> There are people who don't agree with what we do ... There's people who are saying this is wrong, but that's their idea of what's wrong ... not what we're actually doing is wrong. That's the difference ... We're doing it as best we can, and as humanely and fairly as we can ... About the press stuff – the bad practices come from bad training, people not being shown stuff properly, or having it as a job rather than a way of life.

In opposing 'job' to 'way of life' this statement reflects pigmen's unanimous resistance to the derogatory misconception that the work is unskilled and 'anyone can do it'. For them, the role entails complete commitment. On the pig farm human and animal workers all 'live in'; given that a tied cottage (and the risk and dependency this entails) is often part of the pigman's employment deal, stockmanship figures as a totalising lifestyle.

Set against this background of disaffection, 'traceability', 'transparency' and 'provenance' have become food buzzwords over the past decade, with low food miles and short supply chains posited as ideals in the project of reducing distances between stages in the supply chain, and between producers and consumers. The 'Horsegate'[4] meat adulteration scandal of 2013 provided an extreme example of the risks posed by over-complex food supply chains – especially where meat is concerned – and reaction to this event revealed the strength of public interest in the issue of food accountability and associated animal welfare.

Although some current retailing practices are allowing consumers increased access to information concerning the 'where', the 'who' and the 'how' of meat production, the backstory of meat-making is still heavily edited. That said, some pig farmers (often those operating outdoor systems) are steadily assuming increased public presence, allowing themselves to be clearly identified on meat packaging. However, this strategy both conceals the often vicarious nature of farmers' relationships with pigs as well as obscuring the presence of pigmen themselves. The 'invisibility' of livestock has been documented by Tovey (2003) and pigmen's own 'invisibility' was confirmed by an industry consultant who told me that, in contrast to pigs, whose performance figures are obsessively recorded, no statistical or demographic data on pigmen is collected. Estimates of the total number of stockmen working across all species range between 185,000[5] and 292,000 (Farm Animal Welfare Council, 2007: 6), but exact numbers of pigmen remain unspecified.

Speaking of the National Pig Association (NPA), one pigman explained how he saw the organisation as 'a sort of NFU[6] for pig farmers; there's no mouthpiece, nothing like that for us ... We don't have a special union.'[7] To clarify, the division of labour in scale livestock production dictates that farmers fulfil managerial, bureaucratic and public relations duties, while behind-the-scenes pigmen undertake the artisanal, manual work of making pigs.

Splitting the difference

Pigs and pork; the two are riven, bodily and linguistically, literally and symbolically; the very terminology reinforces an absolute conceptual and physical divide between live animals and commodified meat products. Meat manufacture makes the fundamental connection between a sow and a shrink-wrapped pack of sausages disappear; pigs get lost in the transformations and translations of meat marketing. Similarly, the physical spaces separating pig farms, pork production sites and the places in which pork is consumed literally embody the notions of disconnection and separation with which this chapter is concerned. Contexts of pork production and consumption readily suggest a variety of discontinuities, polarities, disjunctions. For example, the lives of urban meat-eaters and rural meat-makers rarely coincide; farmers and urban shoppers do not mix. Wide geographical gaps exist between pig breeding sheds and supermarket meat aisles, killing lines and kitchens; muckheaps and farm effluvia exist in a seemingly different world from the polished glass and steel of the sanitised meat counter. The private space of the pig farm, firmly closed to outsiders, contrasts sharply with the open-to-all, 24/7 public domains of meat consumption: butchers' shops, restaurants and fast-food outlets.

Against the contextualising distances, disparities and disaffections described above, I take the pigman's uncompromising claim about ruthlessness as a point of incision to get deeper under the skin of the pig industry and explore the specificity of pigmen's relationships with pigs. In exploring the detail of how 'ruthlessness' is actually constituted within intensive pig production, I show how the idiom of detachment is mobilised and calibrated by pigmen themselves as they hold alternating phases of human–animal connection and disconnection in tension. In so doing, I acknowledge that any attempt to positively rehabilitate the ethics of such detachment within lay perceptions is liable to be beset with difficulties.

Short stays: structured separations

The following brief outline of the working logistics on the intensive 'farrow to finish'[8] pig unit that hosted my fieldwork is included to provide a sense of the fragmentary nature of the production line itself, and to illustrate how fragmentation and division of labour provide the framework in which relationships between pigmen and pigs are constructed. The tri-partite organisation described follows a widely used pig-production template.

In industry terms this unit is categorised as 'medium' sized, supporting a breeding herd of 400 sows and eight boars, and a slaughter herd of 3,500. Every week it sends around 200 pigs for slaughter fulfilling a contract with a major retail chain. Quality assurance reports arising from quarterly inspections by a pig vet and data analyst characterise the unit as 'exemplary' in terms of productivity and welfare. The entire herd is cared for by three full-time stockmen and a part-timer, all men. Each full-timer has responsibility for a particular segment of production, and each possesses specialised husbandry skills relevant to the animals on his 'yard'. The pig population is split into two discrete elements; 'breedstock' (comprised of boars, gilts[9] and sows), and the 'pigs'[10] or 'slaughter herd' comprising all the progeny: piglets, growing pigs and finishers. The term 'pig-unit' is something of a misnomer implying a single unified space, but in reality the unit is divided into three linked spaces with the two herds distributed between them in purpose-built, stage-specific accommodation. The service yard[11] houses boars, 'in pig' (pregnant) sows and gilts, and newly weaned sows awaiting reimpregnation. The farrowing and weaning yard is where sows/gilts give birth, and where newly weaned piglets are housed in 'nursery' sheds. The finishing-yard accommodates growing pigs until they attain a predetermined slaughter weight.

Dominated by vast hangar-like barns, countless metal gates and pens, concrete, walled and railed walkways, the pig unit's ambience is harshly utilitarian. The size of the operation, spread across several acres, means that the 'production line' is long and neither its beginning, end nor middle, are discernible to the uninformed eye. The pace, intensity and continuity of production, and the sheer numbers of animals involved, seem at first to preclude any opportunity for closeness with the pigs. Batches, or detachments, of pigs are always arriving or departing. The details of every piglet's birth are carefully logged, as are their projected slaughter dates. There is a machine-like predetermined order to the movements every animal undertakes, and for pigs, there are no jobs for life. Every stay is short term: for example, once breeding sows have produced their sixth or seventh litter at three years of age, their fertility declines and they are sent for slaughter, destined for sausage production. The service-yard manager explained the lifespan of pigs: 'The gestation period for a sow is 3 months, 3 weeks, 3 days: 115 days. Our pigs ... are achieving 90 kilos live-weight in 151days.' Therefore the production lead time is short with the journey from service-house to serving-dish being accomplished in a total of just under nine months. In this environment, production coheres, not despite, but precisely *because* it consists of a series of staged separations: this is the dynamic by which the transformation from animal to commodity, pig to pork is effected.

Detachment, docility and discipline

Chapter length does not permit exhaustive description of the daily routines of pigmen and pigs,[12] but to summarise, every pig's lifespan is divided into a series of clearly demarcated production episodes, each of which is literally timed and spaced. Strict timetabling, which fuses temporal rhythm, and the kind of social discipline practiced in institutional settings applies in the pig unit's workings. Drawing relevantly on Foucault's (1978: 139) notion of 'bio-power', understood as 'techniques or "disciplines" designed to manipulate human bodies and transform them into docile and productive subjects', Novek (2005) examines the discipline involved in intensive livestock systems. Classically, such disciplinary techniques were mobilised in hospitals, barracks, prisons and, importantly to this case, factories. In pig production the adage that 'time equals money' could be coupled with the phrase 'and so does space': Foucault's (1979: 143) idea that 'Each individual has a place and each place has an individual' is apt. Farmers' emphatic attention to the optimisation of space and time is driven by the fiercely competitive market conditions of the trade in pork. The fact that the British pig industry receives no support or grant aid from the government or from the European Union (EU), yet its products must compete with cheap pork imports from EU countries with lower production costs,[13] means that every minute and every square inch count. Every pig unit is an environment where the biological, interior timescales of gestation, birth and growth must synthesise with externally imposed production timetables which are, in turn, dictated by the conditions of competitive global pork trading. Here order, regimentation and regulation, expressed as 'routine' are paramount. In connection with the emphasis on efficient routine, the apparently contradictory concepts of 'passion' and 'self-discipline' are working idioms understood by pigmen to be virtually synonymous.

Novek's portrayal of the pig farm as a disciplinarian institution

Artisanal affection

is persuasive, but this view does not constitute a complete picture. Importantly, Driessen (2010: 1–12), looks beyond the industrial paradigm to draw attention to a plethora of practical and ethical issues which amalgamate in farming practice. Together these constitute a 'mosaic of concerns' among which Driessen cites food security, labour conditions, rural livelihoods and economies, environmental issues and animal wellbeing. Driessen summarises Boltanski and Thevenot's (2006) 'orders of worth', or 'justificatory regimes', which embrace inspiration (creative, emotional, imaginative values), domestic (trust, kinship), renown (honour, recognition, public display), civic (the common good), market (contracts between producers/consumers), and industrial (worth based on efficiency/production) so as to emphasise the immense complexity which ensues when some, or all, of the 'concerns' or 'justificatory regimes' collide. Farming thus involves mixed motives, and is conducted within multiple orders of worth, figuring the mosaic as 'the site of tragic choices, for instance between consumer autonomy and animal wellbeing, or … between farmer safety and the intrinsic values of animals'. What Driessen makes clear is that farmers – and, I argue, stockmen – neither possess nor subscribe to a predetermined collective set of professional ethics. Instead, the moral agency they exercise emerges from the particularities of their individual work situations, as well from the influence of external societal factors. Put another way, difficult ethical choices about livestock treatment are made on a 'mix and match' basis in response to an almost infinite number of variables. As a consequence of the sheer volatility of these factors, the kinds of relationships stockmen share with animals are always in flux, always multifariously intermixed, and far more complex than has been suspected hitherto.

To illustrate the newly emerging scope of knowledge concerning stockmen's relationships with animals, I draw on Wilkie's (2010: 173) proposal that one of the impacts of the division of labour in the livestock industry is a corresponding division of workers' attitudes towards animals. Wilkie (2005: 218) notes how 'the various stages of the production process provide workers with a range of opportunities to interact with their animals, and each stage sets constraints on the nature of that contact'. She acknowledges that 'the degree and kind of emotional involvement with each type of animal is not static and can vary as the animal's perceived status changes and the nature of the interspecies relationship strengthens or weakens' (2005: 181). Animal husbandry thus involves emotional versatility, a perpetual oscillation between instrumental and affective attitudes, an idea supported by English et al. (1992: 27, 36) for whom stockmanship consists of a 'jigsaw puzzle' of affective fragments distributed among the various roles that a stockman assumes in relation to his animals; during different production stages pigmen may act as pigs' leaders, carers or even their peers. The diversity of these roles emphasises how affective adaptability and flexibility are prime stockmanship skills. Emotional resourcefulness, whose cultivation requires time and dedication, figures as the quintessential occupational attribute: it is the core of the job, the part which not just anyone can do as I show in the ethnography that follows.

Detailing the kinds 'affinity' and 'aloofness' implicit in this role-switching Wilkie (2005: 218–219; 2010: 181) provides a fourfold model, paraphrased below:

> 'Attached-attachment' or 'strong emotional attachment' (emotional intensity, ascription of pet-like status to individual de-commodified livestock animals).

> 'Concerned attachment' or 'emotional affinity' (personal, enduring relationships extended towards individual breed-stock animals who are not regarded as part of a de-personalised cohort).

> 'Concerned detachment' or 'emotional detachment' (impersonal concern towards commodity animals who are handled with care yet reduced to tool-like status).

> 'Detached-detachment' or 'emotional aloofness' (distance from de-individuated, commodified animals destined for consumption).

Although her account mobilises rich ethnographic data, Wilkie recognises that her own ability to specify exactly what 'close' or 'knowing' relationships with livestock really entail, especially in industrial farming contexts, is hampered by the industry's own reluctance to communicate openly about its methods, a stance which has 'contributed to a perceptible lack of information from the perspectives of those who actually work with livestock' (2010: 184). When planning fieldwork industry professionals warned me that I would never gain admittance to an intensive unit because the dual causes underlying farmers' reluctance to admit inquisitive outsiders run deep. First, following calamitous disease epidemics, real anxiety and vigilance persist in relation to maintaining bio-security. Second, many farmers and stockmen had horror stories to tell concerning unwelcome approaches from animal activists. The 2012 suicide of a Norfolk farmer[14] following serious cruelty allegations by Animal Equality provides an extreme example, but activist interest fuels many farmers' determination to keep their farm property and practices private. The lack of transparency arising from such concerns directly obstructs the acquisition of knowledge about the means by which stock-

Artisanal affection

men mobilise the intertwining functions of empathy and detachment. Although Wilkie alerts us to the existence of 'detached-detachment', the self-protective farmer attitudes I mention may have contributed to preventing her ethnographic data from fully penetrating or capturing this contentious and doubly compounded property's practical applications, its proclivities or its latent values.

Ethnography: managing pigs – managing emotions

This section moves away from the wide-angle contextualising view of the industry to focus on pigmen's first-hand experience. The ethnographic data it offers was generated in 2013 during individual semi-structured interviews with three highly experienced pigmen: David[15] (foreman/service yard manager), Tom (farrowing/weaning yard manager), and Nathan (finishing yard manager), all long-standing colleagues on the unit described previously. My earlier research with these stockmen paid attention to human–pig empathisation and proximity.[16] By contrast, these interviews invited the pigmen to identify and consider varieties of distance. This data questions the assumption that empathy and business-led instrumentality inevitably figure as mutually cancelling opposites. By considering examples of the detached elements of pigmen's professional behaviours, I show how pigmen's practices of cultivating distance between themselves and pigs may take unforeseen forms, or produce unanticipated consequences for both human and animal workers. I do not claim that views expressed by the participants capture the range of every stockman's professional outlook, but my long-term research suggests that they are typical and current among pigmen.

Rather than first discussing their day-to-day management of pigs, all three interviewees spontaneously homed in on the topic of production-led pig euthanasia and the responsibilities and effects this practice imposed. (Sick or deformed piglets are despatched by a sharp blow to the head, whereas adult pigs are 'given a single injection of lead', that is, shot.) In large herd populations mortalities caused by disease, injury or accident are inevitable. David told me how he understood killing as:

> Part of life; it's reality … I see this cycle in my job all the time … I have to think of it every day. We nurture stuff and we have to kill it … When I kill something I do it … to save pain and suffering … and also economically there's no sense in keeping a pig that won't make it through the system.

The dichotomy between caring, keeping things alive, averting suffering and 'being businesslike' both reinforced and qualified the initial claim made by David about being 'ruthless' in his work. Tom's thoughts coincided with David's:

> I find it hard to despatch … smaller pigs, than I do older pigs. I think that's just a natural instinct that it's harder to despatch a day-old piglet – probably because they're a small, vulnerable animal. It's just part of what I do. It makes it easier that it is part of the production, because I know that I have to do that for the rest of the production to carry on, so it's easier to do that than to let something go on and suffer later on.

When asked about the effect that carrying out euthanasia had on him, David said, 'When I kill something, I lose; there's just something inside that changes a little bit … You lose a little bit of yourself. You're maybe not quite such a, I dunno, a complete person.' He went on to explain how for him taking a life is 'a very personal thing … very intimate. [...] Nothing can be done to that thing ever again … There would never be that closeness again.' Here the most intense intimacy with the animal occur precisely at the moment of killing, at the ultimate rupture between human and animal. The pigman loses not merely a commoditised pig, a number on a profit and loss account, but also the relationship that he had with the living animal, and crucially, a part of himself.

Such long-term repetition of killing and associated loss of selfhood prospectively figure as highly pernicious. If the process were solely subtractive, the pigman would inevitably reach a state of total emotional impoverishment, so how are the deleterious effects of the work assuaged? An answer may lie in the fact that, in holding life and death in almost symmetrical relations, stockworkers simultaneously maintain an acceptable balance between positive and negative aspects of the work. The weekly replacement of slaughter pigs with a supply of newborns[17] suggests a correspondence between the regeneration of the herd and a concomitant restitution of pigmen's compromised selfhood. An anecdote of David's lends weight to this idea. Speaking of a newly-retired slaughterman, he described how this man's professional experience came at great personal expense: 'He felt quite empty after a lifetime of killing things.' When asked if his experience differed from the slaughterman's David said that he could 'spread' himself and be 'very nurturing and very ruthless at the same time'. He gave this example of killing a piglet: 'Within a split second I'm picking another pig up which is fit and healthy and helping that to get on the teat to survive … I've just put that deformed pig down, and I then have another one to help, that makes me feel better.'

Nathan also reflected on the highly personalised encounter that killing involves:

> If it's a lame one I often feel guilty about having to shoot them because they're as bright as a button, mentally. They're looking up at you – 'What are you doing?' – sort of thing and I'm thinking 'I'm not allowed to send you to slaughter and you're not going to get any better so I've got to do this.' And in your mind you're saying 'I'm really sorry about this, but I've got to do this.' But there are other times when a pig is clearly pretty sick ... Even though you're killing it, you feel as though you're helping it; you're doing a good thing.

He described how other routine tasks induced deeply felt emotive response:

> There are times when I feel really guilty because ... sometimes you have to mix [finishers] up because of space issues ... You know you've just put three pigs in a pen of ten and they're going to get picked on. You feel really guilty ... That is the one thing I hate the most ... I really wish I didn't have to ... There's no choice. It's because the slaughterhouses want a specific size of pig, so if I had my way I'd keep them all in family groups all the way through to slaughter, then just put the whole lot out whether they weigh a hundred kilos, seventy kilos. But the slaughterhouses don't like that.

Like the sheep-farmers and racehorse producers studied by Gray (1998) and Cassidy (2002) respectively, many pigmen insist that the ability to empathise with pigs is an innate, inherited attribute, and that their artisanal expert practice of animal- husbandry is unviable for those not 'bred' to it. Perhaps this idea partially expresses pigmen's recognition that the exact relationship between empathy and detachment is enigmatic, almost impossible to quantify verbally. However, this faith in genetic predisposition has to be reconciled with the harsh realities of commercial production. These accounts show how the requirement to make swift alternations between nurturing/affective and destructive/aloof acts imposes highly contradictory demands, a conflict succinctly captured by David's reference to being 'at loggerheads with yourself'. Paradoxically, he also asserted that his ruthlessness and his caring 'don't come from two different mes'. The interviewees all articulate the discomfiture they feel about 'dehumanising' aspects of the work; being a less 'complete person', a condition which they present as antithetical to the empathetic, 'natural instinct' or more fully human drive to preserve life. The interviewees' statements show how commodification, which objectifies and ultimately de-animalises pigs[18] is paralleled by an element of dehumanisation for the stockmen involved. Such partial dehumanisation does not necessarily translate into bad stockmanship involving cruelty or indifference to pigs: to figure stockmen's detachment or self-distancing from pigs in such simplistic terms would miss the point that mobilisation and management of the inter-relationship between attached/detached behaviours is fundamental to the culture of stockmanship.

The statements reveal how pigmen use compound, overlapping justificatory rationales in attempting to alleviate the emotional burden imposed by their work. Their justifications coincide with several of Boltanski and Thevenot's (2006) 'orders of worth': industrial worth – for production efficiency; market worth – to fulfil contractual arrangements; civic worth – doing good for pigs, employers, meat processors and consumers; domestic worth – extending positive sentiments and care towards pigs who figure as co-workers or 'kin'. Rather than offering ways of offloading blame or scapegoating others, their justifications function as vital distancing tactics intended to self-insulate the pigmen from negative emotional impact caused by conflictual and erosive aspects of the work.

However, these insulation tactics are neither total nor infallible. In acknowledging their responsibilities, and the concomitant emotional challenges they face, the pigmen collectively point towards acute self-awareness of ethical dimensions implicit in their work and in so doing they reveal their socially incommodious position as intermediaries (linking farmer, abattoir and consumer) who must do the difficult work of performing animal-averse procedures assigned to them by off-farm agencies. Their situation corresponds with Hughes's (1962) concept of 'dirty workers', a group to whom society first delegates 'degrading' work before denigrating both the work it has mandated and disparaging those who perform it. Hughes (1958) defines dirty work as physically disgusting, presenting social affront to workers' dignity and being counter to moral conceptions – conditions which apply powerfully to pig-stockmanship, as do Douglas's 2002 theorisations concerning dirt as taboo. Douglas traces societal preoccupations with separating pure/impure, clean/dirty to show how negative qualities are projected on to those associated with dirt. In developing these theories Ashforth and Kreiner (1999) observe that although dirty work's stigma inflicts damage on worker status and credibility, it also contributes to the formation of strong occupation-based subcultures which facilitate workers' own positive understanding of what their job is and why it matters.

Such subcultures provide dirty workers with the valuable social resource of a collective defence mechanism which moderates the stigma's impact. Viewed against this theoretical backdrop, pigmen's mobilisation of justifications of worth and their frequent allusions to the '*culture* of stockmanship' together emerge as important devices for recasting their role in positive terms. A different distancing tactic emerged when Tom

Artisanal affection

claimed to deliberately resist closeness to the pigs. He maintained that: 'What I'm doing is a production of an end product ... so I don't feel like I have to *de*tach myself from them, because – like, I'm probably not *a*ttached at the beginning.' Similarly, David spoke of making a conscious effort not to 'play' or 'make too much of fuss' of boars or piglets who want to 'be friendly'. He said, 'I know that they will have to go away, so I don't let myself get too close.'

Both men's statements reveal the existence of carefully constructed emotional boundaries; the fact that human–pig relationships must inevitably be short term and finite both constrains and predetermines the intensity of relations just as Wilkie (2005: 217–218) proposes. However, pigmen's spontaneous deviations from their self-imposed prohibition on friendliness partially destabilise this idea. Affective proximity is revealed in the intimately affectionate appellations which are habitually used to address the sows. Piglets are referred to as 'Charlie' or 'Chubby', and David often personified the boars as his 'workmates'. During interview he made several telling Freudian slips in referring to pigs as 'people'. Similarly, closeness was disclosed via non-verbal clues in the consistently firm but considerate way that I saw pigs handled. Other kinds of closeness are formally authorised. For example, the commonly used industry directive to 'be the boar' reminds pigmen to administer boar-like stimulatory behaviour during artificial insemination so as to promote strong oestrus and optimise fertilisation of a sow's ova: more conceptions equal more pigs, more profit. Being the boar involves lending body weight by applying palm-pressure on a sow's back, or scratching her shoulders. Positive mutual physical contact of this kind, aimed at maximising productivity, incidentally averts mutual affective disengagement between pigman and sow.

Responding to the popular presupposition that scale production by default militates against animals receiving individual care, all three men repeatedly referred to stress-inducing time pressures. Nathan made the point that his job involved routine work, times when he was 'just doing the job' automatically, and phases when he was 'very conscious of all that was going on'. Similarly, Tom distinguished between carrying out automated or technologically assisted tasks ('pushing buttons' to adjust heat, ventilation, light or to deliver piglet feed), and more 'hands-on' care (assisting sows during difficult births, carrying out postnatal procedures on newborn piglets). He explained how on busy days he integrates routine whole-herd tasks with setting time aside to look after individuals:

> I go to that sow, look after [a] litter, pick up muck, then come back to make sure she's still farrowing OK ... she's not ... to feel that I'm rushed.

> As far as she's concerned she's getting on with it and I'm helping her. [I] don't have the time to individualise each pig. I have a hundred crates with a hundred sows, so at least a thousand pigs to look after, so have to spread time across the whole lot, so if there's a pen of sick pigs, you give them as much attention as you can, but you mustn't give them all the attention because obviously you've got older, bigger pigs that are doing without your attention. It has to be a happy medium between doing both. [I'm] less hands on with the pigs than with the sows ... I feel the same feelings for the sows as I do the pigs ... It doesn't mean there's a lack of care, it just means the care has to be shared out between everything.

This statement draws attention to the demands set by combining automated and manual stockmanship techniques while delivering whole-herd and individual attention across different categories, ages and stages of pigs. The notion of 'spreading', or distribution of care, shows how the pigman does not indiscriminately deploy the insensitive, non-compassionate or wholly exploitative 'detached-detachment' that Wilkie notes, but rather a 'dual detachment'. He does not choose between being detached from *all* pigs as opposed to being attached to *all*, or *some*, pigs. Instead, his work consists of a perpetual oscillation between detaching from the whole herd so as to nurture the individual, and separating from the individual so as to care for the whole herd. Reconciling these concurrent, and often stress-inducing demands, involves the self-discipline of time management and strict compliance with routine, which in this context together figure as another important distancing tactic. Inasmuch as this 'spreading' strategy promotes the equal disbursement of care shared among single pigs and many pigs, it simultaneously offers pigmen another justification of worth since it promotes their confidence in the concept of working for the 'common good' of the entire herd.

When asked if or how apprentices are trained to deal with stockwork's emotional challenges, all three interviewees said that they had never received any formal preparation: 'Nothing's taught'; 'You're not told anything'; 'You're not told how to deal with anything.' Nathan spoke of the anxiety he felt the first time he watched a vet perform an autopsy. He anticipated a colleague asking if he was OK, but when no one did he realised what was expected of him:

> [I] really braced myself for it inside, and more or less said 'I don't care what I see. It's not going to affect me. I'm going to be big and brave here. I'm going to prove to them that I can put up with this.' ... I was so determined to prove myself to be capable ... I was so psyched up. You know it's coming and you're preparing yourself all the time.

Despite pig stockmanship being a heavily male-dominated profession, Nathan insisted that the resolve he described was motivated less by his own machismo, or by masculine peer pressure, or by the fear of 'mickey-taking', and more by a determination to prove his possession of *comprehensive* capability. Seen like this, self-protective bracing up/psyching up function as manifestations of professional pride rather than as expressions or indicators or either personal weakness or cold indifference.

'Feeling rules' and ruling feelings

Revisiting the topic of killing, Nathan described how, when several pigs need to be despatched, he 'steels' himself and shoots them in quick succession. He said that spacing out killings would 'make you feel terrible … drive you nuts'. The frequency with which the idiom of 'steeling up' was used by the three men implied that all of them experienced a sense of personal risk concerning the consequences of failure to arm themselves against incapacitating psychological or emotional harm. For Nathan the ability to separate mentally, to 'go into your own little place in your mind to take yourself away from reality a bit and [and] block everything out' was vital for his own well-being. David alluded to the issue of burdensome guilt when he said that he often 'berated' himself about the pigs he had killed. The conscious effort involved in balancing out 'good' and 'bad', and in creating distance between himself and the destructive aspects of his work was made obvious when he said: 'I take on board the guilt thing about killing things.... To keep my own sanity, I need to realise that I have done a lot of good and helped a lot of animals.' When asked what might happen if he could not achieve this by using detaching or distancing strategies, he was unequivocal: 'You need detachment. If you didn't have it you'd be psychopathic.' Tom endorsed this idea:

> If someone [over-attaches], it would be very, very hard and they wouldn't do the job for long because you just couldn't. I don't feel that you could do the job properly because you just wouldn't be able to distinguish between what needs to be done, and what you'd like to be doing, or what you *feel* you'd like to be doing.

Goffman (1990a) and Hochschild (1979) have shown how feeling is regulated in their respective studies of 'impression management' and the presentation of emotion in the workplace. Both discuss how individuals operate 'feeling rules' to control how they appear to others. In the pigmen's accounts steeling, bracing and psyching up figure as important emotion rules. These appear to be less about self- hardening desensitisation and more concerned with the means by which pigmen erect self-protective emotional boundaries while maintaining what Tronto (2005) identifies as the ethical elements of care: attentiveness, responsibility, competence and responsiveness. 'Steeling' and compassionate 'softening' thus emerge, and merge, as complementary and interdependent rather than oppositional attributes.

Inter-relationships between 'care ethics' and emotion management have been explored by Noddings (1984), Kittay (1999) and Held (2005), who link the concept of care with feminised, virtuous and dutiful labour – qualities compatible with pigmen's principled attitudes towards taking pride in 'work well done' and 'passionate' engagement with both their role and their charges. While pig stockmanship is predominantly 'men's work', it paradoxically consists largely in constructing relationships figuring pigmen as domestic carers and pigs as dependants. However, destructive acts of pig euthanasia, which compromise pigmen's sense of being fully human, have an unexpected parallel since nurturing and caregiving also seem capable of disrupting pigmen's sense of masculinity. Together, the subtractive effects of caring and killing bear out Goffman's (1990b) concept of 'spoiled identity' since they both compromise pigmen's positive self-perception. Goffman (1990b: 12) relevantly defines the spoiled identity of a stigmatised person as 'reduced ... from a whole and usual person to a tainted, discounted one', an idea applicable to the pigmen's sense of depletion as being neither wholly male, nor a complete person. The social distancing of pigmen, coupled with the gender-based self-distanciation I describe, together constitute another powerful order of occupation-based detachment.

Critical attention has been given to the disciplining of pigs,[19] but less is mentioned about pigmen's self-discipline, and while animal advocates concentrate on welfare costs incurred by livestock in capitalist production, to date, virtually no recognition has been given to parallel qualitative human costs. However, pigmen's experiences of conflict and their consequent need to create distance from both its causes and effects are not unique. Drawing on Gieryn's (1983) concept of boundary maintenance, Hunter (2005: 254–261) analyses the prevalence of emotional conflict and use of emotion rules among trainee midwives. Her identification of the clash midwives experience between being 'with woman' or 'with institution' (being intimate, empathetic, intuitive towards women in labour, as opposed to dispassionately obeying the hospital's procedural rules) resonates with the way that pigmen negotiate being 'with pig' (giving humane individual care) or 'with business' (complying with profit-led commercial dynamics). This dichotomy is powerfully evidenced in the work of Tom, the farrowing manager, in particular because, for him, pig-husbandry consists largely in pig-midwifery. The idea of his working between being 'with sow' or 'with business' is reinforced by his description of returning to labouring sows at night to provide additional individual care.

Importantly, Hunter also notes how unwritten rules are established during midwifery training, and shows that when such rules cannot be adhered to, blame, guilt and self-criticism are internalised by trainees who rarely acknowledge their own support needs. This internalisation process correlates closely with the pigmen's accounts of how they deal with work-induced guilt. For pigmen, the 'social invisibility' of farm-workers noted by Newby (1977) comes replete with an institutionalised and unmentionable 'emotional invisibility'. Unlike the midwives who practise 'discursive resistance' by discussing problematic issues together, pigmen rarely have access to peer reassurance originating outside their own unit. Their resultant personalisation of guilt reinforces senses of isolation from both colleagues and wider society.

In attempting to get beyond defamatory stereotypes, this study reveals how pigmen perceive their self-image: they self-characterise as guilty and proud, humanely caring and instrumentally businesslike. Despite these conceptual rifts, each of the interviewees showed that detachment and attachment both contribute to a unified work ethic. Rather than seeing these features as polar opposites, they insisted on their being 'interlinked', and 'on a continuum' – ideas suggesting mutual enfolding of the two. The data disclose how conscientious pigmen uphold the ethical elements of empathic care identified by Tronto (2005) and confirms how these are neither overshadowed nor cancelled out by the intermittent need to create distance. The mismatch between what Tom says (never attaching so as to avoid detaching) and what he does (voluntarily giving extra care after-hours) perhaps serves as the most powerful example of the complete articulation that pigmen effect between attachment and detachment.

Although the ethnography illustrates how the pig sector's workers adopt behaviours which coincide in varying degrees with all four of Wilkie's affective categories, my data suggest that there are no grounds for automatically ascribing the category of 'detached-detachment' to the human–animal relationships pertaining in intensive pig production. The fact that pigmen constantly move between, and adopt, elements of all four affective categories destabilises the possibility either of keeping categories separate, or of pigeonholing emotions or behaviours. This chapter builds on Wilkie's insights and extends her typology by showing in detail how the qualities that pigmen must propagate and maintain in order to perform their work – namely compassion, empathy, emotional detachment and social distance/proximity – are inextricably interwoven. In contrast to Wilkie's categories which separate detachment from attachment, my data show how compassion and empathy are embedded within various practices of detachment. Informed by pigmen's own accounts of their work I argue for the existence and inseparability of various nuanced forms of 'detached compassion' and 'empathetic distance'.

Conclusion

The chapter contends that any presumption that pig production is dominated by detachment's negative or detrimental aspects is unsustainable. Properly deployed, detachment offers mutual benefits for livestock workers and livestock. I have shown the importance pigmen ascribe to their detached behaviours: being detached contributes to staving off emotional bankruptcy, preserving mental and ethical equilibrium and enabling a sense of being both human and humane in a socially isolating workplace where people are heavily outnumbered by animals. Pigmen validate the cultivation and control of detachment on the grounds that it offers means to ensure objectivity and promote clear judgement on the often difficult ethical choices they face.

Alongside detachment's positive aspects the chapter also acknowledges how negative stigmatisation and self-alienation experienced by many pigmen emerge as strongly marked occupational features. Importantly, these features need rectification if the pig sector is to solve the linked problems of damaged public image and an impending recruitment crisis. Driessen (2010: 14) proposes that if *farmers*' ability 'to take part in ethical debates is questioned, a choice is already made on whose terms these debates are performed, and what constitutes ... meaningful debate' – an idea equally applicable to stockmen. My data proves that these workers are completely capable of rational explanation of what appears to many observers as a duplicitous or ambiguous attitude towards livestock.

These findings contribute to the broader anthropology of working worlds involving expert practice by providing concrete examples of the effects generated when internalised, innate, intuitive capabilities of workers collide with externally imposed business-led demand. The unique ethnographic material I offer opens up areas of uncharted anthropological territory to demonstrate how, rather than being emotionally blunted or devoid of feeling, unseen workers operating beyond the social pale sharpen their sensibilities to effect means to contend with the complex and ambiguous occupational demands they face. The academic reach of this idea is capable of extension beyond the interstitial space of the farm which exists between human and animal realms: it would bear application in other working environments where affect, detachment and proximity operate as coexistent forces and in contexts where the logic and functionality of denigrated workers' occupational knowledges deserve attention and retrieval.

By documenting the first-hand experiences of a group of workers for whom closely interwoven relations between attachment and detachment are paramount, the chapter transcends the limitations of existing (mis) understandings of commercial agricultural practice. If present opacities, human 'invisibilities', or animal 'disappearances' are to be neither perpetuated nor replaced with a different set of misperceptions, then analyses of detachment's function, as offered in this chapter, offer a valuable contribution to broad academic debate around the ethics of food production.

The chapter has focused on reciprocities between making things and making selves, separating from things and relinquishing aspects of the self, processes that stress the indivisible relationship between expert manual practice and emotional aptitude. My contention that artisanal work may be constructive (producing things) as well as reductive (depleting the maker) in almost equal measure opens the way for further scholarship which re-examines interactions between not just detachment and attachment themselves but, by extension, entanglements between occupational prestige and opprobrium, ignominy and respect.

During this account of managing pigs and managing emotions the subtexts of craft and craftsmanship have surfaced repeatedly: many pigmen think of themselves as craftsmen and I have shown how their attachment to pigs emerges as an artisanal affection. My account builds on existing theory to suggest that the complex physical and perceptual processes of making and unmaking I describe thus transcend the notion of mindless mechanical production, figuring instead as highly deliberative. Just as pigmen refine the craft skills of manual dexterity, visual acuity, tool use, calculative ability and working to specification, so too do they shape and hone affection and aloofness, dovetailing them to fit pig farming's purposes. In a working world where the onus rests on holding yourself apart while holding yourself together, one pigman's definition of detachment as 'a survival strategy' is far more than a mere figure of speech.

Notes

1 Following livestock industry conventions, I use the terms 'stockman' and 'pigman' interchangeably. The term 'pigman' is prevalent in the industry and reflects the fact that the 'hands-on' segment of pig production in Britain is largely male dominated. At the numerous farms I visited during fieldwork I did

not encounter any women directly engaged in pig stockmanship. That said, the industry routinely employs women in specialist veterinary, managerial, advisory and facilitatory roles.
2. See www.ciwf.org.uk/what_we_do/pigs/default.aspx; wwww.factoryfarming.org.uk/pigs.html; www.viva.org.uk/what-we-do/latest-updates/cruel-britannia (all accessed 14.11.13).
3. See Karpf (2001) and www.bbc.co.uk/news/uk-england-cumbria-12471373 (accessed 14.11.13).
4. See British Veterinary Association (2013); and Lawrence (2013).
5. www.ukagriculture.com (accessed 14.11.13).
6. National Farmers Union.
7. NPA claims to be 'the voice of the British pig industry'.
8. 'Farrowing' is the specialised term for birth of piglets, and 'finishing' refers to fattening pigs in the final production stage.
9. Gilts are young adult females yet to give birth to their first litters.
10. When pigmen speak of 'pigs', they refer exclusively to animals destined for slaughter.
11. 'Service' is the term used for impregnation, whether by the boar or by artificial insemination.
12. See Baker (2010) for my detailed account of spatio-temporal organisation on a farrowing-yard.
13. British farmers consistently claim that they produce animals to higher welfare specifications than their European counterparts: higher welfare systems are more expensive to implement.
14. www.bbc.co.uk/news/uk-england-norfolk-17404304 (accessed 14.11.13).
15. All pseudonyms.
16. I provide an extended account of pigmen's empathy with pigs in Baker (2011).
17. Weekly numbers of piglets born slightly exceeds numbers sold.
18. See Vialles (1994) for an account of the final stages of de-animalisation within abattoir contexts.
19. See Novek (2005); Coppin (2003).

References

Adams, Carol, 1990, *The Sexual Politics of Meat*. New York: Continuum.

Ashforth, B. E. and Kreiner, G. E., 1999, 'How can you do it?': Dirty Work and the Challenge of Constructing a Positive Identity. *Academy of Management Review*, 24(3): 413–434.

Baker, Kim, 2010, *Species of Time: Sows, Stockmen, and Labour*, www.gold.ac.uk/anthropology/garp/GARP16_web.pdf (accessed 18.11.13).

Baker, Kim, 2011, Making Meat: People, Property and Pigs in East Anglia, Chapter 4, Be the Boar, 151–70 (PhD thesis: Goldsmiths, University of London).

Boltanski, Luc and Thevenot, Laurent, 2006[1991], *On Justification: The Economies of Worth*, Princeton, NJ: Princeton University Press.

British Veterinary Association, 2013, Comment: Horsemeat and the Food Chain veterinaryrecord.bmj.com/content/172/8/194.full (accessed 19.11.13).
Cassidy, Rebecca, 2002, *The Sport of Kings: Kinship, Class and Thoroughbred Breeding in Newmarket.* Cambridge: Cambridge University Press.
Coppin, Dawn, 2003, Foucauldian Hog Futures: The Birth of Mega-Hog Farms. *Sociology Quarterly* 44: 597–616.
Davis, David, 1984, Good People Doing Dirty Work: A Study of Social Isolation. *Symbolic Interaction* 7(2): 233–247.
Douglas, Mary, 2002[1966], *Purity and Danger: An Analysis of the Concept of Pollution and Taboo.* London: Routledge.
Driessen, Clemens, 2010, Farmers Engaged in Deliberative Practices; An Ethnographic Exploration of the Mosaic of Concerns in Livestock Agriculture. http://edepot.wur.nl/ 159370 (accessed 25.11.13).
English, Peter, Gethyn Burgess, Ricardo Segundo and Dunne, John, 1992, *Stockmanship. Improving the Care of the Pig and Other Livestock.* Ipswich: Farming Press.
Farm Animal Welfare Council (FAWC), 2007, *FAWC Report on Stockmanship and Farm Animal Welfare.* London: Farm Animal Welfare Council.
Foucault, Michel, 1978, *The History of Sexuality*, vol. 1., trans. Robert Hurley. New York: Pantheon Books.
Foucault, Michel, 1979, *Discipline and Punish: The Birth of the Prison*, trans. Alan Sheridan. New York: Vintage Books.
Gieryn, Thomas F., 1983, Boundary-work and the Demarcation of Science from Non-Science: Strains and Interests in the Professional Ideologies of Scientists. *American Sociological Review* 46(6): 781–795.
Goffman, Erving, 1990a[1959], *The Presentation of Self in Everyday Life.* London: Penguin.
Goffman, Erving, 1990b[1963], *Stigma. Notes on the Management of Spoiled Identity.* London: Penguin.
Gray, John, 1998, Family Farms in the Scottish Borders: A Practical Definition by Hill Sheep Farmers. *Journal of Rural Studies* 14(3): 341–356.
Harrison, Ruth, 1964, *Animal Machines.* London: Vincent Stuart Ltd.
Held, Virginia, 2005, *The Ethics of Care.* Oxford: Oxford University Press.
Hemsworth, Paul H., 2003, Human–Animal Interactions in Livestock Production, *Applied Animal Behaviour Science* 81(3): 185–198.
Hochschild, Arlie R., 1979 Emotion Work, Feeling Rules, and Social Structure. *American Journal of Sociology* 85(3): 551–575.
Hughes, Everett C., 1958, *Men and Their Work.* Glencoe IL: Free Press.
Hughes, Everett C., 1962, Good People and Dirty Work. *Social Problems* 10: 3–11.
Hunter, Billie, 2005, Emotion Work and Boundary Maintenance in hospital-based midwifery *Midwifery* 21: 253–266.
Karpf, Ann, 2001, Farmers' Grief Leaves us all Bereft. www.theguardian.com/uk/2001/apr/12/footandmouth.comment (accessed 13.1.14).

Kittay, Eva, 1999, *Love's Labour: Essays on Women, Equality and Dependency.* New York: Routledge.

Lave, Jean and Wenger, Etienne, 1991, *Situated Learning: Legitimate Peripheral Participation.* Cambridge: Cambridge University Press.

Lawrence, Felicity, 2013, Where did the 29% Horse in your Tesco Burger Come From? www.theguardian.com/uk-news/2013/oct/22/horsemeat-scandal-guardian-investigation-public-secrecy (accessed 18.11.13).

Mayfield, L. E., Bennett, R. M, Tranter, R. B., Wooldridge, M. J., 2007, Consumption Of Welfare- Friendly Food Products In Great Britain, Italy And Sweden, And How It May Be Influenced By Consumer Attitudes To, And Behaviour Towards, Animal Welfare Attributes. *International Journal of Sociology of Food and Agriculture* 15(3): 59–73.

Miele, Mara and Bock, Bettina, 2007, Editorial: Competing Discourses of Farm Animal Welfare and Agri-Food Restructuring. *International Journal of Sociology of Food and Agriculture* 15(3): 1–7.

Newby, Howard, 1977, *The Deferential Worker. A Study of Farm Workers in East Anglia*, London: Allen Lane.

Noddings, Nel, 1984, *Caring: A Feminine Approach to Ethics and Moral Education.* Berkeley: University of California Press.

Novek, Joel, 2005, Pigs and People: Sociological Perspectives on the Discipline of Nonhuman Animals in Intensive Confinement. *Sociology of Animals* 13: 221–244.

Regan, Tom, 2001, *Defending Animal Rights*, Illinois: University of Illinois Press.

Singer, Peter, 1976, *Animal Liberation*, London: Jonathan Cape.

Tovey, Hilary, 2002, Risk, Morality and the Sociology of Animals – Reflections on the Foot and Mouth Outbreak in Ireland. *Irish Journal of Sociology* 12(1): 3–42.

Tovey, Hilary, 2003, Theorising Nature and Society in Sociology: The Invisibility of Animals, *Sociologia Rurali*, 43(3): 196–215.

Tronto, Joan, 2005, An Ethic of Care, In Ann Cudd and Robin Andreasen, eds, *Feminist Theory: A Philosophical Anthropology.* Oxford: Blackwell Publishing, pp. 251–264.

Vialles, Noelie, 1994, *Animal to Edible.* Cambridge: Cambridge University Press.

Wacquant, Lois, 2004, *Body and Soul: Notebooks of an Apprentice Boxer.* Oxford: Oxford University Press.

Wilkie, Rhoda, 2005, Sentient Commodities and Productive Paradoxes: The Ambiguous Nature of Human Livestock Relations in Northeast Scotland. *Journal of Rural Studies* 21: 213–30.

Wilkie, Rhoda, 2010, *Livestock/Deadstock. Working with Farm Animals from Birth to Slaughter.* Philadelphia, PA: Temple University Press.

Websites

www.bbc.co.uk/news/uk-england-cumbria-12471373 (accessed 14.11.13).
www.bbc.co.uk/news/uk-england-norfolk-17404304 (accessed 14.11.13).
www.ciwf.org.uk/what_we_do/pigs/default.aspx (accessed 14.11.13).
www.factoryfarming.org.uk/pigs.html www.ukagriculture.com (accessed 14.11.13).
www.ukagriculture.com (accessed 14.11.13).
www.viva.org.uk/what-we-do/latest-updates/cruel-britannia (accessed 14.11.13).

4

Professionalism and expertise: comment

Veena Das

I begin by thinking of disengagement as a mode of being in the world as my entry point into the three marvellous chapters on which I have been given the privilege to comment. In a famous essay on Heidegger, Charles Taylor (1993) referred to the short list of twentieth-century scholars (in which he included Merleau-Ponty and Wittgenstein) who had powerfully contested the hold of rationalism on our pictures of what is called thinking. 'Engaged agency' rather than 'disengagement', Taylor argued, required that we take human embodiment as essential to the way our worlds are shaped. But 'being shaped' by such facts as our being embodied creatures or creatures endowed with language was not the same as attributing causality to these conditions – rather, Taylor showed that our expressions (e.g. something lies at hand) appear to make sense only in a world in which humans have *this* kind of body that can grasp things – such projections between the physical and the metaphorical would make no sense to creatures from another kind of planet or from one of Wittgenstein's imaginary tribes. Elsewhere I have argued that the expression, 'forms of life' in Wittgenstein makes available the profound idea that the social and the natural mutually and continuously absorb each other (Das 2014; Han and Das 2015). The natural in this case includes the biological but is not restricted to it – as evident in Wittgenstein's examples of what is 'natural' to the way we count or the 'naturalness' of doing mathematical operations in a certain way and the disputations over some questions but not others as arising from within a form of life.

The three chapters in Part I open a window to asking (from my perspective) the following set of questions. First, since all the three relate to expert knowledge, is detachment necessary to 'expertise' and how does that relate to the picture of thought as 'disengaged' that Taylor characterises as having become embedded in the 'common sense' of our civilisation? Second, how are subjects and objects mutually created: does the rich ethnography of practices tell us something about the relation between expert knowledge and the possibility of criticism as a social practice through possibilities of conjunctions and disjunctions? Finally, how do we relate detachment in the field of technological intervention to the familiar objects of anthropological analysis such as kinship and ritual?

Detachment and disengagement

Two facts of modern reason that seem crucial to understanding the affective investment in objectivity as a mode of thought, are: first, the distrust of ordinary experience as misleading to proper thought; and second, the trust in procedures that would stabilise what would otherwise be fleeting, widely divergent understandings of phenomena. The imperative of disengagement as a condition for scientific research or 'the view from nowhere' as Nagel (1983) formulated it, has come under considerable scrutiny from scholars in science and technology studies who have raised the issue of the disunity of science (are procedures similar in laboratory sciences versus field sciences?), as well as the societal agreements through which scientific facts come to be recognised as 'facts'. The chapters in this section effectively challenge the picture of disengagement in the process of scientific production not by contrasting it with engaged agency but by giving us a different angle on the related idea of detachment in three different fields – that of engineering, surgical intervention and artisan practices of pig rearing for the production of meat. We are invited to consider the differences that emerge among these three different scenes and to ask how the picture of modern reason that Taylor so effectively critiques might be modified by looking at practices rather than forms of abstract argument. Is disengaged reason practised in the same way in the world of transplant surgeons as in the world of engineers or livestock workers? As Knox and Harvey say, the practices of detachment described in the work of engineers building a transnational highway project in Peru are somewhat different to the detachments of scientists in their pursuit and production of stable 'facts'. Knox and Harvey call these practices 'virtuous detachment' since it is only by severing their work from the surrounding relations with persons and materials that engineers are able to carve out an area in which they can intervene. Separating themselves from the toxic aftershocks of their interventions in terms of material consequences for those who are affected by the project or from the social upheavals caused, for instance, by widespread displacement, seems a necessary condition for engineers who engage in large projects such as the one described by these authors. The engineers inhabit the spaces they intervene in for the period of the project in a flurry of intense activity but then they disappear from these social worlds. This modality may bear similarities to public health or development projects instituted by external agencies.

I would add here a note of caution that one cannot construct a strict boundary between pure science and engineering as Knox and Harvey seem to suggest – after all, fields like molecular biology have evolved out of close connections with system engineering that introduced the ideas of robustness in the techniques used (see Keller 1995) – so engineering as a discipline has a laboratory or clinical component that might require different ways in which detachment or disengagement might be practised. The question then shifts to what is specific to infrastructural projects such as building roads and bridges that elicit the practices of virtuous detachment that Knox and Harvey describe. And what does it have in common with the successful performance of transplant surgery or with the practice of artisanal knowledge that turns the pig into a commodity in a factory-like setting?

It seems that one important way in which engineers and transplant surgeons find themselves as embedded in the social is through the regulatory mechanisms within which their expertise is located. For Knox and Harvey, engineering is a pragmatic science – it involves devising technical interventions to bring about concrete and observable social effects. Yet it seems to me that this general definition applies much more, or at least applies differently, to engineering projects that are placed in communities rather than the engineering of new molecules in the lab or in a cancer clinic. We do not get much guidance here on thinking about the specificity of infrastructural projects that are made to stand for engineering as a discipline by general references to pragmatic versus pure science.

What is nicely captured by the chapters on road building as a project and the practice of transplant surgery is that the wider context of legal regulations and technical norms are taken by the practitioners as given. These regulations and norms are, of course, produced through a political process that manages inherent multiplicity, indeterminate outcomes and risk allocation in each case – thus laws that regulate how land might be acquired for public roads or whether a kidney can be donated or sold are subjects of political disputations and parliamentary decisions, but the engineers and surgeons do not see themselves as participating in these politics. The virtuous detachment is done by an explicit distancing from the political process, taking it as a given for the particular outcomes to be produced. In this sense the stabilised protocols of the engineer and the transplant surgeon demonstrate their adherence to procedural reason, but these also carve out a domain in which their responsibility is contained. A surgeon might be faulted for not performing a technical procedure correctly but not for the fact that law does not allow a patient awaiting a transplant operation to buy a kidney even if there were a willing seller.

The relation between the technical and the social, then, is produced through the appearance and disappearance of the social in the making of engineering and clinical projects. The effective mechanisms to distance oneself from the relations in which one is placed constitute the condition of possibility for the outcome to be achieved by the application of expert knowledge. It is in this sense that detachment is seen as 'virtuous' by Knox and Harvey and necessary to achieve the 'moral materiality' essential to surgery itself by McDonald. As an example, McDonald describes how the stance of detachment is essential and has been cultivated in the production of the body and disposition of the surgeon by medical pedagogy. Detachment comes into full view in the surgical theatre but must give way to the re-entry of the social, when, for instance, the contribution of organ donors is publicly recognised and celebrated.

Let us pause here for a moment and ask how the alternating rhythms of social embeddings and disconnections might be seen as growing out of particular forms of life rather than thinking of detachment as the subtraction from the social. First, consider the specificity of the political culture within which Knox and Harvey describe how engineers represent the phase of assessing the feasibility of making a highway in the light of legal and technical norms. In a different kind of political culture, a discussion on the feasibility of an engineering project might have been steeped into a commentary of corruption or kickbacks. In a discussion of public projects in India, the talk would inevitably move to the kickbacks received by politicians, the corruption in the supply of materials and the manipulation of records about labour deployment and sundry other issues that make it impossible to think of the kind of detachment from politics that Knox and Harvey describe (see Shah 2010). Similarly, the work of Lawrence Cohen (1999, 2004) alerts us to the lobbying done by transplant surgeons to legalise the sale of organs in India, or media exposures of some slums as places where the bodies of the poor are made 'bioavailable'. The picture of society as morally integrated through gifts or donations of organs has always rubbed against the periodic revelations about regular illegal markets for the sale of organs in India and other places. One might well argue that while these variations in the social milieu are important, they do not affect the argument about detachment as the stance necessary for the phase in which the engineer is engaged in soil analysis or the transplant surgeon is in the operation theatre.

Here I want to return to Taylor's analysis of the bracketing of what he calls 'background' in the argument about disengaged reason. Taylor argues that the many conditions taken for granted as part of the background are necessary to make our experience intelligible. What makes this stance of detachment intelligible, then, is precisely that which allows technical expertise to flourish. It is what produces the conditions under which corporate responsibility can be evaded or severe inequalities in access to latest medical procedures can be put outside the legitimate concerns of transplant surgeons. Knox and Harvey gesture toward this outcome when they analyse the protests of the people whose farming practices were adversely affected by the displacement of the soil on cultivable land and the way engineers could distance themselves from any responsibility for these outcomes. But surely the social is not so much subtracted as made present through the modality of detachment, much as the state is most present when it refuses to respond to a disaster as has been so poignantly described by Ann Lovell (2011) and Vincanne Adams (2013) in their work on post-Hurricane Katrina New Orleans.

It is very interesting to see that in Crowder's chapter on the artisanal practices of pigmen in a pork producing farm, the context of the wider criticisms of the practices of pig farms is fully present and orients such stances as suspicion toward outsiders as pigmen give an account of their own practices explaining how they cultivate the disposition of ruthless distancing from the acts of killing in which they participate. In this case detachment is first embedded in language – for example, the distance between sausage and sow that protects the consumer from the knowledge of the source of his food; and second, it is present as a particular way of constructing the self when the practices require a certain cruelty or ruthlessness with which the experience of interacting with the living animal is calibrated with the experience of preparing the animal for slaughter. There are interesting resemblances with the anatomy lesson and the mastering of the sensory experiences of revulsion at the production of cadavers or of meat. There is an important theme here of how our expressions (cadaver versus body; pork versus pig) embody a reference to actions that carry a hint of our transactions with death as a condition for the regeneration of life of a certain kind. This is a theme to which I return in the last section.

Subjects and objects

An important contribution of actor-network theory is that it contests the idea of the agent as the knowing subject and objects as those which stand over and against the subject, on whom the subject acts. It is now a commonplace that subjects and objects are reciprocally constitutive.

Actor-network-theory is interested in what things do with us (not just to us) rather than thinking of objects as standing over and against subjects. One way to conceptualise this aspect of thinghood is to track the movements of things in and out of their thinghood and reciprocally to think of persons as also constituted by movements in and out of personhood. Michael Serres (1982) formulated the notion of quasi-objects to suggest entities that are like objects in some ways, for they stabilise social forms that would otherwise be too fleeting to capture, but they are unlike objects in that they circulate and make up a different composite whole (temporarily before they detach again) with subjects to whom they become attached. An analogy Serres uses is that of the furet or the ball as an accessory in the passing of which a game is played through the movements between a 'we' and an 'I'. The essential point that I wish to take from this idea is that of subjects being created through circulation of such quasi-objects or accessories. However, in order to count as a 'ball' in a game of rugby or a 'king' in a game of chess, the game must exist before the accessory can be deployed. Even more fundamentally, as Wittgenstein argued, our forms of life must grow criteria through which we recognise a contest as a game and not a war. Thus while Serres's point about circulation in the production of subjects and objects as having an entangled existence is well taken, it is necessary to see what scaffolding concepts must exist for something to count as an object or an accessory or a game.

Both McDonald and Crowder give exemplary accounts of the way subjects and objects are mutually created in the process of learning how to be a surgeon or a pigman. McDonald's descriptions are not only vivid in their details of the scene of the anatomy lesson – they also show the intersecting histories of representations and creation of particular parts of the body as these become separated from the living body to become cadavers or organs or tissues. The body is not one thing but a multiplicity and the creation of the surgeon's hands or eyes are ontological projects achieved through great attention to the cultivation of certain dispositions in which detachment seems the important outcome. Similarly, a pig is not simply slaughtered at the end of a lifespan or if need arises, as happens in the context of a family's herd of livestock that might also be used for meat. Rather, the entire lifespan is organised around externally imposed rules geared towards the ultimate aim of growing the pig to the right weight when it can be profitably slaughtered. In Crowder's words, 'Every pig-unit is an environment where the biological, interior timescales of gestation, birth, and growth must synthesise with externally imposed production timetables which are in turn dictated by the conditions of competitive global pork trading.' The burden of Crowder's argument is to show how pigmen come to be produced as much as the pigs are produced for the market. The great merit of this chapter is that it never loses sight of the wider contradictions – 'tragic choices' have to be made, says Crowder, between animal welfare and consumer autonomy bringing a mosaic of justificatory discourses and ethical concerns into pig rearing on the farm. It is also interesting to observe the affective conundrums in which Crowder gets entangled as she distances herself from naming her field site as a factory farm; or her insistence that detachment is a learnt skill through which pigmen manage their volatile emotions, refusing to play with piglets or avoiding eye contact when they have to kill a piglet who is unhealthy and becomes a risk that must be eliminated.

Detachment as a disposition has to be cultivated through institutional practices and training of the senses as both these chapters demonstrate so well. Clearly, the boundaries between subjects and objects are constantly shifting – thus McDonald argues that the body is first made into cadaver but annually or biannually, after the cadaver cannot be used any more, it is remade into a social body. One important question that arises here is the way that temporality is conceived. There seems some preference in all three authors for a linear sequential time – for example, a division into phases from feasibility studies to actual construction to the consequences of the road in Knox and Harvey; of the antecedent experience of anatomy lessons and dissections for medical students in order for detached surgeons to be produced; and in terms of externally imposed production schedules for the production process of the pigs. In part, this preference for linear time (despite acknowledgements of the rhythms of the subtraction of the social and the restoration of it) seems to be determined by the idea that there is a single product at the end of the procedures – a road, a functional body, a commodity. Yet if the authors were to think of outcomes as multiple – so the laying of asphalt also produces less cultivable land, or increased communication; the techniques of transplantation might create a market in organs; or the production processes in pig farming might produce unmanageable toxic waste – then this notion of time might have to give way to the incorporation of multiple durations (Crowder already sees the superimposition of natural biological rhythms with socially produced production schedules); of time as crumpled rather than stretched out into clear phases. This might help us to think further about which kinds of objects become accessories (Sanskrit grammar already gives us these two ways of conceptualising objects for each stands in a different relation to the production of agents) and expand the vocabulary of subjects, agents, objects, quasi-objects, accessories, just as taking three different scenes

Professionalism and expertise: comment

of intervention have produced here a rich possibility for thinking of detachment as a multiple rather than a single kind of disposition.

Kinship and ritual as points of comparison

All three chapters begin with the primacy of relations and the way the production of expert knowledge and practice demands a severing of relations for certain purposes. Knox and Harvey explicitly ask how Marilyn Strathern's classic paper on cutting the network (1996) provides a framework for thinking of limits that are imposed to halt what would otherwise be endless proliferations of relations. How far does this reference to relations make kinship a model for thinking of abstract relations in science and technology? Is the process through which people sometimes try to opt out of the endless demands placed by kin, or the sheer exhaustion of having to engage with the complexities of obligations to give and receive, lead to detachment as a disposition that is similar to detachment produced in engineers and surgeons and pigmen? Otherwise said, how do ideas of the everyday inform scientific thinking?

My thoughts are tentative but I am struck by the fact that in all three chapters, the presence of death is like the unstated background through which the argument is foregrounded. Knox and Harvey begin with a fictionalised account of a mining disaster; McDonald's descriptions are explicitly about cadavers and of wresting life-giving potential from dead bodies and undead organs; the ruthlessness cultivated by pigmen is in the service of converting living beings into dead meat for consumption. It is in this larger traffic between life-giving force and the production of death that I would see the possibilities of connections between practices of detachment in the everyday and in these specialised domains. I was reminded of linguistic euphemisms – laboratory animals are never killed, they are always sacrificed – and some remarkable analogies one could make between ritual procedures and scientific protocols. I do not mean to suggest that kinship is a technology but to say that the nearness to death in all these descriptions requires far greater attention to the vulnerability of the rationality established through the practices described here. It is true that Knox and Harvey refer to the vulnerability of science and McDonald might be read as describing procedures that are precisely about controlling vulnerability. Yet by bracketing the whole question of how different contexts – that of the domains of specialists and that of everyday life – are stitched together with reference to the finitude of human existence, I submit that anthropologists end up ignoring a very important dimension of sociality and the urge to escape it from time to time. Like ritual, technical procedures too can produce horror by showing human identity to be vulnerable to complete dissolution. In Stanley Cavell's classic definition of horror: it is the name given to the perception of 'the precariousness of human identity, to the perception that it may be lost or invaded, that we may be or may become, something other than what we are, or take ourselves for' (Cavell 1999: 418–419). It would take another paper to spell out the full implications of the appearance of horror in the anatomy class or in the way in which animals that are food for some might be imagined as companions for others (but see Diamond 2003).

Just as we might think of sacrifice as a way in which we make death present to ourselves, so we might think of modern ways in which death is made present in the scientific-technical enterprise through which we confront who pays the price for the enhanced lives of some others. In everyday life we take resort to an 'ordinary realism' to enable us to dwell with the fragility and vulnerability of life (Laugier 2013) – to the extent that we might think of technical expertise also as unable to escape the perils to which life is subject, perhaps detachment is one expression of this ordinary realism.

References

Adams, Vincanne, 2013, *Markets of Sorrow, Labors of Faith: New Orleans in the Wake of Katrina*. Durham: Duke University Press.

Cavell, Stanley, 1999, *The Claim of Reason: Wittgenstein, Skepticism, Morality, and Tragedy*. Oxford: Oxford University Press.

Cohen, Lawrence, 1999, Where It Hurts: Indian Material for an Ethics of Organ Transplantation. *Daedalaus* 128(4): 135–165.

Cohen, Lawrence, 2004, Operability: Surgery at the Margin of the State. In Veena Das and Deborah Poole, eds, *Anthropology in the Margins of the State: Comparative Ethnographies*. Santa Fe: School of American Research Press, pp. 165–190.

Das, Veena, 2014, Action, Expression, and Everyday Life: Recounting Household Events. In Veena Das, Michael Jackson, Arthur Kleinman and Bhrigupati Singh, eds, *The Ground Between: Anthropologists Engage Philosophy*. . Durham: Duke University Press, pp. 279–306.

Diamond, Cora, 2003, The Difficulty of Reality and the Difficulty of Philosophy. Partial Answers. *Journal of Literature and the History of Ideas* 1(2): 1–26.

Han, Clara, and Das, Veena, 2015, An Anthropology of Living and Dying in the Contemporary World: A Concept Note. In Veena Das and Clara Han, eds, *Anthropology of Living and Dying in the Contemporary World*. Berkeley: University of California Press.

Keller, Evelyn Fox, 1995, *Refiguring Life: Metaphors of Twentieth-century Biology*. New York: Columbia University Press.

Laugier, Sandra, 2013, Veena Das, Wittgenstein et Cavell: le *Care*, l'ordinaire et la folie. In Anne Lovell, S. Pandolfo, V. Das and S. Laugier, eds, *Face aux Désastres: Une conversation à quatre voix sur la folie, le care, et les grandes détresses collectives*. Paris: Les Éditions d'Ithaque, pp. 161–192.

Lovell, Ann, 2011, Debating Life after Disaster. Charity Hospital Babies and Bioscientific Futures in post Katrina New Orleans. *Medical Anthropology Quarterly* 25(2): 254–277.

Nagel, Thomas, 1983, *The View from Nowhere*. New York: Oxford University Press.

Serres, Michael, 1982, *The Parasite*, trans. Lawrence R. Schehr. Baltimore, MD and London: Johns Hopkins University Press.

Shah, Alpa, 2010, *In the Shadows of the State: Indigenous Politics, Environmentalism, and Insurgency in Jharkhand, India*. Durham, NC: Duke University Press.

Strathern, Marilyn, 1996, Cutting the Network. *Journal of the Royal Anthropological Institute* 2(3): 517–535.

Taylor, Charles, 1993, Engaged Agency and Background in Heidegger. In Charles Guignon, ed., *The Cambridge Companion to Heidegger*. Cambridge: Cambridge University Press, pp. 317–336.

Part II
Ritual and religion

5

Engaged disbelief: communities of detachment in Christianity and in the anthropology of Christianity

Joel Robbins

Society is a thing of connections. Few would dispute that this is the foundational background assumption of the social sciences. We might imagine these connections to be fleeting and made anew in each instant, as currently popular nominalist approaches suggest. Or we might imagine them to be enduring and susceptible to concatenation into larger structures, as older, more realist approaches contend. But regardless of how we imagine connections to exist, there is little doubt that as social scientists we tend to focus on them in our analyses. More than that, we tend to value them – to feel, as Pedersen (2009: 1) puts it, that connections are by nature 'Good Things'. Not to be connected – that is anomie, disintegration, the sad spectre of the lonely crowd off bowling alone. Connection is what works best for human beings, is what constitutes society, and it is therefore what we study. The fact that this is the case is what gives an anthropological volume on detachment its novelty and importance.

Of course, if one stops to think about it, its not hard to convince oneself that if connection is so important to social life, some kinds of disconnection or detachment have to play a role as well. We can get to this point in any number ways. Logically, we might imagine that connection makes no sense without something like detachment to define its boundaries. Or ethnographically, we can learn from people in places like Melanesia, as Marilyn Strathern (e.g. 1996) and others have shown, in diverse ways, that efforts to increase attachments in one direction tend to involve detaching from them in others. Or we can look for the moments in more or less classical social theory where the importance of detachment as something other than a defect has risen to the surface of particular discussions. In this vein, we might note Simmel's (1950: 315–316) profound essay on secrecy and secret societies in which he notes in conclusion that

'Concord, harmony, coefficacy, which are unquestionably held to be socialising forces, must nevertheless be interspersed with distance, competition, repulsion, in order to yield the actual configuration of society.' Similarly, we can register Elias's (1987: 3–4) point, made in a work on the sociology of knowledge entitled *Involvement and Detachment*, that 'the very existence of ordered group life depends on the interplay in people's thoughts and actions of impulses in both directions, those that involve and those that detach keeping each other in check'.

Given that we can make a case for the importance of detachment in any of these ways, and probably in others as well (see the Introduction to this volume), we do not have to expend too much effort here legitimising the project of getting the topic on the table. The trick is rather keeping it on the table once we get it there. To do that, we will have to begin to demonstrate both that detachment makes important contributions to social life and that it is as susceptible to close, differentiating analysis as connection has proved to be. We will need, that is, to attend to diverse dynamics of detachment and register the distinctive social work they each accomplish.

This chapter takes up some of these kinds of tasks in the realm of religion. It is worth noting at the outset that this realm is likely to be a hard case for theorists of detachment. At least in the Western (and in this respect profoundly Protestant) imagination, what is more given to forming bonds than faith or belief? To believe *in* some being, to have faith in that being, is to tie yourself to it in a highly committed way (see e.g. Ruel 1997; Robbins 2007). If religion is a matter of belief, then it is nothing if not a matter of connection. This is surely yet another way to cash out the often proposed etymological root of the word 'religion' in **leig*, 'to bind'. For social scientists, the link between religion and connection has evidenced itself both in the assumption that relations of belief are strong ones, and in the claim from Durkheim forward that the bonds between people who share beliefs in the same things – for example, in gods, or ideas or values – are also unusually strong. And this double assumption of a link between religion and connection remains as true today as in the past. For example, some of the currently most important and influential work in the anthropology of religion is focused on religious mediation: the very problem of how to make the presence of deities evident so that people can connect to them and can form communities around these connections (Keane 1997; Meyer 2006; Engelke 2007). If religion is all about connection in the ways I have just listed, we might ask, what room can there be to introduce detachment into discussions on this subject?

I am going to approach the problem raised by the question of how to think about detachment in relation to religion in two ways here. I first want to go over some pretty well-known ground concerning Pentecostal and charismatic Christianity by means of a slightly different path than usual and to use the results of this exercise to make a point about the role of detachment in Christianity more generally and in other monotheistic faiths. I hope this part of the chapter helps us further the task of exploring differences between kinds of detachments and the social roles they can play by laying out one influential religious family of detachment dynamics in very clear terms. I then turn to the relationship between anthropologists who study Christians and the Christians that they study. As it happens, anthropologists often find this relationship somewhat fraught precisely because they worry over the way, as Elias would have it, involvement and detachment balance out on their side of these relationships. In conclusion, I suggest that the points I make about detachment in my discussion of Pentecostal Christianity can help us think through the problems of involvement and detachment anthropologists of Christianity experience in the field, and I will consider how both of these analyses of detachment can contribute to a broader theoretical investigation into the ways social relations are constituted.

Detachment, Christianity and monotheism

There is, by now, a large and growing body of anthropological work on Pentecostal and charismatic Christianity: the kind of Christianity that expects all believers to have access to the Holy Spirit and the various gifts it brings. This work has shown that one of the distinctive feature of Pentecostalism as it is found among many people who have converted to it from non-Christian religions is that it tends not to define their pre-conversion spiritual ontologies as unreal, but rather to insist that converts need to see the spirits that populate those ontologies as wholly evil and to work to detach themselves from them. Very often the work of detachment from non-Christian spirits is self-conscious and highly ritualised, with converts performing a variety of rites to banish spirits from their environment and their bodies. Widespread rites of spiritual warfare, in which believers pray to God to destroy the local spirits that seek to connect with them, and of deliverance, which aim to put an end to the influence of spirits on human beings, constitute an elaborate theatre of detachment – one in which themes of the need for distance and disconnection are continually brought to the fore (for examples see Robbins 2012 on spiritual warfare and Bialecki 2011 on deliverance).

I can illustrate some of the ways detachment from evil spirits becomes an issue for converts to Pentecostal and charismatic Christianity by drawing on my field research with the Urapmin of the West Sepik Province of Papua New Guinea. The Urapmin, who are recent converts to a charismatic form of Christianity, first treat all illnesses by means of Christian prayer. In their healing prayers, people ask God to remove the traditional nature spirits that are the causes all illnesses that do not end in death. The imagery of these prayers focuses on detachment. The nature spirits are understood to cause illness by clinging to their victims. In their prayers, people ask God to tear these spirits off those who are sick and to banish the spirits to hell, from where they will no longer be able to attach themselves to people.

While the need to detach nature spirits from people has been part of Urapmin healing rites since before they became Christian, the emphasis on their banishment and on complete disconnection from them is new. This becomes apparent in sacrificial rites that the Urapmin sometimes practice in relation to the nature spirits. People undertake these sacrificial rites when illnesses linger even after several sessions of healing prayer. Such persistent illness is particularly worrisome when it is a child who is afflicted, since nature spirits can succeed in killing children, though not adults. Thus it is when children have been sick for some time that people will sometimes sacrifice a pig to the offending nature spirit, asking the spirit to take the 'smell' of the pig and release its victim. Urapmin see this rite as potentially unchristian – it is the only rite they recognise as pre-Christian that they still practice, and they undertake it only with great reluctance, and in fact only when Christian mediums proclaim that the Holy Spirit has demanded it. As this suggests, the Urapmin have in many respects Christianised their sacrifices. What is important about these partially Christianised sacrifices for the present argument is a contradiction that now holds between the parts of the rite. The sacrifice itself is something of an exchange with the spirits, aiming to repair relations with them. But the Christian prayers that now surround sacrifice focus, as do the prayers at the centre of other healing rites, on having God destroy the spirits or 'throw them out' of Urapmin territory (see Robbins 2009 for such a prayer and for a more detailed discussion of Urapmin healing rites and sacrifices). The Christian emphasis on detachment is now to the fore in these rituals and it encompasses the lingering traditional sacrificial emphasis on managing relations with nature spirits in sustainable ways.[1]

Beyond their healing rites, Urapmin also sometimes imagine performing larger-scale rituals that would ask God to rid their land of all nature spirits. Urapmin do not have a name for these rites, though they accord globally with recently developed Pentecostal rites of spiritual warfare (DeBernardi 1999; Jorgensen 2005). To this point, the Urapmin have not been able to bring themselves to practise these rituals on a grand scale (though they have tried something similar to banish spirits from a single village). In these rites, Christian Holy Spirit mediums would all work at once not to heal an individual, but to entreat God to chase all the nature spirits away. People's unwillingness to deploy these rites might be taken to say something about how they construe the limits of detachment (as well as, more concretely, about the difficulty of living without any credible explanation for illness) (for more on these imagined rites, see Robbins 2012). But the fact that people can conceive of such rites at all speaks volumes about the fundamental role of detachment in the Pentecostal imagination.

In many places, though not in Urapmin, the Pentecostal drive to detach from local spirits also comes to underwrite similar efforts to disconnect from other people. This happens when Pentecostals see relatives and neighbours who are not converts as impediments to their own efforts at spiritual detachment because they maintain relations with the spirits that help keep the spirits in place, and because, through witchcraft or other evil means, these people sometimes maliciously direct evil spirits to reconnect with Pentecostals who have detached from them. For Pentecostals who come to see their kin and neighbours as aligned with the spirits in this way, often migrants from the countryside to the city, detachment as a social process feeds a kind of individualism that defines people as operating best when they are free of traditional spiritual and social influences.

Birgit Meyer (1998: 195–199) offers several examples of the Pentecostal entwinement of spiritual and social detachment from her work with Ewe charismatics in Ghana. In one case she recounts, a schoolteacher who had found herself unable to marry sourced her difficulties to the spirit Wuve, one of the 'false gods who comes from Satan' and who marries women in their dreams, thereby preventing them from finding human husbands. Wuve had afflicted many women from this teacher's family. The vulnerability of all of these women to Wuve's approaches followed from the fact that the teacher's paternal great-grandfather had long ago successfully approached the spirit to make his infertile wife pregnant. The spirit has troubled this man's female descendants ever since. To detach herself from Wuve, the teacher had for some time stopped participating in family ceremonies, and Meyer met her at a charismatic Christian prayer camp where she sought God's help in separating herself from her family and the link they made between her and this evil spirit (Meyer 1998: 196–197). For many Ghanaian converts, disconnecting from their families and the spiritual legacies they carry become important religious goals.

As I have already noted, the Pentecostal dynamics of detachment I have just discussed are well known. The importance of the Pentecostal promotion of ontological preservation, spiritual disconnection and social disjunction for the study of issues such as conversion and cultural change has already been widely canvassed (Robbins 2004a provides a review). But these materials have not, to this point, been considered as a contribution to the study of detachment per se. When we consider them primarily as instances of detachment, I want to argue, we quickly come to notice that they are not as particular to Pentecostalism as we have imagined. From this point of view, the value Pentecostals place on detachment is at least a common feature of Christianity, and it may well be a mark of monotheistic faiths more generally.

Let me start to make this argument by situating the Pentecostal interest in detachment in relation to Christianity more generally. Christopher Morse is a United Methodist theologian and a Professor at Union Theological Seminary in New York, one of the great institutions of liberal Protestantism. Morse is not, to my knowledge, in any respects a Pentecostal. Yet in a book entitled *Not Every Spirit: A Dogmatics of Christian Disbelief*, Morse (2009) has developed a distinctive theological argument that reveals some surprising similarities between the Pentecostal emphasis on detachment and the way this issue is handled in other branches of the Christian tradition.

As a dogmatics, Morse's book aims to lay out in coherent fashion the fundamental tenets of the Christian faith. What makes it unique, at least to a relatively amateur theological reader like myself, is that it is organised primarily around an orderly set of claims about those things Christians must actively disbelieve, rather than only around an enumeration of those they should actively embrace. Morse takes his warrant for this approach from texts such as 1John 4:1 – 'Beloved, do not believe every spirit, but test the spirits to see whether they are from God; for many false prophets have gone out into the world' (Morse 2009: 3). Toward spirits that one has tested and found false, one is enjoined to practise what Morse (2009: 3) calls 'faithful disbelief' – a disbelief grounded in one's faith in God and based on a recognition that 'having faith in God means that some things are to be refused credence and trust' (2009: 4). Because trust as well as credence is at issue in belief, faithful disbelief is not for Morse equivalent to the primarily intellectual stances of doubt or scepticism, it is rather about refusing to accept the essentially social, relational demands of specific *'claimants ... for our attention and allegiance'* (2009: 8, emphasis in original). During the Roman period in which the Christian confession 'Jesus is Lord' arose, for example, believing it entailed disbelieving the then common claim that 'Caesar is Lord' and attenuating one's political allegiance accordingly (Morse 2009: 13). On Morse's account, Christianity is built on a series of detachments from bonds such as this one that have been created by false beliefs. That is to say, for him Christianity is, in important respects, a religion of detachment.

I want to take two points from this reading of Morse's striking book. The first is that it renders Pentecostalism's strong emphasis on detachment from evil spirits much less exotic than we might have thought it to be in relation to the religious dynamics at the heart of other forms of Christianity. Instead, that emphasis now stands out only for its extensive ritualisation in Pentecostalism. At the level of doctrine, the differences are not so striking – all Christians practise their faith by performing faithful detachments. The second point, though one that Morse does not argue as directly as I do here, is that Christian communities are at least in part formed out of their shared detachments. It is in important respects by faithfully disbelieving the same things that people form themselves into a church. Among the Pentecostals that I study in Papua New Guinea this is clear – people are never more united than when they are asserting the need to detach from evil spirits and are working toward this end in various ritual contexts, such as the Christian healing rites discussed earlier. Morse teaches us that this is probably true in many kinds of Christian churches. In terms of our interest in various dynamics of detachment, we might label this Christian way of forming groups the creation of solidarity through detachment – a unity in rejection that expects of people something quite different than do some of our other models of solidarity.

I will return to solidarity through detachment later. But before I do, I want to widen the lens I am using one more time. Having pulled back from Pentecostalism to find detachment at the heart of Christianity more generally, I want to consider whether we can pull back even further and see similar dynamics of detachment at work in all of the monotheistic faiths in the Abrahamic lineage. My sense that it might be possible and worthwhile comes from my reading of some of the increasingly influential work of Jan Assmann. Assmann is an Egyptologist/social theorist who has developed a set of stimulating arguments about the nature of the Abrahamic traditions by asking what their monotheism looks like from the point of view of the Egyptian polytheism they eventually displaced. From a polytheistic point of view, what is new in monotheism is what Assmann (1997: 1; 2010: 35) calls 'the Mosaic distinction' between 'true and false in religion'. Polytheistic religion, on Assmann's reading, does not distinguish between true and false gods. Instead, it is a social 'technique of translation' between religions and cultures, allowing followers to correlate the gods given one of set of names in one place with those given different names elsewhere by attending to their similar functions (1997: 2–3). By contrast to the open, border-dissolving character of polytheism, Mosaic monotheism represents something new. It is a 'counter-religion' that 'rejects and repudiates everything that went before and what is outside itself as "paganism"' (1997: 3). It is this insistence on the 'negation' of gods other than the One True God that defines monotheism, more than the belief in one god per se (since religions not so given to negation may also imagine one god as the sum of many gods, or as the apex of a hierarchy of gods, without negating those other gods in the process) (Assmann 2010: 31).

In Assmann's view, a similar commitment to negation runs throughout the Abrahamic faiths. As he puts it, the Mosaic negation of false religion underwrites not only the distinction between 'Jews and Gentiles', but also those between 'Christians and pagans' and 'Muslims and unbelievers' (Assmann 1997: 1). As a counter-religion – as a religion that as Morse would have it enjoins followers to practices of faithful disbelief – Christianity thus turns out to be built around dynamics of detachment that it shares with its kindred monotheistic faiths. As students of detachment, then, we have some basis for suspecting that faithful disbelief and its attendant promotion of solidarity through detachment are important social operators in many parts of the world today. Though I cannot pursue it here, this argument opens up the possibility of exploring comparative questions about detachment in Judaism, Christianity and Islam in order both to deepen our understanding of detachment and to explore in new ways the similarities and differences that mark these faiths.

Detachment and the anthropology of Christianity

Peter Sloterdijk (2012) has argued that all scholarship is based on detachment. Intellectual work always requires what he calls, borrowing from Husserl, some kind of epoché – a bracketing of our usual worldly involvements in order to allow for distanced contemplation and reflection. This argument is not wholly new, and of course the ideal of scholarly detachment is, like all ideals, easy to critique for its failure to wholly, or even very thoroughly, guide practice: there are certainly all kinds of arguments available today that suggest that our claims to scholarly detachment are mere pretensions at best, and that at worst they contribute to failures of self-understanding and insight that sometimes mark our work. But Sloterdijk shows that, as an ideal, the notion of scholarly detachment has a long and in many respects noble genealogy, and he reminds us of how much we would stand to lose if we abandoned it entirely (as, for example, current demands for fast 'impact' so often tempt us to do).²

In light of Sloterdijk's argument about the centrality of detachment to academic work, I want in this section to raise the question of what a focus on detachment can teach us about the nature of anthropological fieldwork among Christians. One of the complexities of the attempts anthropologists make to detach from their familiar worldly involvements is that they normatively do so in order to attach themselves to the worldly involvements of others. That is to say, anthropologists quite self-consciously have to balance detachment and attachment. References to the fieldworker as a 'familiar stranger', 'marginal native', and even as a 'participant observer' (a term that is at least gently oxymoronic) indicate that the problem of finding the right relation between involvement and detachment has haunted the conduct of anthropological fieldwork for a long time. A number of figures have regularly stood sentry at the borders of bad practice in this regard, warning us of the kinds of relations of under-detachment or over-involvement we do not want to have with those whom we study. On the side of too little engagement stands the tourist, while on the more crowded side of too much involvement we traditionally find the government officer and the missionary (Clifford 2003; see also Cashell 2009 on tourism and detachment). Today, NGO workers must be counted somewhere in this mix as well, though my own formation occurred just a bit too early in relation to the rise of NGOs for me to have good intuitions of exactly where to place them.

But just as all anthropologists who give the matter any thought have to contend with the unusual mixture of involvement and detachment that characterises the social relations through which they do their work, anthropologists of Christianity face some particular problems in this regard. Although anthropologists of Christianity have not yet written much about all but one of these problems, they often discuss them among themselves. Their discussions most often turn on three issues. The first has to do with the fact that anthropologists often harbour strong negative feelings about Christianity. For them, Christianity is what Harding (1991) has described as a 'repugnant' cultural other. Since this is the one issue that has been written about a bit, I will not dwell here on the reasons for this response to Christianity – I simply want to register its existence and note that it sometimes causes anthropologists problems in the field, as they find themselves feeling angry at, disappointed with, or alienated from those they study, or at least from the Christian practices that are important to them.

A second problem anthropologists of Christianity face in the field has to do with the difficulty of working with people who are committed to evangelism and who embrace a model of conversion that lays out clearly what someone must do next if they come to truly understand the Christian cosmos. The evangelistic zeal of those they study is a double-edged sword for most anthropologists of Christianity. On the one hand, it often leads Christians to be very welcoming and quick to explain their faith, but on the other it sets up expectations of what constitutes a proper outcome of interaction that most fieldworkers worry they will fail to meet. For the most part, anthropologists feel they successfully navigate the tensions evangelistic interactions raise for them through a mix of honesty and an understanding on the part of most Christians that conversion can be a long time in coming even in the face of committed and prayerful proselytisation. Yet the failure of anthropologists perfectly to play their parts in evangelising interactions further contributes to the sense of distance they feel in relation to those with whom they work.

The third problem is the most complex in its contours and it seems to me to leave anthropologists even more unsettled than the first two. It turns on the discomfort ethnographers feel when it comes to participating in Christian rituals or undertaking other actions (including ways of speaking) they feel indicate a level of Christian commitment they do not truly have. I can offer an example of this kind of discomfort from my own fieldwork. The Urapmin practise a ritual they call a 'Spirit Dance' or 'Spirit Disco'. This ritual aims to cleanse participants of sins they have committed and confessed to God. I will not go much into the details of the rite here (for a full description, see Robbins 2004b). For present purposes, I only need to mention a few key aspects of the ritual. For most participants, Spirit Dances are a long-running (often many hour) circular dance around the inside of the church. During the dance, some dancers begin to shake intensely as they are possessed by the Holy Spirit who enters their bodies to fight with the sins that reside there and eventually throw them out. The dancing is accompanied by steady, rhythmic drumming on traditional Urapmin drums (instruments that are not usually used in any other Christian rituals in Urapmin). At least once during a Spirit dance I must have been tapping my foot along to the incessant beat. Afterwards, a number of people who had noticed this told me in a good humoured but also serious way that it looked like I was starting to 'receive' the Holy Spirit and that I would likely be possessed at a future dance. I responded immediately that I doubted that this was the case. I pointed out that where I came from, in the United States, people often tapped their feet in time to music and that I did this all the time at home. Furthermore, I pointed out that Urapmin dancers never tapped their feet as a prelude to becoming possessed. People were sceptical of my denials of any spiritual influence on my behaviour and said they would wait to see what happened at the next dance. For my part, I stuck to my claims that I was sure the Holy Spirit was not involved in my behaviour.

Why this strong protest that I was more detached from the Spirit Dance than the Urapmin thought I was? Is this not a strange way to carry on for someone practising a field method based on 'building rapport'? For anthropologists of Christianity, this is not a trivial question. Many of them, like me, report feeling hesitant when it comes to participating fully in Christian rituals, or even appearing to do so. In some respects, this complication of anthropological fieldwork with Christians is tied to the previous one of evangelism, since it is in part the evangelical concerns of those with whom one works that lead one to feel dishonest if one implies a greater involvement in Christianity than one really feels one has. But there is more behind fieldworkers' discomfort on this score than simply a worry about appearing to be moving toward conversion when they are not really doing so. As is well documented in the anthropology of Christianity, many Christians define their religion as a matter of holding appropriate beliefs. Even if we accept recent criticisms, including my own, of the assumption that the beliefs involved are always about propositions rather than commitments, we are still left with the fact that Christians place a high value on belief as they understand it (Asad 1993; Ruel 1997; Robbins 2007). In keeping with this, they also place a high value on sincerity – on having one's speech and other action bear out one's true beliefs (Robbins 2001; Keane 2007). Ritual or other religious actions that are insincere – that are not backed by adherence to the beliefs that are expected to ground it – are considered empty at best and deceptive and therefore sinful at worst. Caught in the web of such ideas about belief, anthropologists of Christianity are destined to feel uncomfortable about participating in Christian ritual practice when they do not share the beliefs at its centre. This failure to participate, or to participate fully, produces a further sense of detachment in the field.[3]

All three of the problems I have discussed – the anthropological aversion to Christianity, the difficulties raised by proselytising calls for conversion and the way the centrality of belief in Christian understanding renders participation in its ritual life difficult for anthropologists – can be seen to contribute to a situation in which anthropologists of Christianity routinely find themselves contending with too much detachment in the field. Whatever detachment might be needed for the production of knowledge – the observer side of the participant–observer seesaw – anthropologists of Christianity often feel they have exceeded it and are unable to employ the techniques used by those who study other topics in order to redress the balance. Sure that they do not want to be overly involved missionaries, they come perilously close to occupying the equally unwanted position of chillingly detached tourists.

In concluding this section, I want to suggest that perhaps a recognition of Christianity's own investment in dynamics of detachment might help us find a way to address, or at least differently understand, the situation of anthropologists of Christianity in the field. In the simplest terms, my proposal is that if we cannot always align our beliefs with those of the people we study – despite the importance that they themselves place on belief – perhaps we should explore aligning our faithful disbeliefs with theirs. Perhaps, that is to say, we can find our solidarity in shared detachments rather than attachments. As Morse (2009: 75) puts it in considering how to handle the differences between various Christian churches in his dogmatics, there can be 'an ecumenicity that arises out of shared disbelief'. We already know that sharing disbelief is an important Christian technique for producing internal bonds, perhaps it can work across boundaries of faith as well.

I have to confess that I am not yet sure how this would work – my proposal is more of a hunch than a worked out programme at the moment. But one can imagine that when confronted with Christians praying to God to banish spirits of sickness, we can share their contention that ill health is not worthy of our allegiance. Similarly, when they pray for wealth, we can share their rejection of the spirit of poverty. More ambitiously, we might generally share the common Christian disbelief in the idea that the world as it is represents the best of all possible ones, or that it is destined to remain the same forever. Admittedly, even if we take this tack, our sense of involvement is unlikely to be complete. We might sometimes, for example, worry that by our lights the means some Christians have chosen for overcoming what they reject may not be the most efficient ones for meeting their goals. But at least we could find a way of focusing on areas of some shared commitment. And we would do so in a way that Christians themselves recognise as important: the commitment to detach from that to which one should not be connected.

Coda

Let me close with a bit of an auto-critique. At the outset I mentioned that it is not that hard to raise issues of detachment in anthropology – to put this topic, as I rather colloquially phrased it, on the table. But I added that, given the importance of connection in social theory, it would likely be hard to keep detachment in focus for very long. I have a sense that in just this way I have had some predictable difficulties staying focused on detachment in this chapter, and it might be worthwhile to make these difficulties explicit in the context of this volume.

When I was in graduate school, whenever I or my fellow students wanted to sound clever on any subject, we had a handy, well-rehearsed verbal manoeuvre that consisted of saying that whatever we were talking about was 'a social relation'. This produced many profound statements on the order of 'freedom is a social relation', 'meaning is a social relation', 'perception is a social relation', 'the body is a social relation', 'solitude is a social relation' and so on. Sometimes these relational claims turned out to be worth thinking about, sometimes they did not, but always they were easy to make. It was as if the words 'social relation' were a kind of fairy dust that magically lifted the level of any conversation upon which they were sprinkled. My worry for this chapter is that at the most basic level I may have come around to saying something like 'detachment is a social relation'. I hope I have shown through my account of solidarity through detachment one way in which it can be a distinctive kind of social relation, and that I have more originally shown that this kind of social relation turns out to be at the centre of many different kinds of Christianity, and perhaps of monotheistic faiths more generally, and that it might play some role in the construction of anthropological field relations as well. But if turning detachments into relations is a common way social scientists prove they abhor a relational vacuum, I cannot claim to have moved beyond this to build a model of social life on a foundation of absence and disconnection alone. I leave it to others to determine if this represents a healthy sense of the limits of arguments for detachment – a sense that without attention to attachment as well they are destined to fail – or whether, had I gone much further with the notion of detachment on its own, I might have learned even more about the dynamics at the heart of Christian religious life and anthropological fieldwork.

Notes

1 One can offer an even more complex analysis of the role of detachment in Urapmin relations with nature spirits. Spirits only make persons sick when those persons have violated taboos the spirits put in place demanding that Urapmin do not talk loudly, laugh or otherwise disturb spirits when they move around the bush to hunt or garden. In effect, the spirits want as little relationship with the Urapmin as possible, and it is when Urapmin come too close that spirits come even closer and thereby make them sick. So the qualities of spirits as kinds of social beings always raise questions of connection and detachment, even before spirits make people ill. But it remains the case that the kind of permanent detachment people seek through Christian healing (and other Christian rites discussed later in the text) is of a more thorough-going kind than that the spirits try to

establish with their taboos on contact. We see here another illustration of the more general point that attention to different kinds of detachment is a valuable ethnographic project.

2 For further reflections of the complexities of scholarly detachment, see Candea (2013).

3 I think there is at least a partial irony in this dilemma that has to do with recognising how influenced by Christianity anthropologists already are when they feel bad about engaging in ritual participation without sharing what they take to be the other participants' beliefs. That is to say, our very discomfort over our detachment from Christians by virtue of our lack of belief, and the limits this discomfort sets to fully engaged participation, indicate that we have achieved some measure of success in coming to inhabit a Christian view of the nature of religious life – like the people we are studying, we have adopted the position that belief and sincerity are critical to the conduct of ritual. We are therefore quite close to those we work with at the very moment when, in forgoing ritual participation, we move to detach ourselves from them most directly. But I cannot pursue this argument further here.

References

Asad, Talal, 1993, *Genealogies of Religion: Discipline and Reasons of Power in Christianity and Islam.* Baltimore, MD: Johns Hopkins University Press.

Assmann, Jan, 1997, *Moses the Egyptian: the Memory of Egypt in Western Monotheism.* Cambridge, MA: Harvard University Press.

Assmann, Jan, 2010 *The Price of Monotheism*, trans. R. Savage. Stanford, CA: Stanford University Press.

Bialecki, Jon, 2011, No Caller ID for the Soul: Demonization, Charisms, and the Unstable Subject of Protestant Language Ideology. *Anthropological Quarterly* 84(3): 679–704.

Candea, Matei, 2013, Suspending Belief: Epoché in Animal Behavior Science. *American Anthropologist* 115(3): 423–436.

Cashell, Kieran, 2009, *Aftershock: The Ethics of Contemporary Transgressive Art.* London: I. B. Tauris.

Clifford, James, 2003, *On the Edges of Anthropology (Interviews).* Chicago: Prickly Paradigm Press.

DeBernardi, Jean, 1999, Spiritual Warfare and Territorial Spirits: The Globalization and Localisation of a 'Practical Theology'. *Religious Studies and Theology* 18(2): 66–96.

Elias, Norbert, 1987, *Involvement and Detachment*, trans. E. Jephcott. Oxford: Basil Blackwell.

Engelke, Matthew, 2007, *A Problem of Presence: Beyond Scripture in an African Church.* Berkeley: University of California Press.

Harding, Susan, 1991, Representing Fundamentalism: The Problem of the Repugnant Cultural Other. *Social Research* 58(2): 373–393.

Jorgensen, Dan, 2005, Third Wave Evangelism and the Politics of the Global in Papua New Guinea: Spiritual Warfare and the Recreation of Place in Telefolmin. *Oceania* 75(4): 444–461.

Keane, Webb, 1997, Religious Language. *Annual Review of Anthropology* 26: 47–71.

Keane, Webb, 2007, *Christian Moderns: Freedom and Fetish in the Mission Encounter*. Berkeley: University of California Press.

Meyer, Birgit, 1998, 'Make a Complete Break with the Past': Memory and Postcolonial Modernity in Ghanaian Pentecostal Discourse. In R. Werbner, ed., *Memory and the Postcolony: African Anthropology and the Critique of Power*. London: Zed Books, pp. 182–208.

Meyer, Birgit, 2006, Impossible Representations: Pentecostalism, Vision, and Video Technology in Ghana. In B. Meyer and A. Moors, eds, *Religion, Media, and the Public Sphere*. Bloomington, ID: University of Indiana Press, pp. 290–312.

Morse, Christopher, 2009, *Not Every Spirit: A Dogmatics of Christian Disbelief*. New York: T. & T. Clark.

Pedersen, Morton Axel, 2009, Detaching the Spirits in Mongolia: A Post-Relational Analysis. Unpublished paper.

Robbins, Joel, 2001, God is Nothing But Talk: Modernity, Language and Prayer in a Papua New Guinea Society. *American Anthropologist* 103(4): 901–912.

Robbins, Joel, 2004a, The Globalization of Pentecostal and Charismatic Christianity. *Annual Review of Anthropology* 33: 117–143.

Robbins, Joel, 2004b, *Becoming Sinners: Christianity and Moral Torment in a Papua New Guinea Society*. Berkeley, CA: University of California Press.

Robbins, Joel, 2007, Continuity Thinking and the Problem of Christian Culture: Belief, Time and the Anthropology of Christianity. *Current Anthropology* 48(1): 5–38.

Robbins, Joel, 2009 Conversion, Hierarchy, and Cultural Change: Value and Syncretism in the Globalization of Pentecostal and charismatic Christianity. In K. M. Rio and O. H. Smedal, eds, *Hierarchy: Persistence and Transformation in Social Formations*. New York: Berghahn, pp. 65–88.

Robbins, Joel, 2012, On Enchanting Science and Disenchanting Nature: Spiritual Warfare in North America and Papua New Guinea. In C. M. Tucker, ed. *Nature, Science, and Religion: Intersections Shaping Society and the Environment*. Santa Fe: School for Advance Research Press, pp. 45–64.

Ruel, Malcolm, 1997, *Belief, Ritual and the Securing of Life: Reflexive Essays on a Bantu Religion*. Leiden: E. J. Brill.

Simmel, Georg, 1950, *The Sociology of Georg Simmel*, trans. K. H. Wolff. New York: The Free Press.

Sloterdijk, Peter, 2012, *The Art of Philosophy: Wisdom as Practice*. New York: Columbia University Press.

Strathern, Marilyn, 1996, Cutting the Network. *Journal of the Royal Anthropological Institute* 2(3): 517–535.

6

Detachment and ethical regard

James Laidlaw

The agenda presented to contributors by the editors of this volume is to see detachment as a positive aspect of social arrangements. Detachment might always be problematic to achieve, might indeed only ever be approached and never reached entirely, but this only invites us to enquire into the various ways people might go about trying to establish and maintain it. Doing so will always depend upon definite kinds of institutions and practices, and it takes work of various kinds, and these, the suggestion is, are amenable to ethnographic analysis. Our editors present this agenda as an alternative to the all-too-common reflex in much of the social sciences merely of denouncing any claims to anything like detachment as necessarily ideological: ideological both in the sense of being false, since underlying any appearance of detachment must be a reality of hidden entanglements, and ideological also in the sense of being motivated, a disguise for 'real' social-political engagements and commitments.

At its simplest, this invitation to take detachment seriously as an ethnographic reality requires, I think, an appreciation that sociality cannot be understood, in a simple quantitative sense, as a matter of more or less interconnectedness. It is not simply the case that to be *more connected* to more other people and things is necessarily to have more of a single unambiguously good thing that we can call 'relationality' or 'engagement'. The line of thought guiding this volume, then, invites us to consider that sociality may not be a matter simply of more connections, and that disconnections of various kinds may also be essential to it. The attenuation or even the cutting of relations may have positive aspects: positive both in the sense that detachment is not merely an absence of connection – there may be various kinds of definite *content* to detachment, and these different forms need describing – and positive also in the sense that these various forms of detachment might be sought as desirable states of affairs.

An example would be Candea's (2010) observation, in his study of human–animal relations in the Kalahari meerkat project, that for scientists to cultivate a stance of detachment towards the animals they study is not necessarily a gesture of moral disregard, as proponents of 'engagement' in science studies and human–animal relations, and more broadly those influenced by Levinas's ethical teachings have tended to assume.

So already the apparently simple injunction to take detachment seriously ethnographically involves several claims: the claim that detachment is not merely an absence, the claim that it might have variable forms, and the claim that it might not have a negative, or even a merely neutral, ethical quality.

Now in scientific research, and in public administration, it has often been claimed that detachment is a moral virtue (Du Gay 2000), and that the kinds of detachment called for in these domains approximate disinterest or even indifference as between possible outcomes. Justice is represented as a blindfolded figure, the implication being that it carries through its impartial process wherever it might lead. Detachment and compassion are in obvious tension. In Buddhism, on the other hand, it has always been an axiom that the supreme detachment achieved by the greatest saints is somehow combined with infinite and universal compassion, although Buddhists trying to learn meditation have not always found this a straightforward combination to achieve in practice.

One crude thought one might have, then, is that one could distinguish the kinds of detachment that are cultivated in different domains – science, bureaucracy, religion – in terms of their ethical and affective qualities, or that different cultures/societies might value detachment in different ways. But I want to suggest that neither such thought will do. Instead, I try to show that within a single local religious tradition – Shvetambar Jainism in north India – we find practices devoted to achieving different forms of detachment, and that their differing ethical qualities make sense in terms of their formal characteristics.

Let me first introduce a different ethnographic example. In the 1990s, reflecting on the genocidal conflicts then taking place in the former Yugoslavia, the anthropologist F. G. Bailey (1996) compared the situation there with what he had witnessed during fieldwork in Orissa in eastern India in the late 1950s. He was struck by similarities, but also by the decisively different outcome. Like much of the former Yugoslavia, the village where Bailey worked had been divided between separate and unequal communities, and at the time of his fieldwork the relations between these communities were destabilised locally by the fact that they were being politicised at state and national level. Low-caste Panos found themselves receiving powerful political patronage. The higher castes found that even using formerly standard disparaging terms to describe their lower-caste neighbours would be subject to legal sanctions, and that they could no longer exclude them from using the village well or access to village temples, and so on. Bailey observes that this politicisation led to identities being understood on all sides in increasingly moralised and essentialised terms. The preconditions for violent conflict were clearly developing, and in other parts of India, as well as in comparable situations such as the Balkans, violent conflict frequently resulted from just these kinds of processes. So Bailey's book asks: what were the factors that put a brake on those developments in that case? What led people to hold back, not to threaten their opponents' really vital interests, and so to stop short of mutually destructive violence?

Bailey does not attribute this fortunate outcome to any very admirable characteristics. It is not that these villagers fell back on generations of good neighbourliness, mutual understanding, or on Levinasian ethical regard for the Other: quite the contrary. His book is called *The Civility of Indifference* and the claim is that members of the opposing groups came to their conflict from a background of treating each other in frankly instrumental ways. They regarded each other pragmatically, mostly as means to their own ends. Now this attitude is plainly in the classic sense amoral. Most will find it a melancholy thought that anything good could come of it. But Bailey's ethnography is fairly persuasive, and his reasoning seems sound too when he points out that this attitude of detached indifference, unlovely as it might be, at least has the merit of precluding the kind of impassioned moralism – and demonisation – that fuels collective violence. Precisely because these groups were not morally significant to each other, no one's sense of self-worth depended on any specific relations being established or maintained with the other. If they denied each other intrinsic respect, consideration or trust, equally and for just that reason they did not become possessed of burning hatred or rage either. Nothing the other did could provoke emotions of that intensity. They just did not matter to each other enough.

So detachment, or as Bailey puts it 'benign indifference', can be seen as a minor virtue (on this see Lillehammer 2014), because it enables coexistence even where there are real divergences or conflicts of interest: not a very heart-warming kind of sociality, to be sure, but something, nevertheless, for which in some circumstances people have good cause to be grateful. The lesson I draw from this is not just that detachment has positive contents which might be various, and not just that the apparently negative fact of detachment need not mean amoral indifference (which is what I think Candea's meerkat-watchers show us), but also that even where detachment does indeed involve amoral indifference, this might positively enable a certain limited kind (but then again all kinds are limited) of sociality. So different forms of detachment, we may conjecture, have different social correlates and different ethical qualities.

I want now to describe three different exercises in the cultivation of detachment, from my own ethnographic fieldwork on Jainism in north India, mostly in the city of Jaipur. These examples, I hope, will illustrate what I think might be some general forms that detachment can take, prospectively in non-religious as well as religious domains, and I end with a somewhat formal characterisation of these three cases, with a view to accounting for their different moral qualities, by which I mean the kinds of ethical regard the work involved in achieving these forms of detachment presupposes or promotes.

When the future Lord Buddha left his home and family and embarked on his search for spiritual enlightenment, he joined, and travelled for a while with, an existing group of ascetics. Traditional Buddhist representations of him towards the end of this period of his life show him as a skeletally thin figure, reduced almost to skin and bone by his efforts to purify his soul through fasting and other austerities. Eventually, he concluded that the means this group were relying on to pursue enlightenment were simply not working. The 'Middle Way' the Buddha then worked out and followed lay between the worldly life of householders and this other 'extremist' path. Almost certainly this Buddhist story is a competitor's partisan (but as we shall see not wholly fictitious) representation of Jainism.

Today, Jain renouncers still live and travel from place to place in small groups, living a mendicant life, practising and teaching their austere and difficult path to salvation. Their lay following is a small minority in India, mostly fairly prosperous urban and trading communities, together with growing populations overseas (ethnographic studies include Banks 1992; Laidlaw 1995; Babb 1996; Cort 2001; Kelting 2001).

The most conspicuous feature of Jain practice is *ahimsa* or non-violence, which lies behind most of the details of the renouncers' monastic code of conduct, and also deeply affects lay religious practice. The pursuit of non-violence is so far-reaching for Jains because their teachings have it that the world is thoroughly suffused with living things, what they nowadays often refer to as 'bacteria' or 'germs' in the air, water, fire and earth, as well as other life forms such as plants, insects and animals, all of which have souls that are fundamentally like those of human beings. Indeed, all humans have lived former lives in various of these other kinds of body. In such a pervasively inhabited world, it is simply impossible to live without impinging harmfully on other living things. Even plants, drawing sustenance from the soil, thereby harm other living things. Yet harming other living things is what causes our own souls to be trapped in the cycle of death and rebirth, suffering the karmic effects of these sins in successive births. To escape this and to achieve enlightenment and liberation begins with avoiding gross and obvious forms of physical violence – in practices such as vegetarianism – but proceeds through an infinity of steps of progressive self-restraint (Laidlaw 1995: 151–189).

The institutions of formal monastic life for both men and women prescribe lifelong celibate renunciation, and the reverence accorded to renouncers by their lay Jain devotees rests on the spiritual authority, in part on the sheer difficulty, of that path. So renouncers have no home or possessions of their own, they move from place to place, carrying with them their very few possessions such as alms bowls, which have been donated by lay followers. They brush the ground before them as they walk, gently removing insects from their path. They cover their faces while speaking, so as to minimise harm to creatures in the air. They learn to sleep lightly and lying still, and in general to avoid any unnecessary or careless physical motion. For lay families many elements of renouncers' discipline are recommended, either permanently or more commonly for limited periods when people take on temporary voluntary vows to practise restraint, or when they fast, either for a connected period or, over much longer periods, on specified days of the week or month, or when they take part in a residential retreat (Laidlaw 1995: 53–64).

Key to all of these technologies of self-transformation is cultivating freedom from attachment: attachment not only to material possessions but also to all existing personal and social ties and relationships, and to the mental states – the thoughts and feelings – that go with those ties. In fact, all likes and dislikes, desires and aversions, hopes and fears: all are obstacles to spiritual progress. It is these mental attachments that drive the unenlightened as they go about their everyday lives to behave in careless and unrestrained ways that routinely lead them heedlessly to slaughter unseen living things in untold numbers. Jain ascetic practice – a variety of forms of meditation, confession, fasting and other austerities – cultivates both the perception of the world as pervasively inhabited, and the disposition to control and constrain one's actions in light of that perception, and so to avoid harming other living things (Laidlaw 1995: 190–229).

So on now to those three specific events and practices in which Jains seek to *cultivate* detachment. The first is Paryushan (see Laidlaw 1995:

275–286; also Banks 1992: 176–84; Cort 2001: ch. 6), an annual weeklong series of ceremonies during the summer rains, and the only point in the year when virtually all lay Jains, even the normally least religiously observant, fast and participate in some of the other forms of asceticism which the more committed practise regularly throughout the year.

In the city of Jaipur, where Jains dominate the large business and trading community (the most conspicuous trade is an international market for precious and semi-precious stones), every morning of Paryushan there are lengthy sermons by renouncers, preceded for most people by a visit to the local temple, and many also participate in collective rites of meditation or confession. Young men might only stay at the sermons for a little while most days, before rushing on to attend to their businesses, but most older men and pretty well all of the women will spend much of the morning in religious devotions. Many people take on extra dietary restrictions for the whole period, excluding foods like green and root vegetables, tea or sugar from their diets, or not eating or drinking at all during hours of darkness. During the last and culminating day of the ceremonies (Samvatsari), almost everyone fasts.

As is the usual way with Jain fasts (Laidlaw 1995: 216–229), this means neither eating nor drinking anything at all from about an hour before sunset the evening before the day of the fast, continuing through the night and the whole of the day itself, until an hour after sunrise the following day. Children and the elderly and infirm may drink boiled water during the fast, but most people take nothing at all.

The day begins with those for whom this is the last of several days' continuous fasting being taken in procession through the streets to a preaching hall, to receive the blessings of renouncers. In a substantial local Jain community, such as in Jaipur city, each year several people, especially but not exclusively unmarried and recently married young women, will complete an eight-day fast at this time.

The morning is spent with the whole local community crammed in the preaching hall, in which neither electric lights nor fans are turned on, to prevent any insects from being harmed, listening to the recitation in the original Prakrit of a canonical text (the *Kalpa Sutra*) describing the life of Lord Mahavira, the Jain equivalent and elder contemporary of the Buddha.

The afternoon is spent in the same building participating in a three-hour rite of collective confession (*pratikraman*, see Laidlaw 1995: 204–215), again involving recitation in an ancient language, in which an exhaustive list of possible faults is recited (most of this takes the form of an enumeration of all the many forms of life one might intentionally or unintentionally have harmed) accompanied by endlessly repeated series of bodily postures to be held for periods at a time, mostly standing, crouching and prostrating.

As the day goes on, this austerely controlled and rather gruelling experience of serious and thorough withdrawal from all harmful interaction with other living things is intruded upon as noise from the street outside becomes steadily louder. The reason for this is that this Jain ceremony coincides with a very different Hindu festival. Ganesh Caturthi is a day of devotion to the elephant-headed remover of obstacles, Lord Shiva's son Ganesh-ji. The festival, as it is currently celebrated, is not very old, having its roots in late nineteenth century neo-traditionalist nationalism in western India, and with a fairly clear pan-Hindu and anti-Muslim subtext (Courtright 1985). It has spread through much of the country now. In a large city such as Jaipur, it involves noisy processions of a Ganesh-ji statue made each year for the festival, and a substantial fair whose attractions bring many thousands of people in from surrounding villages. The festivities are organised and funded by voluntary committees of the commercial district's leading merchants and shopkeepers – in Jaipur mostly the high-caste Hindu colleagues and competitors of Jain businesses. The Jain merchants themselves mostly make donations towards the expenses, but do not take an active part in the organisation.

And lay Jains also participate in the festival itself, but also in notably qualified and disengaged ways. Hindu homes all have a small image of Ganesh-ji above the entrance, and Jain homes have these too. It would be unthinkable to slight the deity on this day. He is generally benevolent and helpful, and Jain merchants also invoke him as they open new business account books ever year, but he is also a trickster and a vengeful deity when crossed. During this festival, then, a simple ceremony of worship (*puja*) is offered to all these images, but whereas for Hindu families this is an integral part of a day-long veneration of the deity, for Jains it is a short, simple act of deferential acknowledgement, mostly performed between the long elaborate text recitation in the morning and confession in the afternoon, when they go home for a short while in the interval where lunch does not occur.

The Ganesh-ji festival represents rather vividly all the material and sensual aspects of life from which the Jains, even if only for the duration of their own holy days, are setting themselves carefully apart. But they have lives to lead the rest of the year, and neighbours to get on with, and in a similar spirit to their worship of Ganesh-ji at home, many Jains also make a brief, if sometimes rather exhausted appearance at the festivities in the streets. To the neutral observer, they might appear to be participating on the same terms as their Hindu neighbours. They will be dressed and comport themselves in the same way and will take in the various sights and attractions, though obviously they will not eat or drink anything. But their participation, though scrupulously courteous and apparently unmarked, is from their own perspective, on account of its coincidence and sharp contrast with Paryushan, seen in an entirely different and very qualified light.

So in so far as Paryushan is, for lay Jains, a brief experience of something like renouncers' ascetic discipline, and therefore an experience of detachment from their domestic life as householders, Ganesh Caturthi serves rather vividly as a representation of just what marks them off from their majority Hindu neighbours. What for the latter is a 'religious' festival, for Jains is exactly what 'religion' teaches and enables them to transcend. From their Jain perspective, they know that what their Hindu neighbours think of as religion, is in fact thoroughly this-worldly and 'social'.

Yet they also participate in it. The gesture is reminiscent in some respects of Erving Goffman's account (1963, 1971) of 'civil inattention': that brief engagement, with mutual registering and adjustment, which enables strangers passing in the street not to walk into each other, without any contact or acknowledgement that would invite or require actual interaction. If the other were not present, there would be no need for these barely perceptible adjustments, but the other is present – in urban life unknown others always will be – and sustaining detachment from them requires this particular kind of very minimal engagement. The difference is that Goffman's civil inattention is typically a *mutual* accommodation; in this case a small but relatively privileged minority makes an accommodation, in the form of a discreetly disengaged participation, without the qualified and disengaged nature of that participation being visible to the other side.

My second example of Jain practices where detachment is cultivated is the renouncers' alms-gathering (Laidlaw 1995: 289–323; 2000). Elaborate rules govern how this is conducted. The basic idea is that all cooking, involving as it does use of water and fire and chopping things up, is inherently violent, as it causes the deaths of many living things, so renouncers seek to receive food from lay households without incurring any of the responsibility for this violence, and indeed without incurring any obligation, as receipt of hospitality and a gift of food would ordinarily do as a matter of course. In order to maintain this detachment, renouncers must 'graze', as cattle do, accepting a little food from each of several families, so little that no one will have to go without as a result, all of that food having been prepared for the family itself and not with the renouncers in mind. And to ensure that no one will prepare more food to replace that which has been given to the renouncers – for then the latter would bear responsibility for the violence involved in that – they must gather this food after cooking has finished and shortly before the families are due to eat.

In any case, they cannot *ask* for any of this from anyone. They should present themselves silently at the door of lay Jain houses. If no one notices and invites them in, they should move on, and if unsuccessful at just a few households, or if any of the households they do visit break the rules in any way – if they see any prohibited foods in evidence, for instance – then they are supposed to come back empty-handed.

Family members place food, taken straight from their cooking pots, into the renouncers' alms bowls. It is both meritorious and an affirmation of the family's orthopraxy with regard to diet that the renouncers will accept their food, and as hospitality anyway dictates, they always try to urge as much as possible on their guests. But the renouncers do not behave as guests. They do not meet anyone's eyes; they express no gratitude, pleasure or appreciation for what they are given, and indeed never actually express verbally any agreement to receive anything. All they say is 'Enough', 'No more', 'None of that'. They engage in no other conversation or interaction while in the house. On exit, they give a simple two-word blessing, which wishes the householders the fruit of their good deed. After that, they return to where they are staying, and the food collected is combined with that gathered by other members of the group from different households, and all mixed together into an unappetising mass, none of which is identifiable as coming from any specific donor.

A number of points are striking about all this. It is hardly an *interaction* at all. The householders are engaged in performing generous hospitality as best they can, and from their point of view their hosts' reluctance to receive not only confirms the latter's austerity, and therefore the merit in giving to them, but also that the household has been as generous as it possibly can.

But the renouncers do everything *not* to be the recipient of anything that resembles normal hospitality. In taking only what could not be missed, and in combining it all together, they ensure that they consume no one thing that anyone has given them. And they do not even refer to it as 'food'. The images used by renouncers to describe and explain the rules governing the process strikingly do not portray it as an interaction either. They say they are like a cow, taking the top of the grass without damaging the plant, or like a bee gathering pollen from flowers.

And in an important sense these images are just. What has taken place has not really been an interaction. The renouncers have received the food they need, but without incurring any obligation and without compromising their detachment from all the sinful, violent processes of production and reproduction that householders are necessarily embroiled in. This, of course, is quite a trick to pull off. Pretty well everywhere, and in South Asia as reliably and affirmatively as anywhere, food transactions create social connection and obligation. In order for the renouncers to be fed and yet, in this respect, for *nothing to happen*, people have to do quite a lot, quite carefully.

Unlike the civil but disengaged accommodation lay Jains make to the Ganesh-ji festival, this exercise in the cultivation of detachment is mutual, and mutually beneficial. The householders receive their blessing and their merit and get to feel good about a generous gift. The renouncers receive their food, but with no attendant responsibility for the violence involved in producing it. And unlike the Jain and Hindu festivals just described, for both parties here the other is not incidental but necessary to the achievement of their own objectives.

The Jain Paryushan does not depend for *its* meaning or efficacy on the existence of the recently adopted Hindu festival, albeit that the counterpoint it provides to the austerity of the Jain celebrations is aesthetically satisfying. Virtually all Hindus taking part in the day's festivities will be entirely unaware that different Jain ceremonies are taking place at all. For the Jains, like the unfamiliar other on Goffman's urban street, the religious-ethnic other here is a contingent happening, something to be accommodated and this is best done, from everyone's point of view, with the minimum interaction possible and even without overt recognition that an accommodation has in fact taken place. It is best achieved in, and conducive to the reproduction of, a spirit of indifference.

The same is not true of the alms-gathering, where neither can achieve their objectives without the other, and so neither could even in principle wish the other away, as the walker on Goffman's urban street could quite coherently wish the pavement less crowded. The parties to the alms gathering, by contrast, even as they are in important senses not interacting in meticulously maintained detachment, stand in a relation to each other that is nevertheless ethically and affectively positive.

There are temptations on both sides to break the rules, and it does happen that people do so, but generally *both sides* have an interest in maintaining the proper distance and restraint between them. In this respect this practice is reminiscent of Candea's description of habituation between observers and meerkats. It requires a degree of inter-patience, the patience and restraint to accommodate the other's contrasting projects and purposes, so as to maintain what he nicely calls a 'pact of inaction' (2010: 249).

Inaction is also at issue in my final example. I have said already that fasting is a key Jain ascetic practice and comes in many forms. Several fasts, with specific dietary restrictions for specific periods of time, are re-enactments of those performed by the characters in well-known myths and parables, and people often perform these fasts in the hope that they will benefit in some way that resembles the events in those narratives: health will be restored to them or to a family member, some difficulty will be removed, and so on. Now although this is common, everyone knows it is problematical and hedged round with qualification. The problem is that fasting is supposed to be an expression and a means towards the attainment of equanimity and the reining in of desires. So to perform one in the hope of *fulfilling* a desire is obviously a contradiction. The routine way this is handled is that one is supposed to banish any thought of practical outcomes from one's mind during the fast itself, to think, as Jain idiom puts it, 'only about cleaning one's soul'. A standard analogy (not exclusive of course to Jains) is that when grain is planted and watered grass will also grow around it, and any worldly benefits from fasting should likewise be unintended side effects, even if they are foreseeable (Laidlaw 1995: 225–229).

In the case of routine fasting by ordinary lay people this is all regarded in a fairly relaxed way, but sometimes the question of the relation between motivation and outcome becomes much trickier. From the very beginning of the Jain tradition it has been a highly prestigious possibility for renouncers to undertake a fast to death, and for some hundreds of years this has also been open to lay Jains. The practice is carefully distinguished from suicide: it requires the permission of a senior renouncer, must not be undertaken in a state of grief, rage or despair, and proceeds by a gradual reduction in what one eats, with increasing lengths of time spent sitting in meditation, ending in a final vow to fast completely and end one's life in that state. Since, as we have seen, embodied existence *necessarily* involves harm to other living things, concerted attempts to practise restraint and progressively to minimise the harm one causes to others point logically towards this as a fitting *telos*. Salvation is conceived as the rebirth of the soul without a physical body, and this fast – referred to literally as 'meditation-death' – is an anticipation of, as well as a means towards achieving, that end (Laidlaw 2005).

In an obvious sense, however, this is an act of intensely engaged will. It differs from martyrdom in the Abrahamic religious traditions most conspicuously in not depending on any act of persecution by anyone else. It is entirely the result of one's own deliberation, decision and action. But how can you dissolve the will by an act of will? How can you successfully realise a desire to eliminate desire? Are these not, like deciding to believe or asserting relativism, performative contradictions?

This apparent paradox must, indeed, loom over the outset of such a fast, but the point of the rules that govern it, and in particular the point of its being a slow and extended process, is precisely to dissolve it, by turning an action into a state of being: into a state that is entirely disengaged from everything around it, so that the self that completes the process is *detached* from the decisions and acts even of the self that began it.

One fairly obvious device for achieving this are the vows, which have the effect of placing the mental states associated with fasting as an act – intention and decision and will and so on – before and therefore *outside* the state of being defined by each vow as the fast itself. With a vow, you do your intending in advance (Laidlaw 1995: 191–195). But only the very duration of the fast – the progressive elimination of items from the diet, the increasing periods of complete immobility, the experience of one's physical being and impingement on the space around one gradually dwindling, of physical strength and energy fading away and finally, of course, physiological shut-down – only all this long drawn-out process can reconcile the fact that this is something someone does, with the required detachment even from the outcome of the fast itself. This is why the most prestigious of such deaths are those by people who are in perfect health when they embark upon the process. So Jain accounts of these fasts always describe their successful completion in the same terms: he or she greets death as much without eagerness as without reluctance or fear.

These three examples, I suggest, indicate that on these different occasions when Jains seek to cultivate detachment they are aiming at distinctly different things, and not just the same thing to different degrees. They bear out, I think, the intuition that if one looks positively and ethnographically at projects to achieve detachment, rather than regarding them as necessarily ideological, then it becomes clear that detachment is not merely an absence, still less a feint of an absence, but takes definite and variable forms.

Let me try to identify the differences between these forms of detachment. In what ways may detachment be achieved? How, that is, might an affirmation of relation or connection be negated? Like Jonathan Mair (Chapter 1, this volume) and following him also Joanna Cook (2013), I find Jon Elster's (1993) rendition of the Hegelian distinction between external and internal negation useful, though to a slightly different purpose. As Mair remarks, real relationships are typically composed of complex combinations of attempts to establish or assert proximity, similarity or connection in some dimensions and to deny such connections in others. And both the assertions and the denials can be made on different bases, and in different modes. The distinction between external and internal negation helps us to be just a bit more precise about exactly what kinds of denials are in question in specific projects for achieving detachment.

So what is the difference between external and internal negation? External negation applies a negative to the whole of a proposition. So if we begin with a simple affirmation, 'A is related to B', external negation would take the form:

1. NOT (A is related to B).
It is not the case that A is related to B.

Internal negation by contrast places the negative inside the proposition. It attaches the negative sign not to the statement as a whole, but to the act or state asserted in the statement, in this case the fact of being related:

2. A (NOT related to B).
We might paraphrase this (with apologies to the Jedi order) as: it is not-related-to-B that A is.

Because what is being denied in these two forms of negation is subtly different, the kinds of detachment they establish also differ.

Mair uses these terms to distinguish, respectively, the *absence of knowing-relation* to Buddhist doctrine that modernist reformers mistakenly attribute to the 'traditional' Buddhists whom they criticise (A does not know about B), and the actually content-ful and specific *relation of not knowing* which the latter in fact cultivate towards the doctrine (A's relation to B is one of not knowing). Self-consciously modernist reformers accuse other Buddhists of having, in Mair's terms, an external-negation ignorance of the doctrine, but the ignorance of the doctrine those Buddhists actually cultivate is based, as Mair demonstrates, on internal negation. They do not merely 'not know' about the doctrine; they have a reasoned view that knowing it is not possible, and that the proper relation to have to it is, therefore, a humble recognition of its unfathomable depth. From their point of view claiming to know the doctrine, which for reformists is the only imaginable positive relation one could have, and is in principle available to everyone, demonstrates a shallow arrogance that is at the same time a moral and a cognitive failing. So in this case external and internal negation are two incompatible rival characterisations of a single state of affairs: the 'ignorance' of Mongolian Buddhists about Buddhist doctrine. External negation characterises the failing which modernists claim to detect in that state of affairs; internal negation is the positive characterisation of the same, a characterisation for which those modernists' religious understanding does not allow. The modernists misrecognise in the virtue cultivated by others only the absence of a different virtue they themselves claim to possess. Both sets of Buddhists have as an important ethical concern establishing a proper relation to doctrinal knowledge, but whereas in modernist Buddhism the salient negation (to be avoided) is external, for the Mongolian Buddhists whom Mair worked with the ethically significant negation (to be achieved) is internal.

Mair's analysis is, I think, absolutely convincing for the cases he describes. The Jain case we are concerned with here is different and perhaps more complex in just one important respect, in that it does not admit of the thought I canvassed at the beginning of this chapter, that different forms of detachment might neatly correspond to different institutions or social domains or spheres. My claim instead is that distinct detachments based respectively on external and internal negation are *both* positively cultivated by the same Jains. The separation Jains maintain from their Hindu neighbours during Paryushan/Ganesh Caturthi is principally a detachment through external negation, whereas the detachment maintained between renouncers and lay donor families during the alms round works largely through internal negation.

External negation denies connection between two entities, but what it is for them to be unrelated to each other is an unstressed and thinly specified matter. As Mair comments in relation to knowledge claims, the absences external negation asserts must be pretty much all alike in their negativity. What is specified is the two entities between which lack of connection is asserted: it is, specifically, B, to which A is not connected. Our example here of Paryushan and the relation Jains have to Hindus is, I think, an instance of this kind of detachment. Jains mark their non-identity with their Hindu neighbours by their detached stance in relation to the Ganesh-ji festival. They appear to be part of it all, but they set themselves apart from their own point of view.

In some respects this is a paradigm case of identity by means of boundary maintenance, of the kind anthropologists have been familiar with since Fredrick Barth's classic study, *Ethnic Groups and Boundaries* (1969). On this account, ethnic groups are constituted not so much by, as it were, pre-existing substantive characteristics they themselves possess as by the differences they consciously imagine and assert between themselves and specific others. Substantive differences, where they exist, should be thought of on this model as the outcome rather than the precondition of processes of boundary maintenance. In so many of the cases anthropologists have described, this boundary maintenance involves explicitly negative moral evaluation of whatever is on the other side of the boundary: not being like some specific other becomes intrinsic to a group's identity, which is bolstered by morally charged disparagement of those others. So common is this, and so prominent in the relevant anthropological literature, that it might be easy to imagine that ethical condemnation is actually necessary to the process. But while it is indeed extremely common, as Bailey's Orissa example illustrates, it is not inevitable, and it is in this context that moral indifference becomes at least arguably a minor virtue.

The discreet way in which Jains mark themselves off from their neighbours in Paryushan certainly involves aspiring to what they see as a higher virtue, but moral opposition to what they distinguish themselves from is notably absent: first because by their participation in the Ganesh festival, albeit that that participation is qualified, lay Jains overtly identify aspects of their everyday lives with those of their neighbours, and second, because the way they set themselves apart is so studiedly unstated. It is not even to the least degree *addressed* to those from whom detachment is established. Like passers-by in Goffman's street, it is an accommodation and avoidance that is most successful – establishes detachment most unequivocally – in so far as it is invisible to the other and executed with barely conscious indifference.

In contrast with external negation, however, internal negation makes disconnection not merely an absence of connection but a definite positive quality intrinsic to the entity (A) to which it applies. This means that indifference is scarcely a possibility and in our Jain case, indeed, the specific character of that from which each party is detached is intrinsic to their identity in the relation. And further, the ethical regard of the other is necessary for the establishment of that detachment. The renouncers cannot exercise restraint by refusing most of what is offered if the householders do not, in a spirit of reverence, make the most fulsome offering of which they are able. And unless the renouncers do accept something, thereby recognising the household as meritorious, then the virtue the former demonstrate in refusing the rest of what is offered serves as a rebuke rather than as a compliment to the household. So instead of barely engaged indifference, this mutual detachment involves an ongoing negotiation of co-patience in which each party's stance and ethical regard directly implicates the other.

My third example – the fast to death – represents a striving towards yet another ideal, which we might state as:

3. A is not related (even to A)

This is neither internal nor external negation, as defined above. Here, the kind of detachment that is aimed at is not the negation merely of any particular affirmation of any particular attachment. It is a negation that is, so to speak, intransitive. The fact that it seems to involve a logical paradox does not prevent it from being of the first importance as an ideal in Jain religious life. But it does make it difficult to describe. As Cook (2013) rightly points out, of the related case of Thai Buddhist monasticism, there is something not quite right about thinking of there being an agent that 'achieves' this kind of detachment, because in so far as it is achieved, the agent who might be thought of as doing so ceases to be as such. As Cook observes, it is of some help, therefore, to think of the relation between attachment and the state the meditator aims at as constitutive (or as she puts it 'definitive') rather than causal, but it is important also to note that this is so only from the perspective which the striving meditator (and the whole tradition) imaginatively attributes to the saint who has already achieved the ideal. From the vantage point of a novice meditator, as of a pious Jain contemplating embarking on a fast to death, a long path of effortful striving stands between them and this dissolution of paradox. If it is actually achieved, it can only be momentarily and at the end of life.

Two thoughts might usefully be taken away, I think, from this discussion, including from the limit-case of detachment imagined as an absolute intransitive state: first, that the distinction between internal and external negation is no more than a useful starting point in terms of distinguishing the different forms of detachment we might find instantiated in social practices and institutions; but also, second, in relation to the general theme of this volume, that notwithstanding this limitation, it is nevertheless worthwhile for anthropologists to examine further both the logical form and the ethical tenor of aspirations to detachment, as they are expressed and pursued in different institutional and cultural contexts.

References

Babb, Lawrence A., 1996, *Absent Lord: Ascetics and Kings in a Jain Ritual Culture*. Berkeley: University of California Press.

Bailey, F. G., 1996, *The Civility of Indifference: On Domesticating Ethnicity*. Ithaca: Cornell University Press.

Banks, Marcus, 1992, *Organizing Jainism in India and England*. Oxford: Clarendon Press.

Barth, Fredrik (ed.), 1969, *Ethnic Groups and Boundaries*. London: Allen & Unwin.

Candea, Matei, 2010, 'I Fell in Love with Carlos the Meerkat': Engagement and Detachment in Human–Animal Relations. *American Ethnologist* 37: 241–258.

Cook, Joanna, 2013, Directive and Definitive Knowledge: Experiencing

Achievement in a Thai Meditation Monastery. In Nicholas J. Long and Henrietta L. Moore, eds, *The Social Life of Achievement*. Oxford: Berghahn Books, pp. 103–119.

Cort, John E., 2001, *Jains in the World: Religious Values and Ideology in India*. New York: Oxford University Press.

Courtright, Paul B., 1985, *Ganesa: Lord of Obstacles, Lord of Beginnings*. New York: Oxford University Press.

Du Gay, Paul, 2000, *In Praise of Bureaucracy: Weber, Organization, Ethics*. London: Sage.

Elster, Jon, 1993, *Political Psychology*. Cambridge: Cambridge University Press.

Goffman, Erving, 1963, *Behavior in Public Places: Notes on the Social Organization of Gatherings*. New York: Free Press.

Goffman, Erving, 1971, *Relations in Public: Microstudies of the Public Order*. New York: Basic Books.

Kelting, M. Whitney, 2001, *Singing to the Jinas: Jain Women, Mandal Singing, and the Negotiations of Jain Devotion*. New York: Oxford University Press.

Laidlaw, James, 1995, *Riches and Renunciation: Religion, Economy, and Society among the Jains*. Oxford: Clarendon Press.

Laidlaw, James, 2000, A Free Gift Makes No Friends. *Journal of the Royal Anthropological Institute* 6: 617–634.

Laidlaw, James, 2005, A Life Worth Leaving: Fasting to Death as Telos of a Jain Religious Life. *Economy and Society* 34: 178–199.

Lillehammer, Hallvard, 2014, Minding Your Own Business? Understanding Indifference as a Virtue. *Philosophical Perspectives* 28.

7

Detachment, difference and separation: Lévi Strauss at the wedding feast

Caroline Humphrey

The first time I was invited to a wedding, I asked a very perceptive 6-year-old boy what to expect and he replied: 'You will sing, you will weep, you will drink and you will fight!' (Legrain, 2013).

At certain pivotal times in a people's lives there is a publicly ratified realignment of allegiances. On occasions such as marriage, adult baptism and taking or renouncing Buddhist vows, a person is said to 'leave' one set of relations and 'join' another. Such shifts of allegiance never cut off all previous ties, but there is a definite alteration in the public perception of a person's identity. The change is also marked by the eventual quality the actors lend to the occasion. While anthropology has long been concerned with *difference* (between the given sets of relations) and *separation/integration* as important themes in analysing such events (Stafford 2000; Stasch 2009; Empson 2011: 175–181), this chapter draws attention to *detachment*, which I conceive as an active practice that works to stand back from any of the particular associations between which a movement in being made.

As I attempt to show using the example of Buriad weddings, such detachment can operate to greater or lesser degrees. At its least conscious, there is the question of simply being able to manoeuvre adequately through the complex of activities. A person cannot *properly* enact the move from X status to Y status while remaining only within the perspective of X, to be replaced by the perspective of Y. He or she should simultaneously be able also to stand mentally outside – to be in this sense minimally detached – in order to comprehend the consequential sequence of actions in time and to perceive the topology of the relations (their connectedness, boundaries, elasticity, etc.) in which he or she is involved. Yet, simple though this seems, my ethnography suggests that people sometimes do not achieve such detachment, or are apt to drop it and revert to a blind and fierce – or at any rate emotional – attachment to one perspective or preoccupation. Perhaps it is for this reason that it is common at such events to have one or more persons delegated to enact the position of detachment. This has to be someone who has a bank of memories of 'how we do things', whose task is to remind the company of endings and beginnings, to craft an atmosphere of calmness, propriety and happiness, and, above all, to affirm the presence of others and their alternative views. I argue that this more deliberate manifestation of 'active detachment' deserves attention in its own right. It requires distance from one's own perspectives and is to be achieved by means of connection with, and making space for, others' expositions. Such detachment is not only a withdrawal from exclusively self-focused kinds of action, but is a further deliberate practice that has its own effect on others.

Exploring these ideas in relation to Buriad weddings means digging into a space in the anthropology of marriage in Inner Asia. On the one hand is the classic literature of Lévi-Strauss, Leach and Needham that analyses systems of exchange of women. Concerned with structural types (direct, indirect, generalised, restricted, delayed marriage exchanges), with the contradictions in such systems (the contrary flows of bride price and dowry, preferential as distinct from obligatory marriage choices and so forth), it hardly addresses what actually happens in the handover process of these exchanges – at the complex node of interactions generally translated as 'weddings'. On the other hand are countless descriptions of wedding rituals. These are characteristically interested in comparison, in detailing the ethnographer's analysis of the customs of one ethnic group as distinct from another's. Rarely do we find an attempt to integrate the two kinds of analysis, or to penetrate behind the elegant diagrams and investigate the practical, emotional and cosmological dimensions of real life instances of what people do at weddings. An exception is work on China, particularly that of Charles Stafford, who writes about the emotions surrounding marriage. He writes about sons chafing under patriarchal authority, who want a separation from parents they cannot have, contrasted with the sadness of daughters forced into a separation that they cannot avoid (2000: 116–120). However, the broader meeting or confrontation of *all* of these actors (i.e. the complex wedding sequence), which in the Buriad case, amid a public declaration of joyousness, is in fact largely composed of hostile contestations – requires an analysis that is not limited to investigating the view from single positions or roles.

For this reason I would particularly like to differentiate 'detachment' from 'separation'. They are often conflated because in day-to-day

English to detach from something means more or less the same as to separate from it. But unlike these verbal forms, which designate spatial actions, both detachment and separation as abstract nouns refer to stances as well as to the processes of disconnection. Here it seems to me that the two have different connotations. 'Separation' implies a break of connection, and whether people regard this status as positive or not, the term as I use it here remains within the binary of the move from X to non-X, or from X to Y. 'Detachment', on the other hand, implies a third 'place', a distancing from any of the other situated perspectives.

In its general usage in English, the term 'detachment' evokes highly diverse evaluative/affective connotations such as indifference, aloofness, subversive irony, disinterest, calmness, rationalisation, freedom from personal preferences, the religiously defined state of non-attachment and so forth, many of which are explored in this book. In recent decades anthropology has tended to judge detachment negatively, aligning it *inter alia* with the seeming over-objectivity and arbitrariness of Lévi-Straussian structuralism. I suggest, however, that Lévi-Strauss's analysis, at least of marriage alliance, has a certain predictive value and that his kinship diagrams – repellent though anthropology students tend to find them – would not be foreign to Buriads. Their own written genealogies do not look so very different. However, analytical rationalisation, whether done by Buriads or by anthropologists, is not the kind of detachment I discuss in this chapter. The sense of detachment addressed here is a quality of action: the state of awareness of a store of potentially realisable acts or social procedures, and a 'hands-off', non-proprietorial, mode of deployment of them when participating in a complex event. In its most 'concentrated' form such detachment is self-conscious and self-monitoring, and artful in its capacity for creative denaturalisation of social norms.

The idea that one plays a part in a social event, and yet may be only partially involved, has been extensively explored by the French anthropologist Albert Piette (1998, 2010). A brief discussion enables me to situate further the kind of detachment I have in mind by differentiating it from his work. Piette attempts to understand the nature of human presence in festive/ceremonial situations. He points to the anthropological neglect of what he calls the 'minor mode'. This consists of unimportant details, of what is present beside the social relevance of actions – absent-minded thoughts, distraction by peripheral objects, wandering glances, docile lack of attention under the effect of habit, an accidental gesture, or 'blank moments' between sequences of action (Piette 2010: 12). Piette argues, and I would agree with him, that these are inevitable and reveal the human way of being. He remarks that were the 'minor mode' *not* to be present, people would call into question the normality of the participants (2010: 13).

Piette explains the significance of his insight by way of contrasting it with alternative theories of action proposed by Garfinkel, Goffman, Simmel and Bateson. The most pertinent for this chapter is his discussion of Goffman's idea of 'role distance'. In Goffman, where 'the frame' is a set of rules underlying a situation, individuals participate by being fitted to 'roles' within the frame and yet they also manipulate and interpret these roles, for example, by speaking with irony. Such pointed behaviour involves a play of implicit distancing in relation to norms, which constitutes a 'wedge between the individual and his role ... The individual is actually denying not the role but the virtual self that is implied in the role for all accepting performers' (Goffman 1972: 95). Piette rejects this scheme on the grounds that it reduces daily behaviours to socio-strategic goals and fails to account for human indeterminacy and untidiness (Piette 2010: 21). For in Goffman the role-distancing behaviours are seen as intentionally 'saying something' and are, therefore, pertinent to the matter at hand; indeed they are often 'impertinent', which as Piette neatly notes, is only a form of pertinence (1998: 283). Piette himself is interested in the conscious yet non-strategic, those little behaviours that actors can distinguish as 'non-pertinent' and are, therefore, tolerated by the entire company as 'minor' (1998: 279).

Both of these arguments are about distancing, yet surely there is some stance that neither of them covers. The idea of detachment I try to clarify cannot be identified with either 'the minor mode' or 'role distance'. It is not distracted, and it is attentive to the matter at hand. What such detachment is able to do by standing back is to reconfigure more broadly *what the matter is* – more generously, one might say. The idea does not propose a self-oriented subject in the way proposed by Goffman. Nor does it foreground pre-set 'roles' that such a subject is contesting. For the weddings I have observed have to be created – every detail has be decided upon among a number of possibilities, and furthermore even important 'roles' such as bride and groom are to some extent improvised, given that they have to react to the unpredictable activities of diverse other participants whose brief is undetermined. Meanwhile, the more set or ritualised elements of weddings are episodes that are perched, as it were, on a swell of underlying agonistic currents of social precedence, rivalry, honour, ambivalence, enmity, aggression and fear. This is one reason why the detachment I attempt to define should not be entirely conflated with the distance brought about by ritualisation – that is, when given ritual acts are pre-set whatever the meaning or emotion that may (or may not) be given them by the actors – a distance created

Detachment, difference and separation 151

by a deflection of individual intentionality (Humphrey and Laidlaw 1994). Detachment in complex scenarios such as weddings may well have this character in respect of rites, but more broadly it must also establish a way of dealing with, without getting engulfed by, all the rest of what is happening, the unscripted, raw and unpredictable. Since such detachment is not directed towards personal goals – but precisely to the opposite – it has to be clearly differentiated from 'role distance'. It can perhaps be characterised as a cosmopolitan art, one that is capable of enhancing cultural forms by promoting, to quote from Amanda Anderson's study *The Powers of Distance*, 'a self-overcoming that enables attention to others' (2001: 15).

Buriad weddings

This chapter derives most immediately from my experience of two Buriad wedding feasts in summer 2013, one held in the city of Ulan-Ude in Russia and the other in the grasslands outside Nantoon, a large village near Hailar in Inner Mongolia, China (for reasons of space this chapter deals only with the first case). The one urban and 'modern', the other rural and 'traditional', the two weddings were visually and procedurally different. But there was a common understanding of what was going on: a person, the bride, was being handed over from one group of people (her natal kin, the guests) to a different group (the groom's kin, the hosts). The festivities, in both cases numbering hundreds of participants, were the grand centrepiece of an unfinished sequence of activities involving gifts and promises between the two 'sides' (*tal*). The wedding enacted by the two groups is distinct from the civil rite of marriage before a state official, which can take place earlier or afterwards, or even not at all. Immense expenditure is involved. Buriad weddings are the greatest, most sumptuous festivity in a person's life cycle.

Traditional weddings enjoined enactments of congratulation, but also difference, suspicion, competition, mockery, fights, hierarchical subordination, separation, tears and bitter accusations. Today, even though most of these episodes are left out or toned down, Buriad weddings are still famous region-wide for morphing into violence.[1]

Mongols laugh at the following anecdote: two young Buriad men meet and one of them has just been to a wedding. 'What was it like?' enquires his friend. 'Oh, it was great! There was a tremendous fight and the groom got stabbed.'[2] As we shall see, this was not quite just a joke. Buriad participants in online forums are far from unanimous about enjoying weddings. Some describe them as 'a nightmare' because they feel trapped by the obligations, long repetitive speeches, the need to be nice to distant aged kin, having to remember the countless recipients to whom presents are owed and the possibility that the whole thing will descend into a drunken brawl.[3] Others positively enjoy the fighting, the abandonment of self-control and the vanishing of detachment. I suggest that in the face of such feelings, and despite the historical watering-down, the successful wedding is magical. It has to operate against itself, that is to supersede the various acrimonious interests it itself consists of. Somehow, the participants have to achieve two magical effects, first to protect the newly related families from the fortune-threatening dangers of the loss of a member on the one hand and the incorporation of an outsider on the other, and second to ensure the life-vigour of the young couple in the future. In these circumstances, detachment is fragile. In earlier weddings, and even now in remote Buriad regions, appointed elders (*türüü*) of the two sides somehow had to concoct it between them. Now, however, and at the two weddings I observed, a neutral 'master of ceremonies' is employed to help them – a person hired to orchestrate the songs and speeches, maintain a joyous tone and keep the flow of events on track. The new and external character of the master of ceremonies is marked by the fact that he (occasionally she) is known by foreign terms, *tamada* by Buriads in Russia[4] and *daidong*[5] by those in Inner Mongolia. This person must support the elders of each group in their efforts to enchant the entire throng and achieve a balance between them. Their task is not easy and they do not always succeed.

To understand contemporary weddings it is necessary to know something about those of the past, since most families these days attempt to enact some version of earlier customs. The 'traditional wedding' is a beloved topic of Buriad and Mongolian ethnographers and has been described in detail for groups all over Inner Asia (Petri 1925; Baldaev 1959; Basaeva 1980; Naranbat 1992; Galdanova 1992; Ochir and Galdanova 1992; Natsov 1995; Krol' 2008). 'Traditional' describes weddings as they were practised before socialist governments intervened to stop the payment of bride price and the performance of 'superstitious rituals'. This would mean up to the 1930s in the USSR, early 1950s in Inner Mongolia (China), and 1950s–1960s in Mongolia. However, Russian ethnography from well into socialist times (Basaeva 1980) indicates that while socialist '*komsomol* weddings'[6] had become an option, most people in rural areas of Buryatia staunchly adhered to almost all elements of the traditional model into the 1970s. After the end of the Soviet Union, with the economic collapse, weddings became more modest, but from 2000 onwards there has been a boom in elaborate and expensive festivities. They can now take many forms, including a 'European' type, with the bride clad in a long white wedding dress, as well as deliberately Buriad versions with most people wearing national clothing. Sometimes people combine the two. I have seen a wedding video with the white dress visible beneath a bizarrely ballooned-out scarlet Mongolian-style gown. Even 'modern' urban weddings are based on elements of the traditional form.

In brief, the salient facts about such earlier weddings are: the potentially marrying groups had to be established as *different* (i.e. not patrilineal kin for at least seven generations) and preferably living at some distance from one another; 'bride price' was payable after a rite of engagement and before the main wedding; the bride was given a round of send-off parties by her kin, which included ritual humiliation of the groom; she was then taken on a ritualised journey by her kin to the groom's place, where she made obeisance to her father-in-law and the elders of the groom's family; the wedding proper (*hurim*) was now held, with a ceremonial feast (*türe*)[7] and public presentation of the dowry and other gifts; after a libation to the deities and a purification of the yurt, the bride's kin returned home; finally, the bride was re-clothed in married women's attire by the wives of the groom's group and then led to the marital bed. This entire sequence was punctuated with nine 'quarrels' or 'grabbings' (*türe-iin yühen bulyaaldalga*), which were said to have been ordained for all weddings by a Khan in ancient times. These fights, mostly between men of the two sides, were so vivid that descriptions of weddings focus largely on them, for example, Natsov's ethnography (1995) of a wedding he attended among Selenga Buriads in 1940.

Clearly, contests were integral to wedding festivities throughout Mongol lands. They varied in the prescribed number,[8] the items fought over and the different meanings given to similarly named tussles.[9] Even within one small region the 'grabbings' varied, or changed over time. Such differences, as well as short-cuts, elaborations, the addition of prayers addressed to ancestors and spirits of the land, and the involvement of singers, shamans or lamas who performed as they saw fit, indicate that weddings were made up from place to place and did not follow a single pre-given model (though it is true that the spats –whether verbal or physical – between the two sides run through all the descriptions). In all this two features stand out enabling us to make a connection with the diagrams of Lévi-Strauss and Leach. First of all, the bride's side is expected, if not to win all of these contests, invariably to discomfort, humiliate and thus subordinate the groom's. And second, not all of the fights were between the adult men of the two sides. On occasion other actors were involved, including women, old people and children, and some of the 'grabbings' happened between groups on one side. How can this be explained?

The alliance situation – fighting, exchanging, putting down

Among many groups of Buriads the ideal marriage was with a girl from the mother's natal patrilineage (*nagasnar*) and brides were repeatedly taken from the same groups over generations (Petri 1925: 27–28; Baldaev 1959: 24–26, 29; Galdanova 1992: 115–116). It was strictly forbidden for a man to take a wife from within his own lineage (the 'warm' *haluun* people) while marriages with *zee* (girls of the father's sister's daughter category) was rare and disfavoured (Manzhigeev 1960: 50–51) or altogether forbidden (Petri 1925: 12; Baldaev 1959: 18). Thus there emerges from many descriptions, by authors who cannot have read a word of Lévi-Strauss, the lineaments of 'generalised exchange', with women moving from one group of males to another and onwards to a third, and so on, while bride price moved in the other direction. The explanation given by Buriads to Krol' for this marriage preference, confirmed by Manzhigeev who was himself Buriad, was the idea that since you have to marry with a 'foreign' (*hari*) group anyway, it might as well be with a group your elders had previously dealt with – that is, the mother's kin (1960: 43). The key point in relation to any given wedding, however, is that this group (*nagasnar*) are regarded as senior and must be shown deep respect. 'Even the *nagasa*'s yellow dog is a *nagasa*' (and must therefore be respected) is a popular Buriad saying.

The enactment of a wedding, however, concentrated a conceptual impasse that is glossed over in the idea of 'generalised exchange'. The prescribed contests were fights between equal groups over some prize, raiding one another for valuable items, or verbal contests over honour, but they were interlaced with a phenomenon of a different order, 'systemic' (or pre-supposed) hierarchy, the notional precedence of the wife givers over the wife receivers. Added to this was the issue of prestations, given or promised. Lévi-Strauss calls 'absurd' the notion that women are exchanged for goods (1969: 238), yet the tension caused by the coexistence of non-equivalent flows surfaced in the Buriad wedding. It is evident, for example, in the different names for the prestation (money, livestock and goods) given by the groom's side. A conceptual ambiguity is seen from the fact that it was sometimes called literally 'the price of the bride' (*basagan-u üne*), suggesting the equality of a bargain, but more commonly was termed 'offering of horses' (*aduu baril*) or simply *baril*, which is any offering from a lower to a higher person in hierarchical mode. The potentiality of switching between several disparate rationales in one event creates, I suggest, a key instability of the wedding, its tendency to jolt between rival battles and scenes of destined subordination, and sometimes to curdle both in the same action.

Several elements of the wedding pitted the two groups against one another as equals competing for fortune, prosperity and renown. The use of a matchmaker (*juuch* – the same word used for an ambassador between two khanates), the selection by each side of their own authoritative and talented elder as 'leader' (*türüü*) to make their case through oratory and repartee, the prayers said by shamans or lamas to the ancestral land-gods of each place to guarantee protection, the 'fight for the sun' midway on the journey between the two homes and the raids to grab some fortune-producing prize are all examples of this. But other essential elements consisted of enforced submission. The bride was literally torn from the arms of her sisters and girlfriends by the men of her own group, who had accepted the groom's offering of money and livestock and therefore had to hand her over to him. This physical subordination of the daughter/sisters by their brothers/uncles was in one sense destined by the idea of the reproduction process internal to the group (unmarried women remaining at home were thought to bring terrible misfortune, like evil spirits), but at the same time the struggle followed the exchange logic of the equal alliance between in-laws. Meanwhile, the bride's side had already shown its 'hierarchical' supremacy over the entire marriage. This can be seen from the fact that the lavish parties for the bride before she departed were called 'games' (*naadan*),[10] described by Galdanova as 'orgiastic' (2002: 149), during which the nights were 'obligatorily spent in pairs, and the bride would take the first opportunity to enjoy the pleasures of love in the greatest measure' (Krol' 2008: 86). It is recorded that the bride's appointed wedding elder presided calmly over all this, giving the tacit approval of the lineage to the goings on. Not only was it generally assumed that the bride would not be a virgin when she eventually reached the groom, but the young men of her own side knew that one of them might be the father of her first child.

It can be added to this that the groom's kin were often unable to pay the bride price in full by the due date. Thus the superiority of being creditors might be added to the disdainful repartee of the bride group's encounters with the groom's on the journey, their haughty requests for more presents and money from the groom's people, countered by the hot-headed 'grabbings' by the other side. At the extreme, these demands could lead to the groom's side yelling, 'We don't want her anyway! Take her away!'[11] Such was the substance of the passage of the girl from one status to another. Whether she was happy to marry or not, the bride had to resist separation: she wailed and sang bitter songs of accusation against her parents – against the very exchange logic in which she was a counter.[12] Once taken into the groom's home she was subordinated to a different round of hierarchic activities that placed her as foreign, incipiently polluting and obliged to perform humble services, the lowest in the household – and yet she was also the nourisher, the giver of life and fortune (*heshig*). Her precarious and ambivalent position, analysed in detail by Empson (2011), is epitomised in the Bayad Mongol custom whereby the new bride had to bow to and 'feed' (with fat collected from households in her own settlement) not only her father-in-law, his gods and his hearth-fire, but also his dog. She sat on the ground with her gown spread out and a little milk was poured in her lap. While she bowed to the dog, which was tied with a ribbon to show it was *heshigtei* ('with fortune'), it lapped up the milk (Ochir and Galdanova 1992: 45).

It is at this point that we again meet Lévi-Strauss, or rather a neglected implication of the generalised exchange pattern he identified. For overseeing the (partial) incorporation of the bride (*ber*) were the older women married in to the groom's family (*bergen*, pl. *berged*). The *ber* was kept at arms' length by the senior men, but she was suffocatingly embraced by the *berged*: they re-plaited her hair into the fashion for married women, re-dressed her, could give her a new name, led her to make her bows, officiated at the key rite of joining her hand to that of the groom, made up the marital bed, undressed the pair and one *bergen* might even lie down together with them in the bed to 'give advice' (Sodnomtseren 1975: 60). But who were these wives? In the ideal case of general matrilateral cross-cousin marriage they would be none other than *nagasa* women from the groom's mother's kin, and indeed from the same broad kin group as the young bride herself. The existence of a related 'brides' group' within the patrilineage of the husband is discussed by Nanzatov and Sodnompilova (2013), who argue that since brides often arrived with a substantial dowry (not only domestic goods but also livestock, and in the richest families in the pre-revolutionary era also gold, silver and even a servant), all of which was their own property and could be removed in the case of divorce, these wives could collectively form a substantial, mutually supportive counterpart to the men of the groom's lineage (2013: 16–17).

The 'wedding leaders' and detachment

It should be clear from the above description that the Buriad wedding was a tensely concentrated affair, the knotting, untying and re-knotting of many strands of relations. Yet 'knotting' may give the impression of a firmness that was not always present – the ties could burst apart, the contests become real fights, the bride could refuse even at the last moment and the groom when finally face to face with the bride might take a dislike to her and send her back. In these volatile circumstances it is notable that many of the episodes of the wedding took place not in ordinary language but in verse or song (Baldaev 1959; Naranbat 1992). These were performed not by the marriage protagonists themselves but by singers (*duuch*) and experts in verbal repartee (*helmerch*) chosen by the two sides. Presiding over each group's honourable enactment were the designated *hudyn türüü* ('leaders of groups allied by marriage'), alternatively called *hurimyn türüü* ('wedding leaders').

The description by Naranbat (1992) of the Urad Mongol wedding is illuminating, since from it one can glimpse something of what detachment meant in the case of the *hurimyn türüü*. I can say this because I happen to know Naranbat, who is an Urad, a former Buddhist lama, and now a professor in Höhhot in Inner Mongolia. He is a witty speaker and a polished, versatile singer, and has himself been engaged as a singer or *hurimyn türüü* at many weddings. Unlike other descriptions of weddings, Narabat's downplays the contests and his account dwells most on the series of prayers, rites and, above all, songs. He begins by stating that the Urad wedding cannot take place without *each* side making a prior sacrifice to common master-deities of the land. He cites the relevant prayer requesting the protection of the spirit-inspiration (*sülde*) of Muna Mountain, which is the highest peak of a long ridge, with its counterpart the Yellow River dominates the entire Urad landscape (Humphrey and Ujeed 2013: 185–223). Thus each *hurimyn türüü*, in charge of such a rite, is broadening the vision of the participants to encompass the wider spiritual realm that both 'sides' inhabit.

Naranbat's account is dominated by the marshalling of the episodes of the wedding, the dovetailing of one activity with another, and the management of time. For example, he writes that when the groom's group arrives to fetch the bride, and after there has been an aggressive trial of the groom's strength, three songs should be sung:

> While these songs are being sung they give presents to the groom [list of presents]. The 'giving of presents' must not last longer than the songs. In is not necessary to finish all of the songs – if the giving of presents finishes after the first song, then they may start the farewell song 'Altai Khangai'. As soon as this ends the guests get ready to depart, and the bride starts to cry. (1992: 63–64)

Detachment is seen here, it seems to me, not just in the objectivising, naming and ordering of action-elements out of the flow, as generally happens in ritualisation. It is also evident in a certain non-possessive relation of the actors to these elements. They are not so much (or not only) elements that should be performed as items that, not being fully mine, are acknowledged as common to all. This is particularly the case for the songs and verses in the memory-stores of the 'wedding leader' and the other people chosen to perform, for such people have to be able to master the repertoires of both sides. In *this* wedding the leader will perform as haughty bride-giver, but in the *next* one, when his group is the receiver, he will have to be equally competent in the other cycle.

This knowledge pertaining to the overall good, the mastery over the swerving of fortune, is not held by everyone; it is this competence that makes an elder the right person to be chosen as wedding leader. We can see here, I think, in the wedding leader's relation to the songs and rites something analogous to the idea of 'poor use' (*usus pauper*) described by Giorgio Agamben in his analysis of the 'highest poverty' as conceptualised by Franciscan theologians.[13] They contrasted 'use' to 'property' ('the right of domination' *ius domini*). Enjoined as monks to live in poverty, yet being an institutionalised order with lands and wealth of various kinds, the Franciscans argued against their detractors that their relation to goods – which I interpret as 'detached' – was that they used but did not own them: 'wanting to have nothing of their own as the interior act, and using the thing as not one's own as the exterior act' (Agamben 2013: 127). Of course the Buriad leader-elders had nothing like this ideology, but in this light we could, nevertheless, see them as 'using' the common stock of the songs and rites of their social world. Ordinary participants might mostly act in the mode of 'property' (grabbing, devouring, accumulating), but wedding propriety specified numerous occasions for them too where the correct behaviour was to make only fleeting contact with a thing. This 'minimal use' is most evident in the custom, when a drink is offered, of sipping it and returning the cup to the donor – an act that is replicated from person to person round the company and repeated countless times in any feast. The detachment implied by such 'drinking but not really drinking' is a renunciation of immediate gratification, a self-overcoming that enables attention to the presence of others.

A present-day wedding: difference, separation, fights and detachment

In turning to present-day weddings I suggest that despite modifications – notably a radical decrease in the number of rituals – the key elements of difference, separation and fights are just as pronounced as earlier and active detachment if anything is more evident. The argument will develop in stages, starting with the presentation of kin difference in an educated urban setting.

In summer 2013 a couple, not in their first youth and both lecturers at an engineering college in Ulan-Ude, celebrated their marriage. The groom came from Kurumkan, a remote mountainous valley in the north, and the bride originated from the Khori Buriads of Aga, a steppe area far to the east. This 'modern' wedding feast was held in neutral territory, a large rented hall in the capital city of Ulan-Ude, midway between the two districts. Invited by distant relatives on the bride's side, we were shepherded to one side of the hall. Meanwhile, buses were drawing up outside disbursing the groom's relatives and friends, who clustered at the other side. Glances were cast across the space, and I overheard remarks such as '... from Kurumkan – ha, ha, no wonder they look so countrified!' Jolly music was playing and there was a long wait while various dignitaries arrived with their entourages, among which almost unnoticed were the bride and groom. We were then seated at long tables holding 60–70 people each, the bride's side tables separated from the groom's by an open space. The marital couple with their four parents were seated at a small table facing this space. I was informed that the elders sitting at the head of each of the tables were the 'wedding leaders' (*hurimyn türüü*).

As dishes began to be served, the *tamada* (master of ceremonies) appeared, a jaunty young man wielding a microphone. His zone of operation was in the space between the two sets of tables, and one by one he called on the wedding dignitaries to make speeches. These *türüü* were numerous, consisting of a man and a woman representing each lineage – the inclusion of women, I was told, being evidence of modernity. First were the leaders of the groom's father's clan, who proclaimed the excellent qualities of his lineage, named its famous ancestors, their deeds and qualities, and declared how good it was that one of their sons was getting married. In flowery language they then complimented the excellent in-laws-to-be of Aga. Next were the *türüü* of the groom's mother's clan. Then it was the turn of the bride's father's clan, then the leader of the bride's mother's brother's clan (the *nagasa* clan). To my surprise, but dawning recognition, the speeches culminated with the exposition of the qualities of the *nagasa*'s *nagasa* clan – the most respected relatives of all, the wife givers of the wife givers (earlier called 'the great *nagasa*', Petri 1925: 28). Lévi-Strauss would surely have been delighted to see his scheme so clearly exposed. But what he might not have predicted was the difference *in kind* between the various groups arrayed in the hall, and a tension arising from the fact that their dissimilar qualities were jostling for admiration (on which, more below).

The bride and groom sat mutely while less polished, more emotional speeches came from their parents. The bride's mother was near to tears, but the *tamada* insisted she take her turn. Teachers, work bosses, school friends and aged relatives followed. Now came the time for general present giving (the 'bride price' and dowry having been handed over earlier) and each notable gift was announced to the hall.[14] The bride's father said he was giving his daughter a farewell gift of three cows and a necklace. Her face crumpled with emotion as she took the jewels from his hand. Round the hall, people smiled approvingly. This moment of separation was all that I observed. People now rose from their seats and went to the top table to offer their gifts – envelopes with money. All of this took a long time, while the company ate and drank their way through the feast, listening with half an ear to jokes from the *tamada* and watching the entertainments he orchestrated (a singer, children from a dancing school, etc.). Rather suddenly, we rose to go. The bride's side are said to be 'guests' and should not outstay their welcome. I was told that young people from both sides would stay to party through the night and that that was when many weddings dissolved into fighting.

In fact, for many Buriads a wedding involves anticipation of a fight. A few years ago two Buriad girlfriends were hitchhiking on the road from Kurumkan to Ulan-Ude. They hailed a lorry, and when it stopped they climbed into the covered area at the back. What a shock! A heap of men's bloodied bodies were lying there. The girls realised the men were not dead when one groaned. It emerged that they were a party of relatives who had travelled all the way from their home in Ust'-Orda, at least three days on uncomfortable roads, to take part in a wedding – and a fight – in Kurumkan. Now they were on their way home. The girls relaxed when they understood this completely normal situation.[15]

Many small incidents might provoke fisticuffs, but I was told of a deeper explanation given by western Buriads: the suspicion that the visitors were not paying the necessary respect to the ancestors and land spirits of the hosts. This fear was revealed to my colleague, Istvan Santha, who was living in a groom's village among Ekhirit Buriads at the time (1990s). A group of heralds had been sent out to the *barisa* (wayside shrine) to wait for the bride's party, but they had taken a different route and thus by-passed the sacred spot. The fear immediately arose that the visitors were disregarding the vital interests of the hosts: for the propitiation at the *barisa* of the ancestor-land spirits is essential to avoid misfortune and raise life-energy. The wedding was then carried out in an atmosphere of aggression: each of the bride's men provided himself with a bodyguard and they went about only in pairs, even to the latrine. The tension only lightened when the groom's side were able to demonstrate their inherited virtues, when their leaders showed through their knowledge of history, songs and improvisations that they embodied the wonderful qualities of the ancestors and *had this accepted* by the guests.

The acceptance is not easy to contrive. For ancestral lines (in western Buriad *udkha*, in other areas *ug*) are not alike: one may be famed for bravery in war, another for shamanic powers, another for prosperity in herding and so forth, qualities inherited through both social and biological fathers. The *türüü* take pride in being able to demonstrate that they know about the various branching lines. In the past they were punished if they faltered, for to get it wrong was to tempt fate and the wrath of forgotten spirits. The *türüü* are also expected to exemplify the particular qualities of the patriline they represent. The result is that any wedding will present, jousting for attention, a multi-coloured array of differences that are conceptualised as *essential*[16] but are also seen as constituent parts of a wider 'Buriad people' that the elders do their best to evoke.

Returning to the urban wedding, the *tamada* (master of ceremonies) has a completely unaligned, position. Long discussion goes into finding such a person, who must not only not belong to either side, but should have the cosmopolitan competence to charm the entire company of workmates, and so on, of diverse post-Soviet backgrounds. This is why a person of mixed background is often chosen, such as Kazakh-Buriad, or Russian-Khamnigan, or professional actors, singers or dancers. Agencies advertise the services of *tamada* – on whom 'the entire atmosphere of your event depends' – who can sing not only Buriad and Russian songs but also 'foreign songs of the 1980s–90s!'[17] Responding to complaints on Buriad websites that such masters of ceremony were offhand, or too self-regarding or simply got plastered, one woman posted that she had found the perfect solution for her son's wedding: a clown, a person without pretensions, who kept everyone merry for the whole night.[18]

The jokes of the *tamada* bubble above existential dangers inherent in weddings. It is not just that social difference (otherness) evokes suspicion and aggression, but there also is a heightened occult risk to all those assembled. Incorrect performance will anger the ancestors and other spirits, while a beautiful wedding gives them joy. The wedding is conceptualised as the inverse of death.[19] It is timed to coincide with an auspicious day and, among western Buriads, with the maximum ascent of the sun.[20] Yet the denizens of darkness, the ancestors, are also present at weddings, called in by the prayers and songs – they feast and drink as a ghostly throng along with the living.[21] The wedding is thus a most serious matter, not only because its celebration of life is a closely interpenetrating 'response' to death, but also because it is chancy in relation to life itself. For the risks of life concentrated into this event are many: not only may one side or the other inadvertently anger the ancestors but the whole venture of creating new life may turn awry. Many Buriad marriages end in divorce and/or childlessness. The bride may not be able to adapt to the inherent 'ancestral' qualities of the new place; the groom may feel simmering resentment if his bride is made the more alien by being pregnant by another man even if he also thereby knows he has married a fertile women. The tensions (economic, for prestige, for honour) can spill over into further hostilities within either camp, even threatening the stability of other marriages.[22] All of this is 'the way things are', always anticipated as a possibility. The contriving of harmony and order at the wedding is thus a great responsibility and it falls primarily on the 'wedding leaders'.

Lengthy discussion goes into the choice of leaders by the parents. According to one experienced woman:[23]

> There is a series of unwritten, but strictly followed, rules regarding the candidature of *türüü*. They must be blood kin, middle-aged or elderly, respected in society, irreproachable in family life, professionally successful, and having fully healthy and prosperous children. [...] I was often present at agitated discussions of who to choose among our relatives. People would point out that one elder drank too much and might bring us into disrepute; another was already on his third wife – and would even two be acceptable? A third reputable kinsman had no children. Another respected woman had been observed in deceiving her husband – how could she be a wedding leader? Once our relatives quarrelled over the candidature of a highly respected woman. She was a widow, who had several successful children but also one unfortunate son – we had to reject her. Of course we hope she never heard about our discussion, but who knows?
>
> As far as I can understand the high demands made of wedding leaders stem from the preservative function they have regarding the new family and the lineage itself – because people believe that the faults of the *türüü*, the chosen representatives of the lineage, will compromise it, and that their wrongs (along with illnesses, bad family atmosphere, etc.) will pass into the new family and harm our future.

Thus the wedding leaders have to be exemplary figures who must 'magically' transfer their lineage qualities to the next generation, and they do so with their mastery of the relations between ancestors, elders and the bridal couple relations at the wedding. My informant also noted that all the appointed leaders of both sides for a given wedding meet beforehand to hold a rite of 'mutual acquaintance'.[24] This demonstrates the importance of acquiring an overall perspective on the event. At the same time, we may surmise, the completeness of the *türüü* as fully adequate social persons provides an impregnable platform from which they may enact detachment in the drama to come.

Conclusion

I have argued that enacting detachment during a complex social event means both to distance oneself from one's own speeches and songs by a particular manner of relating to them and simultaneously to 'use' them in relating to the company at large. If one aspect of such detachment is not being subsumed in a 'property'-like possessiveness, another is a capacity to survey and wield one's own tradition in relation to others.

Amanda Anderson's idea of 'cosmopolitan detachment' (2001: 14) can be adapted to explain the stance of such elders. She writes, for example, that the issue of moral character is central and that she has chosen the word 'detachment', rather than 'distance' or 'objectivity', because this word includes not only a de-naturalising attitude to norms and conventions but also practices of the self (2001: 6). The skill of calm self-restraint – notably, that required of a host, who should be able to craft an appropriately reassuring tone in encounters with strangers – is a practice of the self that is admired and inculcated by Mongol and Buriad parents (Humphrey 2012). Detachment thus connects the personal and the impersonal. This can be seen from Laurent Legrain's description:

> I saw a fight breaking out from a well-started [wedding] party because one of the protagonists kept on singing intentionally out of tune and giggling. The first time he sang this way people admonished him by telling him to sing with respect. The idea of sincerity was totally absent in their reproaches. The purpose of their criticism wasn't to impel him to get into an emotional state that fit with the lyrics of his song … rather they wanted him to support through his song the crafting of the affect of intimacy even if he didn't want to emotionally merge with it. What matters is not to get lost in singing but to be aware of the affect that is crafted and to contribute to its emergence. (Legrain 2013)

This analysis of weddings has described violence as a kind of attachment, or done in the name of belonging/possession, whereas performances of elders are a species of detachment, or done in the name of calm 'use' of tradition for beneficent ends. Yet I have also implied that even the fighting is not totally blind and self-absorbed. For while it narrows its vision to focus on an opponent – whereas detachment opens it to encompass a heterogeneous company – both kinds of action are 'aware' in the sense that they are performative and relational. Here perhaps we should return to Lévi-Strauss, with the observation that both detachment and violence are situational. Anticipated, even planned, fights are provoked by incidents and do not imply a lasting inner hatred. Enacting detachment is likewise done for the occasion. Both emerge from the situation people have placed themselves in – and what is this but the wedding, which is both a pivot in a notional structure as Lévi-Strauss proposes, and also a nexus of unequal and incompatible movements of people and things, as this chapter has tried to describe.

Notes

1 'When there's a wedding all the kin gather together ... it's fun! Though true, you can't get away without a punch-up', Buriad comment on forum. www.buryatia.org/modules.php?name=Forums&file=viewtopic&p=43237, p. 7.
2 Baasanjav Terbish, personal communication.
3 www.buryatia.org/modules.php?name=Forums&file=viewtopic&p=432370, p. 5.
4 *Tamada* is a Georgian word for a toastmaster at a feast. Such a person has to be eloquent, quick-witted and with a good sense of humour, capable of outsmarting competitors in toast-making and regulating the intake of alcohol. The term was borrowed by Russians and subsequently by Buriads during the Soviet period.
5 *Daidong* is a Chinese term meaning 'representative host'.
6 These weddings were organised by the Communist Youth organisation (*komsomol*) from the late 1950s onwards. There was no engagement, no bride price, kin took a lesser role (some of the first subjects in such weddings were orphans), the 'sides' were often formed by brigades of a collective farm, and state and Party officials played the roles of the elders (Tugutov 1965: 26–32).
7 This is a semantically rich word, which also has the meanings of moral principle, state and political alliance (Humphrey and Hürelbaatar 2006: 28–83).
8 The Bayad Mongols prescribed ten contests, different in content from those described by Natsov (Ochir and Galdanova 1992: 38– 51).
9 For example, unlike the Selenga Buriads' 'fight for the sun' on the bridal journey, the Bayad Mongols made the young couple, now at the groom's home, 'prostrate to the yellow sun' by physically forcing down their heads three times while an elder of the groom's side pronounced: 'We worship the yellow sun, we fight for the marrow bone' – probably the same bone that earlier had been the object of a skirmish by the two sides on the wedding journey (Ochir and Galdanova 1992: 41).
10 *Naadan* are sportive festivities imagined as competitive/flirtatious games, and they are widely associated with vitality, sexuality and fertility. For example, the word is also used to refer to the pre-mating dances of animals and birds (Galdanova 2002: 149).
11 Sayana Namsaraeva, personal communication referring to a recent wedding in her family.
12 'Your own ten-year-old child you exchanged for horses, your own twenty-year-old daughter you traded for cows!' 'Father, father, why did you exchange me for a horse? To take revenge on you, I'll bear many children in a foreign clan!' (Baldaev 1959: 107–108).

13 I am grateful to Giovanni Da Col for suggesting Agamben's analysis of 'use' as an analogy here.
14 Aga Buriad weddings are primarily a celebration for the parents; the presents and congratulations are given to them and the grandparents, while the young couple sit in the hall with the guests. http://svadbabur.ru/bur_traditional_svadba.
15 Sayana Namsaraeva, personal communication.
16 Among contemporary Kalmyks, who mainly use the Russian language, it is customary to speak of kin groups not as different 'clans' (*rod*) but as different 'species' (*poroda*) of people. Elvira Churyumova, personal communication.
17 http://vk.com/tamadabur
18 www.buryatia.org/modules.php?name=Forums&file=viewtopic&t=16700&post days=0&postorder=asc&highlight=свадьба&start=15 p. 2.
19 Among Ekhirit Buriads, if someone dies there is a prohibition on holding a wedding during the same year. To dream of a wedding means that a death will ensue (Istvan Santha, personal communication, confirmed by Khangalov (1898)).
20 Just as daylight from sunrise to sunset is the time of human activity – whereas the spirits of the dead rouse themselves at dusk – the wedding should occur in the sunny time between the two great communal sacrifices that constitute meetings with the ancestors in spring and autumn (Galdanova 2002: 148).
21 The dead are also said to make an appearance as skulls, the precious vessels of *sülde* (spiritual energy). There is a Buriad saying, 'At a wedding white skulls roll about' (*hurimda hubhai tolgoi muharyaa*) (Galdanova 2002: 149).
22 At a wedding among Ekhirit Buriads trouble broke out when the groom's people went to the bride's side to make arrangements. The visitors were expected to bring the food and drink for the entire feast, and thus they were in the awkward situation of being hosts in someone else's territory. But the supplies gave out too soon and the groom's people were utterly humiliated. Returning home a huge fight erupted with the kinsfolk left behind: 'Why did you send us out without enough supplies and leave us looking fools?' This culminated in a bitter quarrel between the men and women (their suppliers), during which the father of the groom yelled at his wife, 'That's it! It's time for us to get a divorce!' Istvan Santha, personal communication.
23 Nina Chimitovna Tsybenova, personal communication.
24 The occasion for this rite (Russ. *obyrad spetsial'nogo znakomstva*) is usually when the bride's kin take her dowry to the home of the groom's parents, Nina Chimitovna Tsybenova, personal communication.

References

Agamben, Giorgio, 2013, *The Highest Poverty: Monastic Rules and Form-of-Life*. Translated by Adam Kotsko. Stanford: Stanford University Press.
Anderson, Amanda, 2001, *The Powers of Distance: Cosmopolitanism and the Cultivation of Detachment*. Princeton, NJ: Princeton University Press.
Baldaev, S. P., 1959, *Buryatskie svadebye obryady*. Ulan-Ude: Buryatskoe Knizhnoe Izdatel'stvo.

Basaeva, K. D., 1980, Sovremennye svadebye obryady selenginskikh i barguzinskikh buryat. In K. D. Basaeva, ed., *Byt buryat v nastoyashchem i proshlom.* Ulan-Ude: AN SSSR SO BFION, pp. 15–42.

Empson, Rebecca, 2011, *Harnessing Fortune: Personhood, Memory and Place in Mongolia.* London: British Academy.

Galdanova, G. P., 1992, *Zakamenskie Buriady.* Novosibirsk: Nauka.

Galdanova, G. P., 2002, Svadebnaya i pograbal'no-pominal'naya obryadnost': sotsial'nye i mirovozzrencheskie aspekty, In T. D. Skrynnikova, ed., *Obryady v traditsionnoi kul'ture buryat.* Moscow: Vostochnaya Literatura RAN, pp. 110–156.

Goffman, E., 1972, *Encounters.* London: Allen Lane, Penguin Press.

Humphrey, Caroline, 2012, Hospitality and tone: holding patterns for strangeness in rural Mongolia. *JRAI special issue The Return to Hospitality: Strangers, Guests, and Ambiguous Encounters,* edited by Matei Candea and Giovanni Da Col:63–75.

Humphrey, Caroline and Laidlaw, James, 1994, *The Archetypal Actions of Ritual.* Oxford: Clarendon Press.

Humphrey, Caroline and Hürelbaatar, A., 2006, The Term *törü* in Mongolian History. In David Sneath, ed., *Imperial Statecraft: Political Forms and Techniques of Governance in Inner Asia, 6th–20th Centuries.* Bellingham: Western Washington Press, pp. 263–292.

Humphrey, Caroline and Ujeed, Hürelbaatar, 2012, Fortune in the Wind: An Impersonal Subjectivity. Special Issue of *Social Analysis* (Future and Fortune: Contingency, Morality and Anticipation of Everyday Life, edited by Giovanni Da Col and Caroline Humphrey) 56(2): 152–167.

Humphrey, Caroline and Ujeed, Hürelbaatar, 2013, *A Monastery in Time: The Making of Mongolian Buddhism.* Chicago: Chicago University Press.

Khangalov, Matvei, 1898, Svadebnye obryady, obychai, pover'ya i predaniya, *Etnograficheskoe Obozrenie* 34(1).

Krol', M. A., 2008[1894], *Strannitsy moei zhizni,* edited, with notes and introduction by N. L. Zhukovskaya. Moscow and Jerusalem: Mosty Kul'tury and Gesharim.

Legrain, Laurent, 2013, 'When Things go Amiss'. Introductory paper given at the workshop 'The Hiccups of Everyday Life', Cambridge (unpublished manuscript).

Lévi-Strauss, Claude, 1969[1949], *The Elementary Structures of Kinship,* trans. J. H. Bell and J. R. von Sturmer, ed. Rodney Needham. Boston: Beacon Press.

Manzhigeev, N. M., 1960, *Yangutskii buryatskii rod.* Ulan-Ude: Buryatskoe Knizhnoe Izdatel'stvo.

Nanzatov, B. Z. and Sodnompilova, M. M., 2013, Gruppa "nevestki" v kontseptual'nom universume mongol'skogo obshchestva. *Vestnik BNTs SO RAN* 3(11): 7–18.

Naranbat, U., 1992, Svadebnyi obryad uratov Vnutrennei Mongolii. In K. M. Gerasimova, ed., *Traditsionnaya obryadnost' mongol'skikh narodov.* Novosibirsk: Nauka, pp. 56–70.

Natsov, G.-D., 1995, *Materialy po istorii i kul'ture buryat*. Ulan-Ude: RAN SO BNTs.

Ochir, A. and Galdanova, G. P., 1992, Svadebnaya obryadnost' baitov MNR. In K. M. Gerasimova, ed., *Traditsionnaya obryadnost' mongol'skikh narodov*. Novosibirsk: Nauka, pp. 24–55.

Petri, B. E., 1925, *Brachnye normy severnykh buryat*. Irkutsk: Gublit.

Piette, Albert, 1998, De la distance au rôle au mode mineur de la réalité: contribution à la sociologie de l'interaction. *Information sur les Sciences Sociales* 37(2): 275–297.

Piette, Albert, 2010, Phenomenology of Details: What Is Anthropology? www.academia.edu/2086786/Phenomenography_of_Details_What_is_Anthropology_

Sodnom Tseren, L., 1975, Myangad yastny zan uiliin tuhai tovch temdeglel, *Studia museologia* (1). Ulaanbaatar. 51–69

Stafford, Charles, 2000, *Separation and Reunion in Modern China*. Cambridge: Cambridge University Press.

Stasch, Rupert, 2009, *The Society of Others: Kinship and Mourning in a West Papuan Place*. Berkeley and Los Angeles: University of California Press.

Tugutov, I. E., 1965, Stanovlenie novykh semeinykh obryadov. In P. T. Khaptaev, ed., *Kul'tura i byt narodov buryatii*. Ulan-Ude: Buryatskoe Knizhnoe Izdatel'stvo, pp. 18–37.

8

Ritual and religion: comment
Michael Carrithers

I am honoured and not a little challenged to comment on three such excellent and engaging chapters. Each speaks very well for itself, so I will not précis them, but instead will use them to support some reflections on what they suggest about our general topic, detachment. Let me start, not with the concept of 'detachment', but with its counterpart, 'relationality'. As I understand it, our editors and organisers of the Detachment Collaboratory began from an unease about that idea, an idea which gathers an otherwise highly disparate range of explanatory styles under a single heading. Versions of relationality might include Marilyn Strathern's ideas about the dividual, and therefore about the way in which people, in Papua New Guinea at least, may seem to be mutually constituted in ways Our notions of individuality in human life may otherwise fail to grasp; or Tim Ingold's Romantic notions of the organic connection between people, things and others living in our common world; or perhaps Bruno Latour's demonstrations of the entangling motility of persons and other beings, such that the supposed individuated autonomy of the merely human disappears. And this list could go on. Each of these in itself has offered a fresh – or at least fresh within the tempo of social science – view on the complex of humans in the world. Beyond these, though, the notion of 'relationality' may seem to foretell an even larger intellectual movement. This is a heady prospect: it might presage a new age, the Age of Relations, or perhaps better the Age of the Rhizome, if we take Deleuze and Guattari's image of incessantly and inexorably ramifying underground connections to typify what might unite Strathern, Ingold, Latour and so many others.

Or put it this way: relationality offers the trope of the New, and We in our civilization are particularly vulnerable to such an appeal, the New being one of the key ways We have of guiding and evaluating

Ourselves and Our doings. It has a satisfying abstractness as a concept, and one attraction of that abstractness is that it offers what Hans Blumenberg called a 'Zu-Viel' (Blumenberg 2007:17), a 'too-much', a capacity to capture more than is needed, and I would add, to expand and engulf more than originally intended. Or, as Bert O. States put it, it is a 'proto-keyword' ready to spread 'on the winds of metaphor' (1996: 1). In this case the metaphor is that of, yes, a rhizome, or at least a spreading tangle, a net perhaps, of ... what? Ideas, persons, animals, things, animate things, person-like animals, thing-like persons, or indeed relations themselves? Such a proto-keyword can stimulate, puzzle, and engage the imagination. Once such a proto-keyword is lodged as a keyword, it can then age into an identifying mark by which writers can identify one another and signal in turn their own reading. And the ideas that go with such a keyword may offer insight as well.

What I have written so far is perhaps more to orient myself than to enlighten you; but it does help me at least to identify what is common to the contributions of Humphrey, Laidlaw, and Robbins here. In the first place, 'detachment' is a much more faithful way than 'relationality' of understanding what these writers are doing, and I mean not what they are doing as writers on the topic of religion, or detachment in religion, but in the first instance in their practice as scholars. For while it is true that Humphrey established relations in some sense with Buriads, Laidlaw with Svetambar Jains, and Robbins with Pentecostals, their activity here, on the written page, is quintessentially detached. It is detached because they are writing as scholars; for the same detachment is a defining trait of any scholar in the human and social sciences. I myself am writing of these three colleagues, members of my own tribe and people with whom I have a relationship. But I am writing in a detached way, as a scholar, however warmly I may praise their work and, metonymically, them. Were I not to do so, I would forsake my membership in our collective. So we are connected, yes, but necessarily detached by constitutive self-definition and disciplined activity.

In his chapter James Laidlaw reminds us that the editors challenged us to 'see detachment as a positive aspect of social arrangements'. To the extent that we see the social arrangement of scholarship as a positive one, then, our very participation in this project affirms our positive view of such detachment. And in fact I organise the rest of this commentary on the three chapters *as if* scholarly detachment were the very model of detachment in social arrangements.

This is a very big '*as if*', for there are other practices of detachment which might have a better claim if we were looking for a single moral or a practical model. But I can at least specify in some detail, as a member of our collective myself, what our detachment amounts to. In the first place, it is founded in a particular kind of pronominal relation: scholars of human social life relate to their subjects in the 1) *third person plural*. In other words, we speak of them as a 'they'; and that is despite the fact that, if 'they' were actually present, it would very likely be highly impolite, and in any case pretty weird, to speak about, or to, our subjects in that way. Then, we address a general audience, so our discourse about our subjects is 2) *elaborated*, in Basil Bernstein's terms, that is, it provides explicit expository detail and background which would be unnecessary, or impolite or slightly unhinged, were they actually present. And third, we assume (though this is subject to ethical considerations) that we can 3) *say anything that is germane* to our argument, even though to speak that way in their presence could often be injurious. For we are 4) *disinterested*, or must play that role.

These four traits represent an 'ideal type', an idea invented by Max Weber to sidestep the messiness of actual social life; but I feel that they do cover much of what anthropological writing has been in the past, and mostly remains at present. In so far as there is a 'social arrangement' involved, that arrangement concerns a relation between scholar and readers/other scholars, and only a very attenuated one with the subjects. This detachment from our subjects begins for most anthropologists while in the field, for there we must act doubly, with engagement with our interlocutors in the second person while rehearsing in our minds and our notes that third-person attitude; while being as nice as to them as possible when face to face, we are planning inwardly to talk about them to someone else in a big way. But note, too, that this detachment has close cousins in North Atlantic societies: we are pleased when our medical doctors treat us with politeness and care rather than rigid detachment when we meet with them, but we freely license them to write in their notes about us, and talk to colleagues about us, in a detached third person.

What light does this ideal type of scholarly detachment throw on these three chapters? I start with Humphrey, and note, first, that she founds her argument in a particular choice of *elaborated* and *germane* detail in Buriad weddings. She mentions, but does not present, the diagrammable kin relations contributing to, and resulting from, the occasion, nor does she explain the logics of exchange involved. She turns instead to 'the practical, emotional ... dimensions of real life instances of what people do at weddings'. This choice in itself colours the scholarly detachment involved, in part because it encompasses information discarded by more formal accounts, but also because it takes a positive line in what Ernest Gellner called 'interpretive charity'. Gellner was not a fan of interpretive charity. Like the southern Baptist preacher and sin, he was 'agin it'. For

Ritual and religion: comment

him, too much empathising, too much following of Their view and Their experience, meant abdicating from the social scientist's stern duty to cut through the natives' self-delusions to the bones of systematic interests among them. And Humphrey evidently feels some of the cogency of such an argument, for she makes an explicit case for her version of detachment, and so for including an account of the tumultuous, conflicted, confused, unscripted and violent currents which threaten continuously to break out in the prescribed order of Buriad weddings. So, right there, we can see straightforwardly that there can be different versions of scholarly detachment. It is not a monolithic practice, but a sheaf of subtly differing forms of detachment.

In the foreground, then, Humphrey shows how the Buriad themselves have responded to the endemic chaos, this infectious lack of self-control, which afflicts their weddings by inventing and installing masters of ceremonies, whose specific role requires a particular style of effective and practical detachment. It may seem faintly absurd to compare that master of ceremonies' detachment to scholarly detachment, but there is one telling contrast that is, I think, interestingly diagnostic of both. For whereas the scholar's detachment is created in large part by a commitment to a third-person perspective on her subjects, the Buriad master of ceremonies is constituted in large part by a commitment in the second-person plural to his or her subjects, all those participating in the wedding. And Humphrey is very clear that this detachment, call it 'second-person' detachment, is constituted, first, by a disinterested even-handedness to all the parties to the wedding, second, by a cordial responsibility to the parties, and third, by a skilled allegiance to the ideals embodied in a successful performance of the wedding. And Humphrey suggests in passing something very important to the argument of this present volume, namely that this specifically Buriad form of necessary detachment embedded in ongoing social practice is compellingly suggestive of analogous forms of such constitutive detachment in many other social settings, such as judges in many societies, and civil servants in bureaucratised societies (I use the word 'constitutive' to mark that such roles are constituted by detachment, and that disinterest as regards those they encounter in that role is their salient feature).

The ideal type of scholarly detachment I set out above might throw light on Humphrey and the Buriad, but Robbins' chapter demonstrates that such scholarly detachment may nevertheless have implications which are seriously discomfiting. The problem is one of sincerity, a value strongly held by the Christians with whom Robbins and others have worked. But sincerity is likewise a value to which members of Our society are especially vulnerable, in that it is an implicit value among Us all. The effect is to dramatise vividly that doubleness – or duplicity? – of consciousness characteristic of fieldwork, where one both participates with apparent sincerity but also stands apart inwardly to observe, which makes what Robbins called the 'gently oxymoronic' phrase, 'participant observer', a surprisingly apt designation.

Now if we were to take such Christian ethnography as the paradigmatic case for fieldworking detachment – please indulge me in this thought experiment – then we might find ourselves in the quintessentially false position of self- and other-betrayal which Adorno thought characterised the modern world as such. He offered a parable for this betrayal: in an apparently innocuous conversation on a train one agrees, perhaps vaguely and for purposes of immediate ease, with a stranger's doubtful or objectionable remarks, even though the logical consequences of such remarks would be in fact to condone murder (Adorno 2001: 29). Writing in 1944 in the United States after escaping from Nazi Germany, one can understand how such an illustration of bad faith might occur to him, though the sense of falseness he evoked has much deeper roots in his thought, life and life-world.

You will likely think it melodramatic to compare the doubled consciousness, and doubled practices, of ethnographic detachment with so sombre a view of self- and other-betrayal, and I would agree. But consider this: at present all ethnographic fieldwork, indeed all social scientific research, must very likely undergo ethical scrutiny before it is sanctioned by the funding body and university involved. This ethical scrutiny entails that, among its many complex considerations, something called 'informed consent' be given by those studied. This practice first arose historically as a reaction to just that world in which Adorno wrote, the world including concentration camp experiments on people. And I can confirm, as someone closely involved in scrutinising ethics applications from the widest possible range that might fall under the rubric of anthropology – biological, primatological, medical, psychological, sociocultural – that the deep distrust of research motive and method which is entailed in the practices of informed consent and ethical scrutiny can invite one to find easily in the most apparently harmless research proposal a threatening site of reckless damage and regardless harm.

How does this affect our view of ethnographers' scholarly detachment? Note that when I laid out that ideal type, it was as a contrast between detachment from one's hosts and politeness towards them. But politeness is not merely a matter of etiquette, but is rather an aspect of the morality (I have elsewhere called it a moral aesthetic) built into human life, however that morality is locally practised. So in suggesting a contrast between second-person and third-person views, I had already hinted that there are limitations that might modify our scholarly detachment. It is not that the draconian extremes of ethical oversight are an inevitable or unavoidable accompaniment of ethnographic detachment. It is rather that whatever form of detachment we practise, it is always inflected by its situation, sprawling between the face-to-face encounters during fieldwork and, later, the encounters between reader and text when the fieldwork's results are published. In that light the continual revisions and expansions of our respective ethical guidelines testify not only to growing institutional mistrust but also to the growing catalogue of possible fieldwork situations and therefore to the ever varying forms of ethnographic detachment.

Laidlaw has preceded me here, for he argues in the preliminary section of his chapter that 'different forms of detachment, we may conjecture, have different social correlates and different ethical qualities'. And he has cast his net over far more than just ethnographers' varied detachments to include both the 'civil indifference', which enables peaceable coexistence of differing groups in a variegated complex society, and the highly refined forms of detachment we meet among Svetambar Jains' practices. These cases illuminate one another and demonstrate more generally, I think, the usefulness of the concept of detachment as a tool for comparative thinking.

Laidlaw illustrates, too, the force that the trope of detachment – detachment as a master image to think and act with – can have in Indic renouncer religions. Jains arguably make more use of the trope, express it in a greater variety of specific imagery, and practise the most varied versions of it, at least by comparison with Buddhism. It is as though Jains had disciplined themselves to stick closely to that single trope and to follow out its logic with single-minded adherence to even the most difficult and thorny conclusions.

Moreover Laidlaw's presentation of the three practices in their setting might be said to be a mental rehearsal, a mental reconstruction for himself and us – the German word is *nachvollziehen* – of the working out of that ascetic logic. In that respect Laidlaw's own ethnographic style falls close to Humphrey's in that he exercises interpretive charity, but he does so with a strict adherence to Jain reasonings, and he adopts an ascetic denial of extraneous, non-Jain, social scientific logics, a denial which Ernest Gellner might have found weak-minded. Yet such disciplined interpretation of Jain experience is perhaps necessary, because Jainism is a version of human possibility which is of such rigorous austerity and extremity that only such a rigorous treatment as Laidlaw's can render it generally accessible in the first instance.

Let me take that thought a step further. We have seen forms of detachment being inevitably coloured by their setting; and we anthropologists often believe, or even hope, that our theorising and explaining is best when coloured by the fieldwork encounter itself; so does it not follow happily that Laidlaw's detached interpretation, adhering strictly to the strictness of Jain practices and reasons, is coloured by his fieldwork experience and the style of Jainism he met?

Laidlaw writes of Svetambar Jains in Jaipur, but consider the contrast with the southern Digambar Jains along the Maharashtra-Karnataka border, who reveal not only a different style of Jainism, but also invite a necessarily different style of interpretation/detachment. Among northern Svetambar Jains, the order of renouncers are relatively well disciplined, have a relatively clear sense of how the preceptor/pupil relationship works, and so possess a reasonably settled means faithfully to reproduce Svetambar teachings and practices. Moreover, the lay Svetambars tend to be relatively well educated, and well educated as well in Jain teachings and practices. Hence both orthodoxy and orthopraxy have fertile grounds in which to flourish, and those grounds are also well prepared for a strong sense of the difference between the usages of Jainism and those of what we have come to call 'Hinduism'. Hence Laidlaw appears entirely justified in representing the delicate matter of Svetambar Jains' relation to Ganesh-ji, for example, just as he does, austerely, as a matter of civil etiquette and a superficial engagement quite beyond the immediate intense self-castigating performance of Jain principles.

The situation of southern Digambars and their renouncers is rather different. The renouncers themselves, permanently naked, do not represent a relatively disciplined body knitted together by pupillary succession, but are, in effect, a loose collection of individual religious virtuosi (for details see Carrithers 1989). They are often relatively uneducated, even in the doctrines of Digambar Jainism, and reverence for them is based almost entirely on the visible manifestation of their heroic asceticism. The laity are relatively uneducated, at least in general, and so are less schooled in the doctrines, and to a degree the practices, of Jainism. And indeed just these matters, the relative ignorance of both the renouncers and great swathes of the laity, and so the laxity of Jain practices, have been a constant concern of more educated southern Digambar Jains for the last few generations.

So the consequence has been that the ethnographer (me) is invited, even compelled, to view Digambar Jainism in a different light, and my detachment took a form different from that which Laidlaw exercises here. The relevant form of detachment became one in which I was to consider the doctrines and practices of Jainism as dissolving at the edges, so to speak, among those of the surrounding populace. This detachment was, in effect, a deliberately impolite one, at least in so far as it went against the preferences of some strictly observant Digambars who are concerned to maintain, or better, create, that strict observance among their fellows. In the same basket with strait-laced self-abnegating monochrome Jainism I offered the highly coloured exuberant practices of circumambient Indic worship (Carrithers 2000). Indeed, the image of 'exuberance' seemed the best way to capture what I met, and 'polytropy', a 'turning to many' religious teachers, practices and gods, the best term to capture this relative blending of southern Digambar Jainism with surrounding practices. In fact it seemed reasonable to use southern Digambar Jain examples to illustrate not a rigorously separate sensibility but attitudes and practices that are more generally South Asian (Carrithers 2000, 2010).

I note that my word count has crept over the ordained figure, so I must take your leave. I do so in hope that I have confirmed that thinking about forms of detachment among the doing of ethnography, as among the doing of other social actions, may lead perhaps to a fresher view on older matters.

References

Adorno, Theodor, 2001[1951], *Minima Moralia: Reflexionen aus dem Beschädigten Leben*. Frankfurt am Main: Suhrkamp Verlag.

Blumenberg, Hans, 2007, *Theorie der Unbegrifflichkeit*. Frankfurt am Main: Suhrkamp Verlag.

Carrithers, Michael, 1989, Naked Ascetics in Southern Digambar Jainism. *Journal of the Royal Anthropological Institute* 24(2): 219–235.

Carrithers, Michael, 2000, On Polytropy: Or the Natural Condition of Spiritual Cosmopolitanism in India: the Digambar Jain case. *Modern Asian Studies* 34(4): 831–861.

Carrithers, Michael, 2010, A Social Form and its Craft-y Use. *Contemporary South Asia* 18(3):253–265.

States, Bert O., 1996, Performance as Metaphor. *Theatre Journal* 48(1): 1–26.

Part III
Detaching and situating knowledge

9

The capacity for re-description

Alberto Corsín Jiménez

When Velázquez took to painting *The Spinners* in c.1657 he had been court painter in the service of King Philip IV for over thirty years. Details of Velázquez's persona and biography are elusive and mysterious. Compared to his contemporaries, his oeuvre is scarce, perhaps because he attended only to royal commissions. In this sense, a great deal of his time as royal painter was spent, for instance, curating the royal art collection. In such a capacity he 'had responsibility for interior design and decoration – placing mirrors, statues, tapestries, and paintings in many rooms, in many royal dwellings, and at the temporary destinations of important royal journeys' (Alpers 2005: 183). His role as a collector of art has often been commented upon when noting how fellow artists – Manet, Picasso – have coincided in describing him as 'the painters' painter'. He made of the royal art collection and museum *his studio*, and his art displays this encompassing of art as technique, narrative, history and ambience. His art self-traps itself in both its aesthetic and environmental designs: 'we might imagine Velázquez', writes Svetlana Alpers of his courtly persona, 'as coolly making his way and his paintings while he is caught up (trapped, perhaps) in the Habsburg court' (Alpers 2005: 162).

Velázquez's work, however, is by no means subdued to courtly interests, as anyone who has ever approached his paintings can attest to. Velázquez's art resists comprehension; it places all sorts of frictions and tensions between the artwork and the spectator. Maybe Velázquez was trapped in the Habsburg court, but he surely managed to trap the court and its courtiers in his paintings too. For Alpers, who follows Ortega y Gasset in this respect (1987), Velázquez's strategic entrapment of himself and his work within courtly politics and affairs evidenced his being 'admirable in his *detachment*, a "genius in the matter of disdain"', for whom '[s]ingularity is valued ... not as the exercise of freedom, but as a resistance to coercion' (Alpers 2005: 162, emphasis added). Velázquez's art functioned thus both as a *trap of* and *a trap for* an ecology of meaning, and it is in this capacity for 'double encompassment' (Wagner 2001: 63) that it afforded a sense of self-detachment for himself. Velázquez succeeded in creating a habitat or environment for his work that enabled his staging a dialogue between the things represented inside a painting and the choreographic displays with which he furnished the royal dwellings. He found a place for himself *in painting* that was at once inside and outside the canvas.

In this chapter I would like to explore some of the consequences that derive from this reading of Velázquez's political and charismatic detachment as an effect of his 'entrapment' in the presentations and representations of courtly life. Velázquez paints courtly life and lives a courtly existence, and his art attempts to capture this recursive displacement in and out of each. We may say that his is an attempt at making 'recursion' itself visible as an aesthetic form and technique. The notion of recursion is an important one that I return to later. For the time being, let me note that in Velázquez's case, this requires, on his part, the design of an environment (a pictorial language, a praxis of interior decoration) with which he furnishes and inhabits the interface between the inside and the outside of a canvas. This interface is an emerging and nebulous space, rarely explored before. Drawing from the pictorial resources employed in the description of insides and the ornamental means with which outsides have traditionally been furnished, Velázquez suddenly realises that he may actually be giving shape to an embryonic *capacity for re-description*.

I am interested in these re-descriptive exercises, in how they are rendered visible, and what their effects are. The *forms* of re-descriptions are important. Some rejoice in their spatiality. They come, we might say, with environments attached. Such is the case with Velázquez, whose work operates as a trap of sorts: a trap that draws you into the pictures and simultaneously draws the pictures out into the world. A trap that environmentalises relations. We see this in more detail in the first part of the chapter, where I return to *The Spinners* and describe some of the very original techniques through which Velázquez invented and introduced aesthetic forms of suspension, displacement and detachment into his work.[1]

An argument I want to put forward is that the work of environmentalising relations – the work of environing the hyphen that holds the 're' and the 'description' together, so to speak – is worth paying attention to. Today the capacity for re-description seems to have been pre-empted by an economy of information that places a premium on *self-description*: descriptions that move by themselves, such as in cybernetic feedback mechanisms where information is recursively enriched and self-enhanced. 'Recursion' itself has in fact become a common analytical trope in social theory of late, and in the second part of the chapter I look at recent transformations in higher education, including developments in the political and aesthetic economy of information, to cast some light on the types of environments that these recursions are effecting. If Velázquez found a singular place for himself in courtly affairs through an aesthetics of *resistance*, it would seem that the politics of information today works through an aesthetics of *irresistibility*.

The chapter concludes with some observations about what it may mean to think of 'detachment', about how to inhabit the hyphen, in these our epistemic times: what traps we may need to deploy to move in and out of description as a critical form. The text as a whole may be read in this spirit too, as a modest attempt to essay some of these contraptions, where 'detachment' is presented not just as an object of analysis, but also as a style of argumentation.

The Spinners

Velázquez's painting is a complex and highly sophisticated representation of the myth of Minerva and Arachne.[2] Ovid's fable of Arachne in the *Metamorphoses* (Book VI, I) is the story of a young girl who challenges the accusation that her great skill as a weaver is owed to the goddess Minerva. Goddess and girl thus enter into a competition to prove their respective skills. Minerva soon realises that Arachne's weaving skills are superior and takes offence at the latter's weaving into her tapestry of an image of the infidelity of the goddess's father, Zeus. The goddess then reprises by famously turning the girl into a spider. The weaver, in other words, spins herself.

The Spinners, however, offers no straightforward representation of Ovid's fable. It provides a stark counterpoint to previous treatments of the theme, mostly of an allegorical nature, for example Ruben's *Minerva and Arachne*, which was very well known to Velázquez, to the extent that he copies it in *Las Meninas*, on the far wall just above his (Velázquez's) own head. But while Velázquez gestures and acknowledges previous takes on the Ovidian story, his pictorial solution is very different.

There are three planes to *The Spinners*. Upfront we encounter a group of five women in a workshop: a woman spinning a wheel, one carding comb and the other three variously assisting the spinners. The background space is itself layered into two, with a theatrical representation of Arachne's fable taking front stage, and a tapestry of Titian's *Rape of Europa* (a painting then in the Spanish royal collection) in the back. As

Figure 1 *The Spinners*, Diego Velázquez, c.1657

is so often with Velázquez, the painting looks unfinished: it employs economical, casual brushstrokes to display a sense of fleetingness and movement, blurring faces and hands, or simply avoiding them, by turning heads away or hiding body parts. Velázquez emulates here Titian's innovative *sprezzatura* brushwork (from *disprezzo*, disrespect or disdain; Alpers 2005: 156), to whom he in fact pays homage in the background tapestry. Moreover, this way of handling painting, Alpers has observed, allows Velázquez to blur, not just specific motifs or objects, but 'representation' as an aesthetic strategy more amply:

> the manner of handling paint is sustained in depicting objects at a very different scale. It is not, to use a term of our times, fractal. Threads of white paint hanging from the large foreground winding-skein are painted with the same strokes that highlight and structure the smaller blue gown farther back. The same quick, economical brush strokes that constitute aspects of large things closer by also describe the small figure farther away. (Alpers 2005: 138–146)

This disrespect for scale and clarity is also extended to his representation of social status and standing. Mythical beings (Minerva and Arachne) are pushed into the back of the painting as women of lower rank are placed up front. The stuff of myth (allegory and representation) is backgrounded while the everyday (manual labouring) takes front stage. As Alpers puts it more generally, 'It is not that he [Velázquez] erases or reverses distinctions, but that he frees pictorial representation from any simple relating of size and importance' (Alpers 2005: 178).

I noted above that among Velázquez's duties as courtly painter was taking responsibility for curating the royal collection. This included assisting with the display of the royal household's collection of tapestries, one of the greatest in the world. Velázquez himself never designed a tapestry, but it could be argued – and Alpers has persuasively done so – that perhaps he conceived of *The Spinners* as a commentary on, and a homage to, the traditions and authors that he cultivated as a painter and curator.

The seventeenth-century painting culture in which Velázquez was trained encouraged and rewarded copying. Students learned by copying the masters; artists competed to participate in the lucrative business of copying religious prints for sale in the New World; and patrons were keen to pay for replicas of great paintings, in particular those in the royal collection (Alpers 2005: 190–192). 'The aura of a work might be increased, not decreased, by copying it' (Alpers 2005: 193). In this context, it is not unimaginable to think of Velázquez as aiming to locate himself within this painting culture, and doing so by painting his own collection of copies, his own gallery. Unlike the tradition of collectors' cabinets paintings, however, where a painting reproduced the canonical system of images wherein it hoped for inclusion,[3] *The Spinners* establishes a conversation about the very nature of painting. Thus, here Velázquez stages a conversation on the art and craft of making images with the masters that inspired him – Titians and Rubens, among others – and whose works he came to know and appreciate not just as an artist but as a collector too:

> This room [the workshop represented in *The Spinners*] is not depicted with paintings hanging on the walls and life going on it. Instead, paintings are brought to life and they are brought together. Uncertainties result: are the figures of Minerva and Arachne in front of or part of the tapestry? what is the relationship of the foreground women to painted myth? The recollection of paintings that were in the palace collection – of Rubens, of Titian, of Tintoretto, of Jan Bruegel and more – is appended to a myth and to the practice of making. Art not as a matter of copying, or of imitating, but as re-creating. In *Las Meninas*, Velázquez depicts himself at work in the studio/museum. In *The Spinners*, he is imagining the experience of it. (Alpers 2005: 218)

With *The Spinners*, then, Velázquez plays off invention and convention inside a painting. He introduces spatial, temporal and narrative displacements that superpose and perturb cultural registers ordinarily kept separate, such as those of myth, theatrical performance, allegory, copying, museum collecting, tapestry or manual labour. He is not so much offering a description (a representation) of how these practices and activities take shape in the world as cracking open the terms through which *they mutually describe each other* in this seventeenth-century world. His is an attempt at showing how descriptions re-describe themselves.

The art of description ...

As noted, little is known of Velázquez the painter. His life is well documented, although historians remain relatively in the dark as to his personal vision and artistic project. His place in courtly affairs has left trails in administrative records and registers but little in the shape of biographical references or personal recollections. In the absence of such evidence it is, of course, moot to ask what may have motivated or shaped his outlook and sensibility. There is considerable consensus among historians that a driving-force in Velázquez's life was his ambition to obtain aristocratic recognition and status. His appointment as royal painter was of course a favourable step in this direction, but it also meant that he was left with less time for painting, for in this role he had to assume responsibility for the interior decoration of the royal household. Some historians have seen in this a source of internal conflict, between his vocation as a painter and his aspirations as courtier, between the artist and the aristocrat (Brown 1986).

Not being an art historian I will not dare to take sides in this debate. But I do wish to pause on the terms through which Velázquez seems to elaborate upon this very distinction – between painter and courtier– in *The Spinners*. We have seen that in this work Velázquez rejoices, not in the separation of offices or roles, but in the art of description, in the effects of mutual describabilities. He displays a deep commitment to exploring and generating the pictorial conditions that allow for 'description' itself to assume different registers and forms, and to move to different effects, inside the painting. 'The ability to constantly re-describe something from another viewpoint', writes Marilyn Strathern, 'produces a displacement effect of a particular kind' (Strathern 1992: 73). She calls this effect 'merography', a typically modern cultural resource where '[p]erspectives themselves are created in the redescriptions' (Strathern 1992: 73).

Although it is an intrepid claim to make, perhaps, in *The Spinners*, Velázquez was experimenting with this embryonic seventeenth-century cultural resource: what descriptive and aesthetic register, he might have challenged himself to think, might this emerging *capacity for re-description* assume? What kind of perspective may Velázquez have been attempting to extricate through this novel and exciting technique?

We can offer some tentative answers: no doubt that of an outstanding artist, the painters' painter, as he came to be known – of course, that of a noble courtier too, his long-standing aspiration. Yet perhaps he was aiming for a middle third also: the perspective of re-description itself, a Baroque in-between that places the person and her world in suspension, and that struggles to make this suspension – this recursion between aesthetic, political and biographical forms – visible. Not adjudication and resolution – now painter, now courtier – but re-description. A middle third capable of trapping the proliferative and wondrous capacities of description as a trapping interface itself.

... and the art of separation

The story of Velázquez's entrapment between his royal duties and his artistic vocation came to mind when reading a recent account by Marilyn Strathern on the changes in the expectations of academic office in UK universities over the past twenty years. The focus of her account is, in her own words, 'the *detachment* of the William Wyse Professorship [WWP] from the headship of the Department [of Social Anthropology in Cambridge]' (Strathern 2009: 127, emphasis added). When the head of department and the holder of the foundation chair coincided, 'there was a performative requirement made of the office-holder *as* the Professor' (Strathern 2009: 130). The university was evident, we might say, through the professor, in her investments towards the advancement of knowledge and her defence of the university's interests. Come the audit turn of the 1990s, however, and the person and the office part ways. 'The person', writes Strathern, 'becomes personalised. The WWP becomes less of an office' (Strathern 2009: 130). The office disappears from view and it is the individual intellectual – the intellectual as an individual – that gains full display.

Strathern's account draws on Paul du Gay's critique of the 'ethics of enthusiasm' that held sway across public sector management in the UK during the turn of the century (du Gay 2000, 2008). Enthused by a moral economy of participatory empowerment and creative management, the new gurus of third-way public administration called forth the abandonment of dusted principles of rule-bound bureaucratic organisation and formalistic impersonality. The aim was to shake the state loose from its unbending formalities and inflect a new entrepreneurial and communicative spirit to the state bureaux.

Du Gay develops this analysis by setting in contrast Max Weber's famous account of bureaucratic organisation with the new ethics of enthusiasm. Despite caricatures to the contrary, Weber's model of bureaucracy in fact stressed the levelling and democratic impulses inherent in the procedural impartiality of bureaucratic administration. As Weber himself put it: 'Bureaucracy inevitably accompanies modern mass democracy', which results from the 'abstract regularity of the execution of authority' (Gerth and Mills 1946: 224). The procedural abstraction of impersonality abducts a society of equals from day-to-day interactions. No matter who you are or where you come from, the bureaucratic machinery will make all people conform into homogeneous administrative categories. The work of the civil service, then, may be mirrored to Archimedean levers. In its formalisation of vocation as a statutory professional goal, the bureaucrat enacts an ethic of organisational-cum-social democracy.

Not vocation but enthusiasm, empathy and care is what the new turn in public administration calls for. Under the auspices of 'responsive' government, the civil servant is to be reconfigured as 'something akin to an enthusiastic, energetic and entrepreneurial "yes-person"' (du Gay 2008: 343). The yes person, however, is likely to irradiate affection and commitment well beyond his constitutional and official mandate: 'office and self become blurred, with committed champions coming to see the office as an extension of themselves' (2008: 345). This, then, is a person who encounters no circumscription or delimitation to her attachments. She lets go of the office in lieu of new annexations. As Strathern had it, the office disappears – it gets detached from the person – but a new person appears in its stead: an enthusiastic individual keen on extending his or her constituency, on embracing new connections, on articulating novel annexations. An individual that grows on attachments.

The detachment of person and office, du Gay tells us following political theorist Michael Walzer, is an instance of the 'art of separation' that lies at the heart of liberalism (Walzer 1984). For Walzer, the craft of liberal politics consists in the institution of walls between social domains previously entangled. With each new wall a new liberty is instituted. Thus, the line drawn between church and state instituted a sphere of religious activity where men were allowed to exercise freedom of religious conscience. As for the rise of office as a corporate identity distinct from dynastic, familial or personal interests, the art of separation worked thus: 'the line that marks off political and social position from familial property creates the sphere of office and then the freedom to compete for bureaucratic and professional place, to lay claim to a vocation, apply for an appointment ... The notion of one's life as one's project probably has its origin here' (Walzer 1984, 316–317).

Interfaces

Walzer observes that the separation of person and office marked a point of inflection in the history of political liberalism. His focus is on the reorganisation of a series of categories of political thought: religious conscience, privacy, property, office, even life itself. These were gradually and historically separated out into the building blocks and fundamental constituents of freedom.

I am intrigued by Walzer's resort to the image of the 'wall' as the technology of separation: 'Liberalism is a world of walls', he wrote, 'and each one creates a new liberty' (Walzer 1984: 315). Walls are a brake to rumour-mongering and conspiratorial politics. They help keep ghosts at bay. But walls may also be used for display and decoration. As we saw in the case of Velázquez's duties as curator, the walls of the royal household became centrepieces of his labours. Moreover, as historians Jonathan Brown and Svetlana Alpers have shown us, Velázquez sacrificed a good deal of *his vocation* – 'the notion of one's life as one's project', as Walzer puts it – on those walls. Velázquez took up the challenge of decorating the palace's walls, with tapestries, sculptures and paintings, in corridors and galleries, as a project in the art of description rather than separation. In this sense, walls may be said to behave more like thresholds or media interfaces than barricades.

Velázquez's experimentation with decoration and description as an interface effect makes sense when seen in the larger context of Baroque society, for a concern with theatrics, illusionism or the sublimation of form were indeed characteristic of Baroque aesthetics. Baroque society was in many respects the first media society. The first articulated expression of a theory of media was produced in the context of Baroque political work, and every theory of media since has been, in practice, a theory of the extensiveness and reach of Baroque effects (Corsín Jiménez 2013: 7–11). The use of 'techniques of incompleteness', such as trompe l'oeil or anamorphosis, or the phenomenal explosion in the use of stage machinery in theatrical representations, all contributed to a dramaturgical conception of social life (Maravall 1986).[4]

Take for example Thomas Hobbes's famous theatrical representation of sovereignty and political organisation. According to Noel Malcolm, Hobbes's famous *imago* of a sovereign body holding in its interior, and pacifying the designs of, a chaotic multitude may have been inspired by an encounter with a dioptric anamorphic device designed by the French Minim friar Jean-François Nicéron (Malcolm 2002). Nicéron's design involved a picture of the faces of twelve Ottoman sultans which, on looking through the viewing-glass tube, converged into the portrait of Louis XIII (Malcolm 2002: 213). In Malcolm's account, the anamorphic lens's capacity to effect a transformation of relations, from multifarious and chaotic to unitary and orderly, would have seduced Hobbes's into imagining a similar iconographic representation for the title page of his book. We could say, therefore, that for Hobbes the lens generated the perspective – the capacity for re-description – from which knowledge of the political surfaced. That most modern of epistemes, 'the political', emerged therefore as an interface-effect: politics is what the world looks like from the point of view of the lens.

I have brought up Hobbes's political theatrics at this stage – the interface-mechanics of his politics – because it is to the Hobbesian theory of sovereignty that Paul du Gay turns to after rehearsing a genealogical study of enthusiasm. He traces the use of the term to the period of religious civil wars in seventeenth century England. Back then, Enthusiasts were members of a fanatical religious sect who in the name of an 'Enthysiasmical' revelation claimed privileged access to divine inspiration and, therefore, an unmediated access to truth (du Gay 2008: 347). As is well known, Hobbes had tremendous contempt for such expressions of religious fervour. His Leviathan was a supreme effort to annihilate all manifestations of religious enthusiasm. For Simon Schaffer, who has commented on the dioptric (anamorphic) effect of the Leviathan's parallax artifice, the capacity to 'see double' (to see the twelve sultans and Louis XIII in duplex perspective) became in fact a first step in the ultimate sublimation of sovereignty as hegemonic vision. In seventeenth-century politics this was easily accomplished because outside the rule of sovereign law, as Hobbes noted, lay only a chaotic state of nature, shaped by suspicion, fear, witchcraft accusations and the mischievous play of invisible phantoms. The rise of Leviathan exterminated the invisible, neatly aligning, in a supreme gesture of political illusionism, the planes of the natural and the phantasmagorical (Schaffer 2005: 202).

Let me recapitulate the interface-effect. The Hobbesian lens allowed for the imagination of sovereignty as an autonomous and self-sufficient political *organon*. It allowed Hobbes to cancel Enthusiasm, but it did so by cancelling or hiding the very artificial design that made the cancellation possible. Not unlike Walzer's use of walls, Hobbes opted to look through, and over, the lens rather than with it. His interest in the effects of Baroque media lay not in the genre of its resistances and disturbances (the dioptric refractions) but in the irresistibility of its political programme. Having jumped over the wall, and left the Enthusiasts behind, the Hobbesian person turned his or her attention to the task of 'extending his or her constituency, on embracing new connections, on articulating novel annexations', as I put it above. An individual that grows on attachments and appropriations. A yes person.[5]

Recursions

I have borrowed the notion of the interface-effect from software and cultural theorist Alexander Galloway (2012). Galloway's is a very suggestive take on software, and the structure of digital data and information in particular, because of his efforts at re-situating the latter in the terrain of allegory and symbolism rather than virtuality and technology. Although Galloway does not trace the interface effects of present-day media technologies back to the Baroque, his description of what interfaces accomplish may, I believe, sustain this link:

> Digital media are exceptionally good at artifice and often the challenge comes in maintaining the distinction between edge and center, a distinction that threatens to collapse at any point like a house of cards. [...] The interface is this state of 'being on the boundary.' It is *that moment where one significant material is understood as distinct from another significant material*. In other words, an interface is not a thing, an interface is always an effect. (Galloway 2012: 33, emphasis added)

The moment when a 'material is understood as distinct from another significant material' – the moment when a material detaches itself from itself – is of course a moment of re-description. Galloway is particularly interested in how this inter-phasing is accomplished by digital media today; how the digital becomes the hyphen, in the terms I used earlier. Our failure to pay attention to this middling effect of media, notes Galloway, reflects the poverty of our critical and conceptual imagination, which appears inexorably bootstrapped to the digital aesthetics of networked and informational capitalism. Software's self-executability (the fact that computer programmes run on their own and do things) conceals the fact that it is at heart a symbolic operation. It expresses almost to perfection the idea of a 'symbol that stands for itself' (Wagner 1986), the symbol that self-eclipses its symbolic provenance:

> Such is the fundamental contradiction: what you see is not what you get. Software is the medium that is not a medium. Information interfaces are always 'unworkable.' Code is never viewed as it is. Instead code must be

compiled, interpreted, parsed, and otherwise driven into hiding by still larger globs of code. Hence the principle of *obfuscation*. But at the same time it is the exceedingly high degree of declarative reflexivity in software that allows it to operate so effectively as source or algorithmic essence – the stating of variables at the outset, the declarations of methods, all before the real 'language' takes place – within a larger software environment always already predestined to parse and execute it. And hence the principle of *reflection*. (Galloway 2012: 69)

Information interfaces thus accomplish the trick of proffering re-descriptions that do not look as such. Re-descriptions without a form! Such apparently formless descriptions – self-descriptions, or descriptions that stand for themselves – have in fact long been the object of anthropological analysis. Thus, for example, Roy Wagner famously glossed the capacity of symbols to simultaneously produce obfuscation and reflection as 'obviation': the meaning and relations that are made 'obvious' by a symbol are one of many that have thenceforth also been 'obviated' (e.g. Wagner 1978). Obviation therefore 'executes' a recursive movement, such that the object of a description offers itself up for re-apperception in a future description. Such a descriptive move becomes a trope for/of perception (Wagner 1986: 33).

I have suggested above that it was this 'for/of' divisor that Velázquez may have been surprised to discover inside the '*cárcel dorada*', the golden prison, of his museum walls (Alpers 2005: 180), and which he spent much of his life interrogating and exploring: how to divide the divisor itself, how to trap it and express it in an aesthetic register and form. Velázquez's pictorial solution to the trap was a form of 'environmentalisation': an exercise in interior decoration where the capacity for re-description *made room* (sometimes quite literally) for allegorical, symbolic, ornamental, material and even theatrical dispositions.

If Galloway's and du Gay's diagnoses of the political and aesthetic economy of information are anything to go by, however, it would seem that the enthusiastic self-executability of information is today leaving no room for re-descriptions. So how can social theory 'occupy' and make room for the nondescript again?

In this context it is perhaps no coincidence that 'recursion' has become a favoured analytical strategy in contemporary social theory. Thus, for example, Chris Kelty speaks of free software engineers' self-grounding of their collaborative efforts – by virtue of writing and coding the communicative infrastructure that supports their exchanges – as the construction of a 'recursive public' (Kelty 2008). Exploring the cult of Ifá divination in Cuba, Martin Holbraad likewise resorts to the idiom of 'recursion' to explain how the inventive definitions – the 'infinitions' (Holbraad 2012: 220) – of the truth-regimes through which Ifá practitioners describe their predicaments must inevitably re-inscribe the truthfulness of anthropological description too. And Sarah Franklin has recently advocated a similar recursive route for anthropological analysis, taking inspiration in the way human development is modelled *in vitro* in stem cell labs (Franklin 2013). Modelling 'man' *in vitro* researchers are afforded the possibility of holding a description of anthropos in suspension, a possibility that opens up in turn the conceptual space for encountering and designing new diagnostic tools.

These moments of infrastructuring, infinition and suspension are reminiscent of Velázquez's re-descriptive exercises, as I have presented them here. They dwell on the culture of invention fuelling every description. Yet I wish to pause for a minute on this inventive moment, on the trope of cultural resourcefulness and prefiguration, figuration ahead of time, that these analytical sensibilities announce and incorporate.

Whereas for Velázquez recursion was an *effect* of his re-descriptive perambulations, the aesthetic of his encounter with the environments of mutual describabilities, it would seem that the status of recursion in contemporary social theory is that of a *methodology* instead: recursion as something we should do to or look for in descriptions, rather than something that descriptions do to us.[6] Now it is not my intention to produce a typology of recursions, let alone a normative classification of recursive usages, but I do think it is worth briefly laying out some of the epistemic components of this methodological strand.

The forefather of the methodological use of recursion in social theory was, of course, Gregory Bateson, who borrowed the epistemics of recursion from cybernetics. In particular, he was drawn to cybernetics' conception of information as a feedback system for the way it enabled him to think of the future and the possible as self-looping environments (Harries-Jones 1995). We experience a therapeutic sense of freedom, Bateson argued, when we sift through information that is layered recursively. In so doing we correspondingly undergo a transformation from self- to ecological consciousness. Recursion does not come with environments attached, but if properly executed all the way through, it releases the environment as consciousness.

I am interested in this therapeutic dimension of information, its status as a symbol that may liberate or restrain cathartic energies, for this understanding of information as an on/off releaser of energy is not how cybernetics was first conceptualised in the 1940s. As Peter Galison has shown, cybernetics emerged from Norbert Wiener and his associates' wartime effort at engineering servomechanisms capable of predicting an enemy aircraft pilot's actions (Galison 1994). The blurring of the human-machine (pilot-weapon) interface in the name of an information loop was modelled on the ontology of an enemy, an enemy that was not defined negatively as other than ourselves, but mysteriously as an informational black box:

> the cybernetic Other is not negatively contrasted with us, nor are we the model upon which the Other is empathetically formed; our understanding of the cybernetic Enemy Other becomes the basis on which we understand ourselves. [...] It is an image of human relations thoroughly grounded in the design and manufacture of wartime servomechanisms and extended, in the ultimate generalization, to a universe of black-box monads. (Galison 1994: 264–265)

The fundamental problem for cybernetics, then, was not the ontology of the Other, nor the nature of our relation to them, but *the Other as instruction*, a recursive function for perpetual self-modelling. Description as executability. Thus the premium that cybernetics placed in defining information as structurally irresistible: an object whose density overcomes every matter of resistance, friction or detachment. Information must be free! Its flow uninterrupted, yes, yes, yes all the way through.

Re-enter the 'yes person', for whom the office was 'an extension of themselves', as du Gay put it (du Gay 2008: 345). The extension, we know now, is informational: the cultural obsession that yes persons evince in their demands for ever more information – information that loops around itself, in the name of audit and transparency – is therefore simply a reflection of their ontological self-formation as replicable beings (beings that aim for the replication of themselves in and through information):

> the image of self-replicators such as computer viruses is breathtaking in its own way. *No environment appears necessary when what is at issue is the replication of communication devices themselves*. It is as though genes did not need to be embodied: what is reproduced is simply the informational capacity itself. Models with a life of their own! (Strathern 1992: 169, emphasis added)

'No environment appears necessary' because recursion is indeed its own model, its own method. Because it is self-delivered (data-streamed) in its transformation from self- to ecological consciousness. In this context, then, perhaps the lessons to be drawn from Velázquez's *Spinners* involve imagining what it may mean to speak from a cultural episteme where information does not exist, whose modernity is Baroque rather than anti-, non- or post-, and where the aesthetic sources of suspension and infinition have to be trapped rather than invented. When the capacity for re-description aims for environing its own hyphen.

Coda

One of reasons why the humanities have received vigorous criticism from quarters concerned with their social and media impact refers to the use they make of unpalatable, opaque, unreadable jargon. How can writings that claim social provenance, the critics argue, stand in no relation of transparency whatsoever to the publics they refer to? Why do some academics insist on making information *resistible*?

In a wonderful essay that takes issue with such criticism, Michael Warner has exposed some of the underlying assumptions that equate clarity with political and popular engagement, and has profiled in turn how an intellectual public may in fact work (Warner 2005). For a start, notes Warner, we miss the point of intellectual engagement if we think social or critical commentary should have immediate effect. Those 'who write [so-called] opaque left theory might very well feel that they are ... writing to a public that does not yet exist, and finding that their language can circulate only in channels hostile to it, they write in a manner designed to be a placeholder for a future public' (Warner 2005: 130). The channels that mediate the relationship between an intellectual and its publics are not simply communicative, nor are they coeval to the writing process. We have come to think of the public as a 'socially expansive audience' to which public intellectuals must relate to 'in horizontal terms' (Warner 2005: 144); an over-enthusiastic crowd hooraying our theoretical exegeses. Yet remember: all enthusiasms end up calling forth an art of separation. We might do better distinguishing, then, between the temporality of politics and the temporality of critical and world-making projects. The latter mobilises an orientation to strangeness and long-term risk that is not to be found in the former (Warner 2005: 150, 158). An orientation, in a sense, that looks for and engages in a deliberate play of baroque displacements or enhancements: postponing completion, exercising estrangement, trapping descriptions. Environmentalising relations.

Let me finish with Weber. In an age of disenchantment, Weber found in the vocational call an ethical escape from the determinism of technical accomplishment and the frenzy of enthusiasm. Vocation poised itself in an ethical space at a complex historical moment, when the production of knowledge was being reconfigured by the rise of individualism and rational self-interest. A hundred years later, the one has caused 'vocation to lapse into dilettantism, the other to harden into professionalism'.

The person and the office, the artist and the courtier, the scholar and the administrator parting ways. This is why political theorist Sheldon Wolin has suggested that to 'survive, the idea of vocation might have to be revoked and replaced by the sobrieties of method or invoked: Invocation as vocation's conscience recalling it to the cross-grained' (Wolin 2000: 6).

In – vocation: to summon and extricate – to detach – new voices, new descriptions. An environment for another hyphen.

Notes

1 Velázquez was in fact participating in a larger Baroque epistemology that discovered the trick of holding forms and effects in mutual suspension (Corsín Jiménez 2013): for example, the Shakespearian trick of writing a play into a play, or the pictorial techniques of trompe l'oeil or anamorphosis, where paintings self-efface a part (or the entirety) of their representational motifs. The play and the trompe l'oeil work as descriptions that detach themselves from themselves yet retain descriptive integrity: aesthetic forms and effects through which the detachment of detachment – a capacity no doubt for re-description – is accomplished.
2 What follows is a close reading of Svetlana Alper's magisterial interpretation of Velázquez's work (Alpers 2005).
3 For example, William van Haecht's *The Gallery of Cornelis van de Geest* (*c.*1628).
4 It is worth noting that the Baroque remains tightly anchored in the episteme of modernity. Thus, art historian Martin Jay has distinguished three 'scopic regimes of modernity': Cartesian perspectivalism; the so-called art of describing, where the viewer is drawn to the surface or material qualities of objects and not their relational disposition in space; and, finally, Baroque or anamorphic modernity (Jay 1988).
5 Perhaps the most famous characterisation of the Hobbesian yes person is Macpherson's 'possessive individual' (1962).
6 I think it is fair to say the exception here would be Kelty (2008), who encounters 'recursion' as an ethnographic quality of how programmers construct their social and technological relations.

References

Alpers, Svetlana, 2005, *The Vexations of Art: Velázquez and Others*. New Haven: Yale University Press.

Brown, Jonathan, 1986, *Velázquez: Painter and Courtier*. New Haven and London: Yale University Press.

Corsín Jiménez, Alberto, 2013, *An Anthropological Trompe L'oeil for a Common World: An Essay on the Economy of Knowledge*. Oxford and New York: Berghahn.

du Gay, Paul, 2000, *In Praise of Bureaucracy: Weber, Organization, Ethics*. London, Thousand Oaks and New Delhi: Sage Publications.

du Gay, Paul, 2008, Without Affection or Enthusiasm: Problems of Involvement and Attachment in 'Responsive' Public Management. *Organization* 15(3): 335–353.

Franklin, Sarah, 2013, In Vitro Anthropos: New Conception Models for a Recursive Anthropology? *Cambridge Anthropology* 31(1): 3–32.

Galison, Peter, 1994, The Ontology of the Enemy: Norbert Wiener and the Cybernetic Vision. *Critical Inquiry* 21(1): 228–266.

Galloway, Alexander R., 2012, *The Interface Effect*. Cambridge, UK and Malden, MA: Polity.

Gerth, H. H. and Mills, C. Wright, 1946, *From Max Weber: Essays in Sociology*. New York: Oxford University Press.

Harries-Jones, Peter., 1995, *A Recursive Vision: Ecological Understanding and Gregory Bateson*. Toronto, Ont.: University of Toronto Press.

Holbraad, Martin, 2012, *Truth in Motion: The Recursive Anthropology of Cuban Divination*. Chicago and London: Chicago University Press.

Jay, Martin, 1988, Scopic Regimes of Modernity. In Hal Foster, ed.,*Vision and Visuality*. Seattle, WA: Bay Press, pp. 3–23.

Kelty, Christopher M., 2008, *Two Bits: The Cultural Significance of Free Software*. Durham, NC and London: Duke University Press.

Macpherson, C. B., 1962, *The Political Theory of Possessive Individualism: Hobbes to Locke*. Oxford: Oxford University Press.

Malcolm, Noel, 2002, *Aspects of Hobbes*. Oxford: Oxford University Press.

Maravall, José Antonio, 1986, *Culture of the Baroque: Analysis of a Historical Structure*. Minneapolis, MN: The University of Minnesota Press.

Ortega y Gasset, José, 1987, *Velázquez*. Madrid: Aguilar.

Schaffer, Simon, 2005, Seeing Double: How to Make up A Phantom Body Politic. In Bruno Latour and Peter Weibel, eds, *Making Things Public: Atmospheres of Democracy*. Boston, MA: The MIT Press, pp. 196–202.

Strathern, Marilyn, 1992, *After Nature: English Kinship in the Late Twentieth Century*. Lewis Henry Morgan Lectures, 1989. Cambridge: Cambridge University Press.

Strathern, Marilyn, 2009, Afterword: The Disappearing of an Office. *Cambridge Anthropology* 28(3): 127–138.

Wagner, Roy, 1978, *Lethal Speech: Daribi Myth as Symbolic Obviation*. Ithaca, NY and London: Cornell University Press.

Wagner, Roy, 1986, *Symbols That Stand for Themselves*. Chicago, IL: Chicago University Press.

Wagner, Roy, 2001, *An Anthropology of the Subject: Holographic Worldview in New Guinea and Its Meaning and Significance for the World of Anthropology*. Berkeley, CA and London: University of California Press.

Walzer, Michael, 1984, Liberalism and the Art of Separation. *Political Theory* 12(3): 315–330.

Warner, Michael, 2005, *Publics and Counterpublics*. London: Zone Books.
Wolin, Sheldon S., 2000, Political Theory: From Vocation to Invocation. In J. A. Frank and J. Tamborino, eds, *Vocations of Political Theory*. Minneapolis: University of Minnesota Press.

10

Test sites: attachments and detachments in community-based ecotourism

Casper Bruun Jensen and Brit Ross Winthereik

Introduction

The ecotourism team has convened in preparation for a meeting with the Vietnamese country director of NatureAid, an international environmental NGO. The small team has worked all morning to finish a presentation intended to demonstrate the progress of ecotourism in Southern Vietnam. Seeking to diminish local inhabitants' dependence on natural resources in the Cat Tien National Park, the ecotourism project aims to introduce an alternative source of income for the villagers. The team hopes to empower communities and prevent forced displacement to other areas. They now aim to get the green light from the country director to upscale this project design to other areas of Vietnam. The challenge is to demonstrate that community-based ecotourism is indeed an effective approach to environmental conservation.

The presentation goes well. 'I am really impressed', says the country director. 'Things have really taken off since your last visit. Last time much had been prepared, but it was all invisible. Now there is a physical thing out there.' This thing is a newly finished long house. If all goes well it will become a successful community owned tourist lodge in the following years.

Built in traditional style of bamboo and rattan, it is not hard to imagine as a centre of community driven, environmentally friendly, tourism. Seen from Hanoi, the long house embodies the potential of a local community taking advantage of new business opportunities. But seen from Cat Tien a local community is harder to get into sight.

Attachments and detachments

As the editors of this volume note, connections and relations are prominent preoccupations in contemporary social theory (see also Candea 2010). Their gambit is that in so far as relations now cover most of the ground of social analysis, this leaves researchers blindsided to diverse forms of disconnection and distance. The interest in detachment and distance as analytical rubric is thus, to a significant extent, a critical response to the sense that 'connectivity' (Pedersen 2013) and 'attachment' (Anderson 2001) are presently overvalued, in analytical as well as normative terms.

While understandable, in light of the undeniable strong focus on connections in science and technology studies (STS) and anthropology, this diagnosis must be taken with a pinch of salt. First, it is not obvious that pro-relational concerns are quite as hegemonic as claimed by critics. After all, a history of social science that includes such diverse sources as Simmel on the stranger (1921), Elias on objectivity and detachment (1956), Bourdieu on distinctions (1987), Luhmann on social differentiation (1987) and Callon on market externalities (1998), suggest an enduring and varied interest not only in how things are related but also in how they are separated. In anthropology, this two-fold orientation is prominently exhibited by Marilyn Strathern, one of the key inspirations for the present interest in detachment. It is noticeable, for example, that in the mid-1990s, she was engaged in developing an analytics of cutting, truncating and detaching, and this not in an effort to replace relational anthropology but as an *integral part of it*.[1]

Importantly, recent critiques tend to disregard the specific reasons that led to the increasing interest in connections and attachments in the first place. Two brief examples make this point. In *The Powers of Distance*, the literary scholar Amanda Anderson (2001) criticises feminists, poststructuralists and pragmatists for their relational orientation. Premised on the claim that all actors are attached to specific contexts and practices, this leads to a view of disinterest as a purely 'illusory ideal' (Anderson 2001: 24). What is thus overlooked is that creating distance is an 'on-going aspiration' for many actors, even if it often remains an 'incomplete achievement' (Anderson 2001: 33).

In contrast to relational approaches, Anderson insists that detachment functions as an important regulative ideal in many practices. Scientists, for example, aim to achieve objectivity premised on detachments from what they study. And policy makers strive to maintain distance from the many interests that clamour for their support and attention. It is precisely the importance of these ideals of distance that are rendered invisible by analyses that prioritise situated relations (see also Candea 2010).

But is this a fair interpretation? It might be said that it was precisely *because of* their keen recognition of the sway held by the ideal of distance over many domains of life (and of the considerable power wielded by this ideal) that it became so important for poststructuralists, pragmatists and others to identify the various attachments that undergirded this regulative ideal, and to examine the interests it supported (e.g. Daston 1992; Poovey 1998). Indeed, the focus on connections and relations did not grow out of a neglect of the normative powers of distance but emerged as a specific type of analytical and political response to such powers (Smith 1997).

Or consider Morten Pedersen's argument in 'The Fetish of Connectivity' (2013). This paper offers as a substantial example of the fetish for connections invoked by his title the cognitive scientist Andy Clark's thesis of an extended and distributed mind. Pedersen's critical commentary fails to note, however, that Clark's arguments were interventions in a long and still ongoing discussion, in which 'the mind' has generally been viewed as unaffected by (and thus detached from) environmental influence. Indeed, Clark's argument would seem much more congenial to ethnographic modes of thought, including Pedersen's own, than the traditional view of disembodied cognition that he challenges. Based on this example it is thus by no means clear that the emphasis on connection is to be regretted. Nor is it obvious that Clark's interest in the mind's connections proves the existence of a general fetish. Both Anderson and Pedersen's arguments thus indicate that the merits of a focus on detachment must hinge on something more specific than an overall critique of situated connections.

To situate our own approach, we recall that one of the minor, if persistent, skirmishes at the intersection of anthropology and STS has centred precisely on how to conceive attachments and detachments. Bruno Latour (1993) defined symmetrical anthropology as premised on a refusal to accept the grand dichotomies that usually separate the West from the rest. Rather than grounding differences in technological superiority or in cognition, Latour argued that they simply pertained to the lengths of networks built by 'the moderns'. Incessant efforts to extend networks by connecting more heterogeneous actors gave moderns their edge over other people.

Marilyn Strathern (1995b) countered that an interest in the extension of networks should not deter the anthropologist from also studying how they are cut (in STS, similar arguments had been made since the early 1990s, by e.g. Star 1991; Lee and Brown 1994). Though money flows, and networks are built around its movements, Strathern wrote, 'Cameroonian businessman and Highlands brides alike would seem to both carry the flow *and to stop it*' (1995b: 518, emphasis in original). Stopping the flow, Strathern argued, creates moments of 'interpretive pause' (Strathern 1995b: 522) that might precipitate more enduring forms of detachment. Perhaps, Strathern wrote, 'Euro-American's voiced concern over limits re-runs Derrida's question of how to "stop" interpretation' (Strathern 1995b: 522). Yet ethnographic examples 'challenge the interpretive possibility of limitlessness: the kinds of interest, social or personal that invite extension also truncate it' (Strathern 1995b: 531).

This is precisely Pedersen's starting point (2013: 198). But whereas Strathern simply notes that an attention to ethnography might diminish the conceptual concerns one might have with limitless networks, Pedersen reverses the point by elevating the problem of connections to a general conceptual level. Rather than following Strathern, his argument can thus be seen as illustrative of the problem she is identifying: that Euro-Americans seem obsessed with the *abstract problem* of limitlessness. Even so, the argument against a connectivity fetish would have purchase, if attachments and detachments were indeed routinely separated in STS and anthropology. But it is by no means clear that they are.

If we want to add an own interpretive pause of our own at this point, it is to highlight what one might think would be obvious: contrary to what, quite oddly, continues to be claimed by critical anthropological commentators, Latour's interest in extendable networks has never precluded, but always depended upon, an interest in how actors also detach from them. For example the guiding thought of his 'Irreductions' (1988) was not that everything always is, not to say should be, related. Rather, it was that we can never know a priori what is related or what will come to be, for 'Nothing is, in and of itself, either equivalent or not equivalent to anything else' (Latour 1988: 168). Indeed, Latour emphasised: 'two forces cannot associate without misunderstanding' (168). Yet efforts to create relations are made, and such acts of commensuration create power: 'since nothing is equivalent, to be strong is to make equivalent' – to bring into relation, to commensurate – "what was not"' (Latour 1988: 168).[2]

It is presumably phrasings like the latter, highlighting trials of strength, which grates an anthropological sensibility keen on retaining the possibility of difference not overcome. But the fact that power often accretes in particular places or actors does not mean that it becomes omnipresent, leaving no gaps in its wake. Indeed, ambitions to keep moving, endlessly extending networks, are so regularly flaunted, the results so fragile and unstable, that they are as indicative of weaknesses as of strength (Latour, 1988: 158). On the pivotal point of whether networks are indeed cut and whether such things as gaps, misunderstanding, de-linkage, severed connections, indifferent co-existence or active efforts to detach are consequential, Strathern and Latour agree: of course they are.

It is no surprise that actor-network theory has quite a keen eye for detachment. After all, Michel Serres, one of Latour's intellectual mentors, had written a book of just that name (Serres, 1989). Spanning the genres of storytelling and philosophy, this short book discussed topics as diverse as rice farming, the life of an old sailor and Diogenes living naked in his barrel in Athens. About rice farming, Serres wrote:

> All is consumed. All is occupied, exploited, filled to the mouth, the rim, the edge. Space is pregnant. Places are full. Each section is full. Full of wheat, rice, soybeans, mulberry trees and linseed crops along the plain ... The land is dense, saturated, bulging, filled to capacity. It chokes. I choke. I feel claustrophobic outside. (Serres, 1989: 4)

Serres identifies in rice farming a positivity too complete. This is a space where there is room for nothing but relation: 'no margin, no gap, no passes, no omission, no waste, no vestiges' (Serres 1989: 5). The network is not cut and the effect is claustrophobic.

In contrast, Serres describes sailors as 'holy' as they set out to sea; at the very moment they take leave of their attachments (Serres 1989: 34). But he immediately qualifies: their holiness is premised on the transience of this detachment, on their eventual return to shore. Staying detached, he suggests, pointing to Diogenes, who lived in his barrel in the midst of society, is no option, except for fanatics. The fanatical attempt to escape the power of social relations by complete detachment merely recreates power in the form of indifferent cynicism (cf. Elias 1956: 236). The point is that almost everything interesting happens in the temporal interplay between attachment and detachment.

That is precisely the starting point for the present discussion. A focus on distance offers no alternative to a relational anthropology; nor does an interest in detachment require one to go *beyond* connections. For, being relationally defined, attachments and detachments cannot themselves be fully disentangled. Yet that does not mean they collapse into identity (Cross 2011: 35–36). Instead, they transform over time and emerge in new constellations (Trundle 2014).

Exploring these ideas, the present chapter examines the interplay of attachment and detachment at the heart of the Cat Tien ecotourism project. Here, a 'regulative ideal' of partnership formed the backdrop for ongoing efforts to relate disparate actors and agendas. However, efforts to relate were matched by equally sustained efforts to detach, not only from other actors but also from project visions and practices.

Ethnography in partnership

Between September 2010 and March 2011, we conducted fieldwork in the Danish branch of the environmental NGO NatureAid. During this period we worked together and individually in Copenhagen. Our general aim was to understand how contemporary development fashions expressed by terms such as partnership, accountability and transparency were put into practice (Jensen and Winthereik 2013; see also Venkatesan and Yarrow 2012). Specifically, we explored how partnership was instantiated in day-to-day NGO operations such as evaluating and monitoring projects unfolding in far away places.

In order to do fieldwork, we had to develop a set of 'terms of reference', spelling out how we would contribute to the improvement of the monitoring and accountability practices of the NGO. These terms defined and circumscribed our ethnographic possibilities. They specified that we were allowed to do participant observation and interviews with NGO employees. In some sense, we were thus invited to monitor the monitors. We did so by participating in meetings, conducting formal and in situ interviews, and simply hanging around the offices.

With reference to Marcus (1998: 20–21, 98–99), we might describe this engagement as an instance of circumstantial activism. This phrase is in fact quite telling. We were impelled to engage in a strange sort of activism, not by choice but incidentally, in order to be allowed to relate. These circumstances were inscribed in our terms of reference. However (as you may have noticed), this way of characterising our obligations in itself introduces a small delay; a tiny gap. After all, one would not refer something which one *fully embraced* or to which one was *wholly committed* as mere circumstance. And, indeed, this partnership was defined as much by our need for detaching, for stepping outside the terms, as by our attachment to them (see also Jensen 2007).

Not surprisingly, this situation was mutual. For while NatureAid members were usually forthcoming and friendly, they stayed clear of us when they were too busy (and they were very busy) or when our interests strayed too far from what they thought we should care about. In short, we wanted to be there and they were happy to have us, but neither wanted each other too much or in just the same way. In this sense, and for that reason, our ethnography in partnership was predicated upon ongoing processes of relating, withdrawing, returning and withholding (Jensen and Winthereik 2012), resembling the 'strategy of deferral' discussed by Kim Fortun in the context of her work with an Indian NGO after Bhopal (Fortun 2001: 252).³

In January 2011, we were invited to join a 12-day review mission to one of NatureAid's projects in Southern Vietnam. Here we would have the chance to observe how projects were actually monitored. The rest of this chapter is based on material Brit generated as observer during the mission and in post-hoc conversations with Eric, the leader of the review mission.

Only temporarily visiting the project site, we were disabled from establishing long-term relations with Vietnamese NGO partners and local villagers. Indeed, as Eric made clear prior to the mission, the relationship between the Danish branch of the NGO and its Vietnamese partners was quite fragile and 'easily disturbed'. He perceived the slow progress as being due to a lack of engagement and adequate involvement on the part of his Vietnamese partners. In particular, Brit was told to be careful about sensitive topics with the Vietnamese staff; and partnership issues in particular were considered sensitive. Thus, she was requested not to speak during meetings and to refrain from arranging formal interviews with the Vietnamese staff or project 'recipients'. She was, however, invited to participate in all meetings and she was often asked by Eric and Magnus, the Danish NGO representatives on the review mission, to jointly reflect on what had happened.

Here we might observe that whereas detachment can easily serve as an inventive *conceptual* rubric in anthropology – as testified by this volume – there are few arguments for the benefits of *ethnographic* detachment. Indeed, ethnography's appetite is generally for as many, and deep, relations as possible. Thus, it has been little surprise that some colleagues have found problematic the set-up just described. It seems too ethnographically brittle. The relations are not robust. There are too many detachments. While there is certainly truth in this, we take the occasion to explore the generative potentials of an ethnographic position specifically defined by a series of enforced detachments. Thus, we turn our detachments into an aspect of method, using it to define a circumscribed ethnographic experimental system (Rheinberger 1994; Ronell 2005: 49).

In one sense, however, our detachment from 'local villagers' located us in a situation analogous to that of the Danish consultants. After all, their work was also premised on hit and run field visits, on inability to speak the local language and on perpetually insufficient time. Involuntarily, then, we were placed smack in the middle of a domain of problems similar to the ones faced by our consultant-informers (see also Jensen 2010c). That domain of problems had to do with how to weave together a heterogeneous set of relations in a situation where detachments also multiplied. It also had to do with detaching from relations that threatened to unravel the project.

Externalising history

Emphasising the history of habitation in Vietnam, the NatureAid team generally referred to the long house built as part of the project as 'traditional'. Even so, no one in the villages knew how to make such a house. In consequence, one set of project activities took the form of study trips to other parts of Vietnam, undertaken to allow villagers to learn how build one.

Villagers' lack of knowledge on this issue cannot be separated from a number of events in recent Vietnamese history, including the resettlement policies of the 1990s. In order to get closer to the relational imaginaries upon which the ecotourism project was premised, as well as the aspects of history these imaginaries externalised, we offer a brief account of these policies.

Until the 1990s, the official Vietnam considered the nomadism of ethnic minorities in the central highlands to be a security problem. This led to the introduction of a population policy designed to survey and control the ethnic populations (Salemink 2000: 126). Oscar Salemink describes the Vietnamese 'sedentarization program' (Salemink 2000: 127) as an attempt to force minorities to give up shifting cultivation. The solution was agricultural resettlement, which entailed forced migration, especially from the North to the South. Some Vietnamese NGO staffers, too, could tell stories of the resettlement of their families. In Dak Lak, the place of the ecotourism project, the situation was similar. Resettlement explains the odd names of the involved villages: Village 4, Village 7 and Village 9.

These policies gave rise to various counter-measures. Internal government criticism of the discourse of 'ethnic problems' led to the ratification of a 1990 resolution pleading 'for a concerted development effort on the basis of respect for local culture and of the "family economy"' (Salemink 2000: 130). The resolution stated that fixed cultivation must be combined with forest protection, and it supported the continuation of a population policy seeking to 'modernise' communes by introducing individual family houses instead of the long houses. (Long houses were never meant for habitation by extended families but the political discourse of 'modernisation' imagined a break with an antiquated form of communal living.)

The 1980s policy 'of breaking up the longhouses, justified as a precondition for economic development' (Salemink 2000: 135), then, was also an attempt to change the life forms of resettled minorities. One consequence was that villagers around Cat Tien Park did not know how to build the long house. Indeed, to Eric, the project manager and head of the review team, the fact that fading or forgotten skills were now going to be remembered, shared, and materialised in a house, illustrated the value of the participatory approach promoted by the project.

But which community did he have in mind? Anthony P. Cohen has argued that community is 'largely a mental construct, whose "objective" manifestations in locality or ethnicity give it credibility' (Cohen 1985: 108). In terms of 'objective manifestations', the people from villages 4, 7 and 9 that came together to build the house certainly shared a certain locality. At the same time, they came from different parts of Vietnam and they lived separately. Further, the house was not meant as a communal space, except in the sense that it would be used to accommodate and entertain visiting tourists. Thus, it was quite uncertain whether community was generally present as a mental-symbolic construct in which people themselves were invested. Indeed, it would be more precise to see the community-oriented imaginary of the project as being due to the imposition of an 'external framework' (Langford 2002: 98). It was the effect of an 'institutional form' that arose in response to Danish funding bodies' focus on participatory approaches and premised on the notion that community is in some sense 'natural'.

Even so, the project's externalisation of Vietnamese history *also* facilitated novel kinds of relation among villagers, the project team, tourist operations and Vietnamese officials. The preliminary externalisation of Vietnamese history thus enabled a number of subsequent efforts to reintegrate communities imagined to have been sundered by resettlement and modernisation. That process went beyond symbolic construction, for community was to be materialised by building the long house together.

Materialising community

The immediate objective of this project, which required a 'community' to build a 'traditional' long house, was to find ways of preventing encroachment into Cat Tien National Park. The preventive measure was the creation of economic opportunities that would make encroachment less appealing for people living on the edge of the park.

The project would build a long house to be used as a lodge, where tourists could sleep, eat, buy handicrafts and enjoy dance performances by 'locals'. This way, it was hoped, villagers would be able to generate income, which would minimise their inclination to 'encroach' on the forest to hunt for animals, collect timber and firewood, or harvest bamboo sprouts.

The Danish and the Vietnamese project managers agreed about this general rationale. They also agreed that the project would lead to the fulfilment of a more general objective:

> The overall objective is to promote community based ecotourism in and around projected areas and strengthen the legal framework of government policy, in order to sustainably use forest resources, to slow down forest degradation and to create incentives for a general shift towards responsible tourism in the tourism industry of Vietnam. (Internal project document)

The ecotourism project, then, aimed to change lifestyles and everyday practices in the villages. Despite this agreement, however, many differences prevailed. Nhi, the Vietnamese project manager spoke about the project's capacity to change the 'habits' of the villagers: 'Habit is their way of life, like when they encroach into the forest.'[4] This view might be seen as not terribly far from an earlier official Vietnamese discourse on the backwardness of resettled minorities. It was, however, dramatically different from the view expressed by Eric, originally trained in anthropology, and a strong advocate of community orientation and participation. He saw the Vietnamese project manager's view as illustrating the generally negative attitude of the ruling classes to indigenous peoples. From his point of view, the problem was not villagers' 'habits' but their oppression by the official national culture and its political system. Arguing that: 'the house is a community guest house, an example of "bottom-up", not guided by the heavy hand of the province', he found in the long house potentials for community and environmental relation making.

Even though Nhi and Eric held different opinions about how and why community-based development mattered, both supported building the long house, because the proposal had been made by the villagers during the inception workshops. Indeed, the main reason for the construction of the long house was that it was the outcome of a participatory, multi-stakeholder approach that respected villagers' wishes while also protecting the precious natural resources of the area.

The ecotourism project thus came into being through negotiated efforts to define an intervention that would both modernise the villagers (but not too much) and build capacity through bottom-up processes, while also formulating a critique of the authoritative state apparatus (again, not too much). In this sense, the project wavered between defining the community in terms of two contradictory subject positions: one assuming 'backward' people, the other a collective of political subjects to be empowered. One way or another, however, the 'community' would have to come together.

Peter Rivière has argued that the terms 'house' and 'village' might be used interchangeably, whereas the notion of 'settlement' should be reserved 'for the geographical location'. He defined 'the residents of such a unit as a "community"' (Rivière 1995: 190). Given that residents were literally missing in the ecotourism project, community in Rivière's sense could hardly be said to exist. While manifestly indifferent to such substantive definition, the ecotourism project aligned more clearly with Cohen's view that 'the symbolic expression of community and its boundaries increase in importance as the actual geo-social boundaries of the community are undermined, blurred or otherwise weakened' (Cohen 1985: 50). It was precisely because there was no substantive community that it was so important to symbolically configure one. But again this would have to be a materialised configuration.

Since our 'experimental system' could not be set up to 'reveal the depths' (Langford 2002: 100) of community in Cat Tien, we are far from certain whether the villagers consider themselves part of an inter-village community. Rather like Jean Langford, in her studies of Ayurvedic medicine, we were required to 'skim the surface ... recording haphazard scraps of instruction' (Langford 2002: 100). One 'scrap of instruction' came from Son, a Vietnamese NGO worker who had grown up and still lived in Dak Lak. According to Son, villagers had never worked together in the way they did to construct the long house. Regardless of the economic success of the ecotourism project, he viewed the simple fact that the long house had made possible such collaboration as a major achievement.

Still, we might say that the villagers responded to an externally imposed 'community', mobilised, in minimal form by the participatory project itself. As the community was invoked where none (perhaps) existed, previous detachments gave way to novel forms of attachment, centred on a no-longer-traditional long house.

Community controversies

The long house was situated on a hill on the border of the national park quite far from the villages. Even if nobody lived on the hill, Nhi and Eric had no trouble imagining a community for the house. But if the community was not characterised by co-residence, what defined it?

'Having no autonomous existence as such', writes Avital Ronell, 'the object is not detachable, independent, or precedent to experimental activity' (Ronell 2005: 44). In our case, this holds on two registers, depending on what we take the object to refer to. Having no autonomous existence as such, the long house was not detachable from the participatory approach that led to its construction. At the same time, having no autonomous existence as such, the envisioned community could not be separated from the long house that was meant to evoke it. In both cases, the ecotourism project itself operated through what Ronell calls experimental activities.[5]

Specifically, the project can be described as an experiment in producing both house and community in such a way that they would *become* detachable from the project. Indeed, one measure of the success of the project would be that it would eventually seem as if it had done nothing to create the community, which would thus have had 'autonomous existence' all along.

Following a lengthy workshop facilitated by the external consultant Son with participation of Magnus and Nhi, the review team invites local project workers and park management for dinner in one of the National Park's restaurants. The dinner was a social event, meant to cement the partnership between the ecotourism project and the park. On the way to the restaurant, Brit tries to interview Magnus about his expectations for the evening but he merely laughs: 'tonight is for celebration, not work.'

At the restaurant the group enters a VIP lounge. There is talk about family matters and praise for the delicious food. But suddenly the conversation at one end of the table turns serious. Eric and Nhi are arguing about the events of the day's workshop. The issue is the form of the benefit-sharing scheme for the long house. The facilitator, Son, had been recruited to address precisely that question and during the workshop he had presented a model for income distribution. Having been absent, at another meeting, Eric is now listening to Nhi's explanation of this model. As Nhi praises the model, Eric's jaw drops in disbelief. He is flabbergasted: the model completely fails to comply with the poverty orientation demanded by the Danish donor.

Son had proposed that every family participating should be allowed to invest according to financial capability. Each would automatically gain membership of a collaborative group that would own the house. According to its means, each household would contribute to a pool of funds to be used to run the house. Seventy per cent of the earnings would be paid back to contributors in proportion to their investment. The model thus assumed that wealthier villagers would gradually lift the poorer out of poverty. Stating that the model is 'fundamentally flawed', Eric is now venting his anger at the notion of 'proportion'.

While park management is getting merrily inebriated at the far end of the table, Eric presses on. 'The idea of limitless investment', he insists, 'goes against donor principles'. According to these principles, projects should *directly* benefit the poorest of the poor. But investment according to capability will mostly directly benefit the richest villagers. Voicing his own concerns over limitlessness, Eric insists that the network is cut. 'What is needed', argues Eric, is 'an upper limit to investment, so that earnings will be equally divided.' Nhi and Son counter that this is not what the villagers wanted, but Eric stands his ground, replying that: 'The poorer people may not even have been at the workshop'.

Any actant, wrote Latour, 'needs faithful allies who accept what they are told, identify themselves with its cause, carry out all the functions that have been defined for them' (Latour 1988: 199). So who speaks for the community and which community do they speak for? Defending Son's model, Nhi defines the community as the set of people present at the workshop. She finds it ironical that Eric, who favours community-based approaches so cavalierly overrules community decisions. Eric, however, is not convinced that the community was represented (or even present) at all. The amicable atmosphere of the dinner has vanished. The experimental system temporarily grinds to a halt.

Business attachments

On the day following the restaurant debacle, the review team regroups, this time without Son and the park management. They decide to shelve Son's model, something of a given, since it goes against donor requirements. Though Nhi is still disgruntled at having organised a participatory workshop, only to find its decisions overruled, the team agrees to work towards a scheme in which all members will invest the same amount. Each family will then reap the same benefits or carry the same loss.

The issue settled, they look forward to meeting Jean-Pierre, a French ex-pat and the CEO of Adventure Tours. They hope to make an arrangement to ensure that his business will include the long house in its portfolio of tourist sites. From the point of view of the project team, this is beneficial since it means that the long house will be marketed more efficiently. As they see it, teaming up with Adventure Tours is crucial for the organisational sustainability and long-term success of the project. Like the relation between the Chambri and Peter Barter, owner of the tourist enterprise Melanesian Explorer, this would be an exchange, where villagers deliver an 'ethnographic experience' in return for a 'business opportunity' (Gewertz and Errington 1991: 55). Having had preliminary discussions at Jean-Pierre's mansion and on his boat, the team hopes to settle the deal.

Here we consider how these discussions shed light on 'the mutual constitution of seemingly disjunctive financial sites' (Ho 2009: 180), such as those of international ecotourism and everyday village life around Cat Tien. If this formulation sounds overly reliant on relational imagery (the sites, for Karen Ho, are seemingly disjunctive but really mutually constituted), we add that these discussions also shed light on different detachments among parties that are part of a single, presumably well-integrated, project.

Magnus and Nhi are having coffee when Jean-Pierre arrives along with a Vietnamese assistant. After chatting about an upcoming triathlon organised by Adventure Tours (the Danish consultants are keen to join), the discussion turns to ecotourism and the relation between the community and the long house. Jean-Pierre speaks enthusiastically about the house as a 'centre for profit'. He is by no means unsympathetic to an investment model that will ensure equal distributions of revenue to the whole community. As the conversation unfolds, however, it becomes obvious that Magnus and Jean-Pierre's visions of community are far apart.

Magnus launches the idea of a benefit-sharing scheme 'owned' by the collaborative group consisting of every family in the villages. Each family will operate 'like a small business'. 'Yes,' Jean-Pierre replies, 'everyone should benefit'. But, he adds, this does not mean they should all be turned into small-scale capitalists. Instead, he thinks in terms of membership and a shared fund. He envisions two systems of revenue to 'feed the fund': one source coming from tourists who pay for tours, another from their engagement in specific activities, like hikes or climbing.

Within this exchange system, it is indeed important to Jean-Pierre that villagers are not defined as small-scale entrepreneurs. The local community is an asset that can be leveraged to culturally sensitive ecotourists. Community funds symbolise authenticity (Cohen 1985) in a way small business does not. The benefit-sharing scheme envisioned by Jean-Pierre also signals that the long house is part of a development project affiliated to NatureAid's well-known brand. For these reasons, he is very reluctant to diminish the 'projectness' of the village, and he is especially keen not to make it too business-like.

We have entered a world of paradoxes: NGO workers are trying to convince this entrepreneur of the benefits of capitalist organisation for community purposes, while he urges detachment from too much capitalism and advocates a community fund to advance his own schemes ...

Magnus suggests that a collaborative group with collective ownership should manage the long house. This group will select a local manager to be supervised by Adventure Tours. From Magnus's point of view this is an elegant solution, which resolves the ownership issue in a way that fits donor requirements. It also solves another problem: the urgent need of project team members to detach from this project and move on. Nhi, for one, has little time left. Soon she will be part of a German project (9m euros) to protect tigers.

In contrast, the continued active involvement of the NGO is important for Jean-Pierre who would prefer NatureAid 'to keep one foot in the project'. More importantly, Jean-Pierre flatly rejects the notion that Adventure Tours will simply *advise* villagers on how to run the Long House. In this matter, he is far more confident about using one of 'his own people'. Thus, he introduces the notion of 'management buy-out', which means that villagers can own the house, but Adventure Tours will purchase the right to keep the place organised and up to standard. Indeed, this is a strong demand, for as Jean-Pierre says: 'If there is no permanent guy down there [i.e. a manager], I will not put one Dong inside the project.'

Both parties need the community, but for different reasons and in different form. NatureAid needs a community capable of 'taking local ownership'. This will allow NatureAid to gradually detach from the project and move elsewhere. However, Adventure Tours needs the community for marketing purposes. At the risk of losing authenticity, the community must not become too attached to tourist capitalism. However, the community also cannot be allowed to remain detached from Adventure Tours in the way envisioned by NatureAid, since this runs counter to Jean-Pierre's ideas of efficient management. The solution is a complicated interweaving, requiring NatureAid's continued involvement and AdventureTours' relative detachment.

Both Jean-Pierre and Magnus mobilise the house as part of their efforts to imagine future community. As the discussions unfold, we are witness to a competition between 'a multiplicity of realities' (Nustad 2011: 90). Nobody yet knows what will come of it all. Neither community nor long house has gained full autonomy. However, as Elizabeth Grosz argues, even as 'time and futurity remains open-ended', 'the past provides a propulsion in directions, unpredictable in advance, that in retrospect have emerged from the unactualized possibilities that it yields' (Grosz 2008: 45). The situation remains experimental, but the negotiations to which we are witness are already generating futures (Jensen 2010a: 31–51, see also 2010b).

If all goes well, the community will gradually come to look as if it had been there all along, as if it was entirely detached from development and business schemes. In that case, anthropologists visiting fifty or 100 years from now might compare the forms of life they encounter with the traditional long-house communities still in evidence as of 2011.

But we are getting ahead of ourselves.

Cultural interruptions

The review team is on its way to a meeting with the manager of the district culture house. Painted in a friendly light yellow, the building offers a pleasant surprise – in advance, Eric had warned about its ugliness. Entering the main building, however, it becomes clearer what makes the culture house unattractive to Eric. This building is where the officially enshrined definition of 'local culture' resides. The house has been furnished as a museum, which offers exhibitions of local ethnic culture. Photo exhibitions show the celebration of the annual forest festival, depicting the brutal ritual killing of a forest buffalo. When Nhi disapprovingly referred to the backwards habits of ethnic minorities, she probably had in mind representations such as these.

Almost taking up as much space as the exhibition is an area where woven bags and other handmade artefacts are for sale. Weaving workshops are organised on a regular basis; there are plans to make a small factory where village women can apply for jobs. In short, this is a setting where local culture and economy is 'manufactured according to specifications laid out by the state' (Fortun 2001: 258).

The culture house manager welcomes us, explaining that this is where local culture is performed. After an assistant has poured the obligatory green tea, Magnus introduces the evaluative purpose of the review mission: 'To think about what been accomplished by the ecotourism project, and to discuss how to collaborate on conservation goals in the future'. He hopes the meeting will ensure 'the continuation of good relations' between the culture house and the long house.

'Delinkage from the operations and institutions of the state [is] neither possible nor desirable' (Fortun 2001: 258), wrote Kim Fortun about the relations between her NGO and the Indian state. De-linkage is neither possible nor desirable for NatureAid either, though the flaws of official Vietnamese approaches to culture seem obvious to the Danish consultants. Continued good relations are crucial. Yet, the good relations that Magnus has in mind entail that the culture house loosens its stranglehold on cultural activities in the area. For the long house to attract tourists, it needs a degree of autonomy.

However, the manager of the culture house does not sympathise with the idea of culture performed outside the jurisdiction of the district. 'The culture house is for culture, singing and dancing', she says. The reason why the district has not yet granted permission to use the long house for accommodation, she says, is due to the suspicion that it will be used for cultural purposes.

Towards the end of the meeting Eric asks: 'What do you envision five years from now?' Smiling, the leader answers, and Nhi translates: 'The culture house will be culture house forever, so she has no plans. The purpose of the culture house is to preserve and restore the cultural traditions of the region.'

Virtualising materiality

After an intensive review trip, the team returns to Hanoi for a final briefing at NatureAid's Vietnamese headquarters. Presenting the project progress, its problems and their possible solutions, Eric's PowerPoint slides show a beautiful photo of the long house. The long house vividly testifies to project achievement and the materialisation of community. Eric highlights that the provincial government is inclined to choose the project as a model for community-based tourism. Since one project objective is to influence the national strategy on ecotourism this is a major breakthrough.

After listening to the presentation, the country director is emphatic: 'We need to record the first steps. Can we communicate to the province that it is good not just to have a plan, but to develop a plan together with local stakeholders?' Nhi replies that a video has already been made; a trainee has documented the entire process of building the house. The country director suggests that the trainee should be commissioned to produce another video showing how the long house is used as part of NatureAid's conservation efforts.

Having traced some of the travails of the long house and its community, this setting offers a final image of the entanglements of attachment and detachment in participatory ecotourism. Detached from the complications of local workshops and business negotiations, in Hanoi the house is once again 'mobilized dynamically' (Manning and Meneley 2008: 288), now as a potent symbol of the promises of ecotourism in general. The house is rendered in virtual form in order to travel and strengthen longer networks, connecting NatureAid's aspirations to Vietnamese policies and creating new project opportunities.

This detachment from specific project realities is by no means naive on NatureAid's part. It is not as if Nhi and Eric have suddenly forgotten the on-the-ground challenges of participatory development. Rather, local projects and national policies are topics each understood 'exclusively in its own terms' (Langford 2002: 125). Whereas the ecotourism project in Cat Tien gives shape to one experimental system, detachment from this system and attachment to Vietnamese environmental policies at large defines another one, quite different in both scale and scope.

In Hanoi, the long house ceases to be a material entity with its own history of problems and possibilities. Like the externalisation of Vietnamese history, which facilitated the project imagination, the specifics of the local project itself are externalised. This enables the transformation of the long house into an abstract promise, a future-generating device (Jensen 2010a). In virtual form, its relation-making capacities can grow exponentially. It seems potentially able to extend over the entire country.

Test sites

We have traced the interplay of attachments and detachments in an ecotourism project run by an environmental NGO and its multiple partners. We consider this project as an experimental test site for the construction of community. It is a test site in which the question of what hangs together with what, and what does not, is constantly thematised, negotiated and acted upon by the involved actors. As we have shown, the operations of this experimental domain required the externalisation of Vietnamese history and the disconnection of certain forms of community. It also entailed particular kinds of disaffiliation among project partners, and interruptions of the link between official Vietnamese conceptions and practices of culture and the activities planned for the long house.

But if the case vividly exhibits the importance of detachment in making new forms of the social, it is equally illustrative of the fact that detachments are not, and cannot be, separated out from relational packages. This is why we have been equally keen to avoid two reductive pitfalls. On the one hand, wielded as a weapon with which to combat anything resembling 'abstraction', 'disconnection' or 'distancing', relational analytics are inscribed with a rather normative and one-sided vision of what sociality consists of. Such an analytics is unable to see how different ways of 'cutting' relations are also ways of making worlds. It can imagine detachment in no other terms than as an inherently problematic reduction of lived world complexities.

On the other hand, no solution can be found in an analytical reversal, which prioritises distancing and disconnection. Generating a mirror image of what it critiques, this provides no analytical vantage point for analysing the temporal interplay of attachments and detachments or for understanding their emergent effects. As our case has suggested, attachments and detachments are both integral dimensions of the complex situations we study.

Writing of Nietzsche's fierce attempt to detach his own philosophy from existing modes of thinking, Avital Ronell noted his cool awareness that 'dependence comes first and always squats in any declaration of independence; so-called independence can never shake loose its origin in dependent states' (Ronell 2005: 142). For Nietzsche, it was always necessary to create a 'test site'; an experimental space that could be used to measure the extent to which he had succeeded in really detaching his own thinking from stale convention.

Inspired by this idea of test sites, we have analysed the ecotourism project as a pragmatic experimental system, in which actors come together while constantly putting their agreements and disagreements on trial. The partners truncate relations, cut loose from history and from one another, only to reattach differently. New forms of relations are invented, tested and sorted alongside new forms of detachments (Jensen 2007, 2014).

Yet, as Nietzsche's case also suggests, setting up test sites is not the prerogative of the people we study. It is a game we are all playing, for to understand the coexistence and effects of relations and detachments, anthropologists too must make experimental systems. In a world where everything we do depends on the particular relations and detachments we make, pure distance is a real option neither in theory nor in practice.

Acknowledgements

Thanks to Steven D. Brown, Eric Harms, Frida Hastrup and Atsuro Morita for comments on various versions of this chapter. We also thank the editors and reviewers for their helpful suggestions. We are particularly thankful to NatureAid Denmark and Vietnam for letting us participate in the challenging work of doing conservation through community based development.

Notes

1 Thus, *The Relation* (1995a) and 'Cutting the Network' (1995b) were both published in 1995.
2 Accordingly, Ingold's (2007: 81) critique of Latour, cited with approval by Pedersen (2013: 203) for positing a view of networks as a 'joining of dots', which make up a 'network of intersecting routes', is completely off the mark, a pure straw man. Given Ingold's own strong ecological-relational inclinations, it is more than a bit curious that Pedersen turns to Ingold for ammunition against Latour's supposed fetish for connections.
3 Fortun's strategy of deferral was deployed by the NGO with which she worked. It offered a way of dealing with the complex tangles of environmental and legal redress following the Bhopal catastrophe. The strategy of deferral to which we

refer was deployed by us 'against' the NGO, while NGO members used similar strategies to hold us at bay.
4 According to Oscar Salemink: 'Usually, such "bad habits" refer to religious practices – superstition, "groundless taboos" (accusations of) sorcery, which are considered to be contrary to modern science – and feasts and sacrifices accompanying life cycle rituals – such as burials and marriages, deemed unhygienic or wasteful' (Salemink 2000: 137).
5 Finally, our ethnography was also set up as a small experimental system, a localised and detached domain of inquiry, which enabled *our* detachment from the tangles of Vietnamese culture and history, and focused our attention much more narrowly on project interactions and their consequences.

References

Anderson, Amanda, 2001, *The Powers of Distance: Cosmopolitanism and the Powers of Detachment*. Princeton, NJ: Princeton University Press.
Bourdieu, Pierre, 1987, *Distinctions: A Social Critique of the Judgments of Taste*. Cambridge, MA: Harvard University Press.
Callon, Michel, 1998, An Essay on Framing and Overflowing: Economic Externalities Revisited by Sociology. In M. Callon, ed., *The Laws of the Market*. Oxford: Blackwell, pp. 244–270.
Candea, Matei, 2010, 'I Fell in Love with Carlos the Meerkat': Engagement and Detachment in Human–Animal Relations. *American Ethnologist* 37(2): 241–258.
Cohen, Anthony P., 1985, *The Symbolic Construction of Community*. Chichester: Ellis-Horwood.
Cross, Jamie, 2011, Detachment as Corporate Ethic: Materializing CSR in the Diamond Supply Chain. *Focaal: Journal of Global and Historical Anthropology* 60: 34–46.
Daston, Lorraine, 1992, Objectivity and the Escape from Perspective. *Social Studies of Science*, 22: 597–618.
Elias, Nobert, 1956, Problems of Involvement and Detachment. *British Journal of Sociology* 7(3): 226–252.
Fortun, Kim, 2001, *Advocacy after Bhopal: Environmentalism, Disaster, New Global Orders*. Chicago, IL: University of Chicago Press.
Gewertz, Deborah and Errington, Frederick, 1991, *Twisted Histories, Altered Contexts: Representing the Chambri in a World System*. Cambridge: Cambridge University of Press.
Grosz, Elizabeth, 2008, Darwin and Feminism: Preliminary Investigations for a Possible Alliance. In S. Alaimo, S. Hekman and M. Hames-Garcia, eds, *Material Feminisms*. Indianapolis: Indiana University Press. pp. 23–52.
Ho, Karen, 2009, Disciplining Investment Bankers, Disciplining the Economy: Wall Street's Institutional Culture of Crisis and the Downsizing of 'Corporate America'. *American Anthropologist* 111(2): 177–189.
Ingold, Tim, 2007, *Lines: A Brief History*. London: Routledge.

Jensen, Casper Bruun, 2007, Sorting Attachments: Usefulness of STS in Health Care Policy and Practice. *Science as Culture* 16(3): 237–251.

Jensen, Casper Bruun, 2010a, Asymmetries of Knowledge: Virtual Ethnography and ICT for Development. *Methodological Innovations* Online 5(1): 72–85.

Jensen, Casper Bruun, 2010b, *Ontologies for Developing Things: Making Health Care Futures Through Technology*. Rotterdam: Sense.

Jensen, Casper Bruun, 2010c, Motion: The Task of Anthropology is to Invent Relations. *Critique of Anthropology* 32(1): 47–53.

Jensen, Casper Bruun, 2014, Continuous Variation: The Conceptual and the Empirical in STS. *Science, Technology and Human Values* 39(2): 192–213.

Jensen, Casper Bruun and Brit Ross Winthereik, 2008, Recursive Partnerships in Global Development Aid. In S. Venkatesan and T. Yarrow, eds, *Differentiating Development: Beyond an Anthropology of Critique*. Oxford: Berghahn, pp. 84–101.

Jensen, Casper Bruun and Brit Ross Winthereik, 2013, *Monitoring Movements in Development Aid: Recursive Partnerships and Infrastructures*. Cambridge, MA and London: MIT Press.

Langford, Jean M., 2002, *Fluent Bodies: Ayurvedic Remedies for Postcolonial Imbalance*. Durham, NC: Duke University Press.

Latour, Bruno, 1988, *The Pasteurization of France*. Cambridge, MA: Harvard University Press.

Latour, Bruno, 1993, *We Have Never Been Modern*. New York: Harvester-Wheatsheaf.

Lee, Nick and Brown, Steven D., 1994, Otherness and the Actor-Network: The Undiscovered Continent. *American Behavioral Scientist* 37(6): 772–790.

Luhmann, Nicklas, 1987, The Evolutionary Differentiation Between Society and Interactio., In J. C. Alexander, B. Giesen, R. Münch and N. J. Smelser eds, *The Micro-Macro Link*. Berkeley, Los Angeles and London: University of California Press, pp. 112–135.

Manning, P. and Meneley, A., 2008, Material Objects in Cosmological Worlds: An Introduction. *Ethnos* 73(3): 285–302.

Marcus, George, 1998, *Ethnography Through Thick and Thin*. Princeton, NJ: Princeton University Press.

Nustad, Knut G., 2011, Performing Natures and Land in the iSimangaliso Wetland Park, South Africa. *Ethnos* 76(1): 88–108.

Pedersen, Morten Axel, 2013, The Fetish of Connectivity. In P. Harvey, E. Casella, H. Knox, C. McLean, E. B. Silva, N. Thoburn and Kath Woodwards, eds,. *Objects and Materials: A Routledge Companion*. London and New York: Routledge. pp. 197–207.

Poovey, Mary, 1998, *A History of the Modern Fact: Problems of Knowledge in the Sciences of Wealth and Society*. Chicago, IL: University of Chicago Press.

Rheinberger, Hans-Jörg, 1994, Experimental Systems: Historiality, Narration, and Deconstruction. *Science in Context* 7(1): 65–81.

Rivière, Peter, 1995, Houses, Places and People: Community and Continuity in

Guiana. In J. Carsten and S. Hugh-Jones, eds, *About the House: Lévi-Strauss and Beyond*. Cambridge: Cambridge University Press, pp. 189–206.

Ronell, Avital, 2005, *The Test Drive*. Urbana, IL: University of Illinois Press.

Salemink, Oscar, 2000, Sedentarization and Selective Preservation Among the Montagnards in the Vietnamese Central Highlands. In J. Michaud, ed., *Turbulent Times and Enduring Peoples: Mountain Minorities in the South-East Asian Massif*. London: Curzon Press, pp. 125–148.

Serres, Michel, 1989, *Detachment*. Athens: Ohio University Press.

Simmel, George, 1921, The Sociological Significance of the Stranger. In R. E. Park and E. W. Burgess, eds, *Introduction to the Science of Sociology*. Chicago: University of Chicago Press, pp. 322–327.

Smith, Barbara Herrnstein, 1997, *Belief and Resistance: Dynamics of Contemporary Intellectual Controversy*. Cambridge, MA: Harvard University Press.

Star, Susan Leigh, 1991, Power, Technology and the Phenomenology of Conventions: On Being Allergic to Onions. In J. Law, ed, *A Sociology of Monsters: Essays on Power, Technology and Domination*. London: Routledge, pp. 29–56.

Strathern, Marilyn, 1995a, Cutting the Network. *Journal of the Royal Anthropological Institute* 2: 517–535.

Strathern, Marilyn, 1995b, *The Relation: Issues in Complexity and Scale*. Cambridge: Prickly Pear Press.

Trundle, Catherine, 2014, *Americans in Tuscany: Charity, Compassion and Belonging*. Oxford: Berghahn.

Venkatesan, Soumhya and Yarrow, Thomas (eds), 2012, *Differentiating Development: Beyond an Anthropology of Critique*. Oxford: Berghahn.

11
Detachment and engagement in mindfulness-based cognitive therapy

Joanna Cook

In her seminal work, *The Powers of Distance*, Amanda Anderson calls for a 'defense of the critical, dialogical, and even emancipatory potential of cultivated detachment' (2001: 177). For Anderson the cultivation of detachment is usefully understood as an 'aspiration' to a distanced view – that is, the intention to distanced perspective through ongoing practices. In Anderson's analysis of Victorian writers, engagement and detachment are revealed to be dialectically constitutive. A 'newly informed partiality' results from practices in cultivated distance (Anderson 2001: 6), which impacts on impersonal goals and moral character alike. Her clarion call is for scholars to explore empirically the concrete aims, forms and effects of modern practices of detachment. What might such a project look like?

I am involved in an ongoing ethnographic work on mindfulness-based cognitive therapy (MBCT) in collaboration with the Mood Disorders Centre at the University of Exeter. This research focuses on the MBCT course for participants, reunion meetings for participants who have completed the 8-week MBCT course, and training for therapists. In this chapter I take up the challenge of ethnographically unpacking the form, telos and value of cultivated detachment in the modern project of MBCT in the UK. In this context, MBCT is a therapeutic pathway for National Health Service (NHS) service users who have suffered from three or more major depressive episodes but who are currently well. Participants learn new modes of relating to experience and internal processes in order to prevent relapse into depression.

Differently valorised forms of detachment are identifiable in the practice of mindfulness for the maintenance of mental health. On the one hand, mindfulness is identified as a practice which is uniquely fit to address depersonalising, distancing and negative aspects of modernity that contribute to the quite astonishing statistics on the increasing prevalence of major depressive episode. On the other hand, the practice of mindfulness demands that participants cultivate a detached perspective in relation to thoughts, feelings and bodily sensations in order to engage more fully in the immediacy of life and avoid becoming lost in the ruminative thought patterns that contribute to relapse. I argue that detachment may be identified both as a symptom of modern malaise and a practice of reflection for practitioners. As a reflective practice it is cultivated intentionally in order to maintain a newly invigorated engagement with life and a healthy relationship with the self on the part of the participant.

As such, my approach chimes with recent analytical approaches that explore detachment as a 'social quality of engaged separation' (Stasch 2003: 325), through ethnographic exploration of the 'labour of division' (Pedersen 2013: 203). The cultivation of detachment may be located in appropriate sociality with others, variously conceived, demanding forms of 'inter-patience' in a 'pact of inaction' (Candea 2010: 249) from all parties, or simultaneously built into the 'social architecture of relations' and the reflexive work required for successful ethical practice (Cross 2011: 36). 'Self-distancing' has been identified as central in the pursuit of forms of knowledge and appropriate sociality. For example, the mutual implication of self-distancing (from the self, as variously understood) and social distancing (from the 'object out there') is one of the key tenets of the modernist scientific gambit (see Daston and Gallison 2007). Where my analysis must differ from these approaches to detachment arises from the particular quality and effects of internal distancing techniques in MBCT.

MBCT participants develop particular kinds of distanced perspective, neither as a suppression of the self, nor as a 'splitting' from the self. Mindfulness training is primarily an introspection technique (Fronsdal 1998; Conze 2003). Inherent to the treatment model is a focus on learning, on the capacity for change and on the potential development of a healthy relationship with the self on the part of the participant. The participant must make an ongoing and concerted effort to develop the self-reflexive detachment necessary to maintain the positions of 'observing subject and observed object' in the dual tasks of self-knowledge and self-monitoring (Pagis 2009: 266; see also Mead 1934; Rosenberg 1979; Gecas and Burke 1995). A foundational premise of MBCT is that through dedicated mindfulness training, participants may develop a position of detached observation in relation to somatic, emotional and cognitive processes. This leads to a greater sense of control and self-acceptance. As such, the locus of detachment here is primarily in the relationship that the participant has with his or her own internal responses. As I hope to show, however, the ethical effect of such work is understood to be reflected in a re-engagement with the immediacy of experience of the world, for its own sake and on its own terms. Here, practices of detachment and engagement are dialogically constitutive.[1] Through the cultivation of a detached perspective, participants strive to engage with the world 'as it is' in the present, unclouded by ruminative thoughts about the past or the future.

Mindfulness and modern malaise

Today, mindfulness is mainstream. Mindfulness-based cognitive therapy has been mandated on the NHS for service users who have suffered three or more depressive episodes; the Mindfulness in Schools Programme is bringing mindfulness meditation to primary and secondary schools across the UK, with a view to promoting the emotional well-being of students; targeted mindfulness initiatives are being trialled in the probation service to prevent repeat offences by violent offenders and sex offenders; mindfulness programmes are being introduced into big business to address very real concerns about workplace stress and to reform institutional cultures in ways that prioritise workers' well-being. An All Party Parliamentarian Committee on Mindfulness was established in May 2014 in Westminster to discuss the potential for introducing mindfulness into public policy in the UK.

Recent books on mindfulness cover topics such as teaching, politics, therapy, parenting, learning, self-compassion and depression. One of the originators of MBCT, Mark Williams, is number one in the Amazon Best Sellers List with his book *Mindfulness: A Practical Guide to Finding Peace in a Frantic World* (2011). Beyond this, mindfulness is a buzzword. It has been the focus of long editorial stories in *Time* magazine, *The Huffington Post*, *The New York Times*, and *The Guardian*, among others; some describing the current focus of interest as heralding a 'Mindfulness Revolution' (*Time*). Media reports are also referencing mindfulness as a way of selling very different stories. For example, a Channel 4 *News* feature on early morning raves in London, at which people dance hard for a few hours before going to work, identified the rave events as part of the 'mindfulness movement'. In short, mindfulness is both ubiquitous and has cachet.

Mindfulness appears to offer a targeted technique for addressing the malaise that plagues modern life: narcissism, atomisation, the collapse of cultural and moral hierarchies, the privatisation of life, the severing of the self from communal relationships and bureaucratisation. A recent editorial in *Time* (Pickert 2014) described the 'Mindfulness Revolution' as a way to 'find peace in a stressed-out, digitally dependent culture': a logical response to the contemporary disorder of 'distraction'. In the *Time* article what distinguishes mindfulness from a 'new age fad' is 'smart marketing' (and the common-sense approach of thinking of the attention as a muscle, that will be strengthened by repeated exercise) and science (here referring to the increasing evidence base exploring the neuroplasticity of the brain; see Davidson et al. 2003; Lazar et al. 2005). If we are able to rewire our brains, and this may be achieved through mindfulness exercises, then we can literally make ourselves 'better' people. By giving oneself fully to what one is doing

> One can work mindfully, parent mindfully and learn mindfully. One can exercise and even eat mindfully. The banking giant Chase now advises customers on how to spend mindfully. (Pickert 2014)

Here, mindfulness becomes a practical and emotional tool for coping with the daily bombardment of information and demands on one's attention. In an article in the *Guardian*, Jemima Kiss, the newspaper's Head of Technology, explored corporate interest in mindfulness. Kiss comments that in business and elsewhere, 'Mindfulness is seen as an enquiry for objectivity, a way to claw back some of the equilibrium of how we exist in the real world, rather than the hyper-mediated place we create for parts of ourselves online' (Kiss 2013).

Mental health conditions account for at least 23 per cent of disease burden (DALYs)[2] in the UK, compared to 16 per cent for cancer and 16 per cent for cardiovascular disease (Mathers and Loncar 2006). Rates of reported depression are steadily and insidiously rising. It is estimated that around 10 per cent of the population will become clinically depressed over the coming year (Williams and Penman 2011: 17). The World Health Organization estimates that depression will be the second largest global health burden by 2020,[3] beating contenders such as heart disease and many forms of cancer for the dubious honour.

So, how is mindfulness understood here? While there are some disagreements about how it should be defined (see Mikulas 2011), in its current iterations in the UK it is understood broadly as 'paying attention in a particular way: on purpose, in the present moment and non-judgementally' (Kabat-Zinn 1994: 4). 'Paying attention' means developing awareness of patterns of thought, feelings and bodily sensations. 'On purpose' means changing the focus and style of attention, and 'non-judgementally in the present moment', means focusing on exactly what is in the present without trying to fix or change it. Here, mindfulness is a practical activity, a way of becoming familiar and friendly with the patterns of the mind and emotional and somatic responses, thereby gaining the possibility of choice in how one behaves, in response to those patterns. By developing perspective on these processes, one thereby transforms them.

MBCT was designed to treat recovered recurrent depressive patients by encouraging dissociation from depressive thought patterns that play an important part in depressive relapse (Ma and Teasdale 2004). It has been widely promoted and supported by the NHS and the National Institute for Clinical Excellence (a non-departmental government body that provides national guidance and advice to improve health and social care) as a cheap and effective treatment for depression.[4] It is taught in groups of 8–12 people led by a trained therapist, over an eight-week period. All participants on the course have a history of depression and have been referred there by their GP. The group meets once a week for two and a half hours. The sessions are built up of introductions, practices, enquiries and poems. They are highly routinised. Each session is followed by 'homework' – guided audio mindfulness practices that participants listen to at home every day, bringing mindful awareness to specified routine activities, and pleasant and unpleasant events calendars. In the penultimate week participants also complete a relapse signature chart and action plan. Key focuses of the eight-week course include developing awareness of what one is doing whilst one is doing it, rather than acting on 'automatic pilot', cultivating a decentred perspective on thoughts, recognising that 'thoughts are just thoughts (even the one's that say they are not)', using awareness and perspective to develop the ability to choose how to respond to a thought or a situation rather than reacting to it in a 'knee-jerk' way, and cultivating a kindly relationship towards oneself.

Reflexivity and self-cultivation

The theory of consciousness that underpins MBCT is that our minds can operate in different modes (Segal et al. 2013). The originators of MBCT distinguish between two modes of mind: 'doing mode' and 'being mode'. The problem-solving capacity that leads to cognitive rumination or avoiding painful or difficult states may in fact trigger and maintain depression. This is understood as a maladaptive aspect of 'doing mode', which maintains patterns that reinforce depression: the strategies that are employed in 'fixing' or solving during a negative mood can reinforce the negative thought patterns that lead to a depressive episode. In contrast, 'being' mode is characterised by direct experience of the present without the need to fix or change anything. In order to enter 'being mode', practitioners must cultivate a decentred perspective and thereby step out of the ruminative, problem-solving cognitive patterns of 'doing mode' that characterise much of normal life.

> In practice, the tendency to enter doing mode is so pervasive (especially when one is learning a new skill such as how to 'be'!) that very simple learning situations have to be set up, and the instructor has to embody being mode more or less constantly in those situations in order to facilitate entry into this mode of mind. (Segal et al. 2013: 75)

The focus of the therapy is not on changing the content of negative thinking but rather is focused on how all experience is processed. Learning to switch from 'doing mode' to 'being mode' is an underlying focus of each of the sessions. Through mindfulness training participants are learning to 'step aside', to 'shift gear', from the problem-solving of 'doing mode' and enter into a completely different way of relating to internal and external states. Thus they approach the patterns they were previously struggling with, in a completely new way, that is through 'being mode'. The development of an ongoing and compassionate decentred perspective from which to view thoughts, feelings and bodily responses is a primary task of mindfulness training.

Awareness of thoughts, feelings and emotions develops over the course of the eight weeks. Being aware of and accepting what is without trying to change it is a challenging exercise for most people. Once the practitioner is able to hold a particular thought, feeling or bodily sensation in awareness he or she is encouraged to relate to it in an accepting and kindly way. In hand-outs in week five participants are reminded that:

> Often, we can be with an arising thought, feeling, or bodily sensation, but in a non-accepting, reactive way. If we like it we tend to hold onto it; we become attached. If we do not like it, because it is painful, unpleasant, or uncomfortable in some way, we tend to contract, to push away out of fear, irritation, or annoyance.

Awareness and acceptance are cultivated through clearly delineated techniques. A body scan, a 3-minute breathing space and mindfulness of the breath are all practices for developing awareness coloured by an attitude of kindness. The practitioner develops awareness of what he or she is experiencing most prominently moment by moment, but also the awareness that she brings to it is gentle and friendly, and brought there intentionally. The practitioner is learning to be aware of things as they are. She is also learning to 'soften' towards them. One technique for doing this during any exercise is to intentionally think to oneself, 'It's OK. Whatever it is, it's OK'; repeating 'It's OK. Whatever it is, it's OK. Let me feel it', if challenging feelings, thoughts or emotions arise.

This kindly awareness is distinguished from resignation it is intended to enable the practitioner to respond skilfully to thoughts or feelings.

This points towards what Allen et al. (2009: 418) describe as 'the dialectical tension between acceptance and change': a productive tension between acceptance of depressive feelings and a desire for change (see also Linehan 1993; Teasdale 1999; Hayes 2004). For the first three weeks of the course, most people find it incredibly difficult to find time for practice and, when they do, to stay with the focus of the practice. Common questions that come up in response to the practice included 'is it alright for me to be giving this time to myself? This feels very self-indulgent', and 'what is the point of this? I feel stupid doing this.' Mindfulness practice became one more thing that each of the participants had to 'do'. The group are told repeatedly that whether they felt the practice was 'good' or 'bad' didn't matter, what mattered was actually practising.

They are instructed that in any sitting period, once they had noticed that the mind had wandered they are to congratulate themselves on once again regaining awareness and 'gently escort' their attention back to the focus of the meditation. The first focus for the development of awareness is through a technique called the body scan – the body being a great way to anchor the awareness in the moment. Training to put the attention in different parts of the body at will also helps to develop an awareness of the feelings of the body. Often the body tenses, the breath quickens and the somatic experiences of feelings are hardly noticed. By focusing on the physical manifestation of emotion in the body, the emotion itself is able to be addressed: through developing awareness of the feeling itself and exploring how it feels in the body the participant is able to approach it in a gentle way, without it being too frightening, or being avoided. By dropping into the body, the practitioner is able to develop an awareness of both the immediate thought and the effect that it has on the body, but importantly, to allow this to be without trying to change it.

This is akin to the significance of reflective thought in Foucault's theory of self-cultivation, that is, in 'active processes of reflective self-formation' (Laidlaw 2014: 101). Importantly, what is meant by 'thought' in Foucault is not limited to the content of thinking, which is recognised as cross-culturally variable. A usual understanding of thought as the daydreams, deliberations, conceptualisations and fantasies that make up the unremitting background chatter of our internal dialogues is expanded here:

> It is what allows one to step back from this way of acting or reacting, to present it to oneself as an object of thought and to question it as to its meaning, its conditions, and its goals. Thought is freedom in relation to

what one does, the motion by which one detaches oneself from it, establishes it as an object, and reflects on it as a problem. (Foucault 1997: 117)

The emphasis for Foucault is on the *capacity* for 'stepping back'. What form and content that 'stepping back' takes is culturally and historically variable but a capacity for reflectiveness is taken by Foucault to be a universal feature of what it is to be human. And it is this capacity that 'establishes the relation with oneself and with others, and constitutes the human being as an ethical subject' (Foucault 1997: 200, cited in Laidlaw 2014: 103).

The meaning of mindfulness in MBCT comes strikingly close to this definition of thought in Foucault's analysis: both rest upon the capacity for reflective consciousness rather than focusing on the substantive content of the mind. Participants are cultivating a detached perspective from which to witness thoughts and feelings as they arise and pass away. Here, then, detachment takes the form of an aspiration towards and training in reflexive self-consciousness. What one is doing in practising mindfulness is learning to witness thoughts, in a non-judgemental and kindly way without attaching to them or reacting to them as if they were real. Metaphors that are used to describe this include watching clouds come and go in a blue sky; thoughts make up the weather pattern but they are not the sky. Another is to watch the thoughts as if one were an audience member at a play or a movie; the story is just a story, it is not real.

It must be emphasised that mindfulness is a practice – it is something that is done again and again as a form of 'training' in order to develop the capacity to witness thoughts and to find what is termed 'a decentred perspective' or 'a different place to stand' in relation to thoughts, feelings and sensations. While it may seem like a piece of fairly well travelled knowledge that thoughts are only thoughts not facts, the ability to actually experience thoughts as impermanent mental occurrences and patterns is one that must be cultivated by most people. Through dedicated mindfulness training the participant learns to see her thoughts as transient and undefining, rather than an accurate reflection of reality. As such she no longer needs to respond to the content of the thoughts in the same way and reduces suffering (Teasdale 1999). This further affects the rumination leading to depressive episodes (Segal et al. 2013), but it takes work. This reflects trends in enlightenment thought in which the possibility for standing back from experience through a kind of 'radical reflexivity' (Taylor 1989: 163) is valued in order that the self might be remade through disciplined work. As Taylor writes, 'What this calls for is the ability to take an instrumental stance to one's given properties, desires, inclinations, tendencies, habits of thought and feeling, so that they can be *worked on*' (Taylor 1989: 159–160; see also McMahan 2008: 201–202). Mindfulness here is understood as a way of cultivating a skilful engagement with life, reconfigured as a technique of self-discovery and self-transformation, as well as physical and mental health.

To see a world in a grain of sand ... or a raisin

Paying attention, in a particular way, on purpose is intended to enable the participant to let go of ruminative thought patterns, conceptualisations, aversions or attachments. This is achieved through practices in detachment, but it is described as leading to an increased engagement with life, transforming the banal activity of the everyday into a vivid appreciation of the ordinary in all of its extraordinariness. Detachment here is cultivated as a means for observation. Rather than being consumed by thoughts the participant is learning to be aware of them; he or she is learning to maintain a detached perspective in order to pay attention in a very particular way. Participants are cultivating a decentred perspective from which to witness thoughts and feelings as they arise and pass away. This is achieved, in part, by learning to focus on the activity that he or she is doing while he or she is doing it; to be 'present' and pay attention to an experience while it is happening. The practitioner must detach from the flow of thoughts, feelings and experiences in order to focus on them as objects of awareness. Experience here takes on a specific value – it is through heightened awareness of the qualities of daily life and events that the relationship with thoughts can be transformed.

In the therapeutic work of MBCT, one of the first exercises that participants encounter is known as 'the raisin exercise'. During the first session of an eight-week course we sat in a circle of comfortable chairs and our teacher gave one or two raisins to each person, which we held in our upturned palms. Returning to her own seat, she settled and held her own raisin in front of her. 'Now,' she began, 'if it feels OK for you, I'd like you to imagine that you've just landed on this planet from Mars. And you've never seen an object like this before.' Flickers of smirks and glances rippled through the group momentarily. 'Take some time to explore this object, to really see it. Examine every aspect of what it looks like, the folds and ridges, the way that the light touches it, the darker hollows, its size.' We began to explore the visual experience of the raisin, spending time doing nothing but 'seeing' this object, as if it were for the first time.

We were then asked to explore the touch of the raisin, how it felt in the hand, the texture, stickiness or firmness, rolling it on the palm or between thumb and forefinger. Next, the smell of the raisin, holding it to the nose and inhaling any aroma while also noticing any changes in the mouth or stomach that came with the fragrance. We were asked to slowly bring the raisin to the mouth, feeling it on the lips and placing it on the tongue, exploring the sensation of it in the mouth before chewing. Finally, we bit into our raisins, noticing the sensations in the mouth, the changing tastes and textures of the raisin and the changing experience of the mouth. Taking time to unhurriedly explore these new sensations before swallowing and becoming aware of the changes in the body as a result of the exercise, we were learning to maintain our attention on the experiences of the 'present moment'.

Reflecting on the experience afterwards, participants' reactions to it were varied. Some questioned the point of it. For others it had been deeply frustrating, with one woman feeling so impatient that she had eaten the raisin almost straight away. For some, it had been approached playfully as an imaginative and entertaining exercise.

In his book, *Coming to our Senses* (2005: 230), Jon Kabat Zinn writes of the raisin exercise:

> Eating dispels all previous concepts we may be harboring about meditation. It immediately places it in the realm of the ordinary, the everyday, the world you already know but are now going to know differently. Eating one raisin very, very slowly allows you to drop right into the knowing in ways that are effortless, totally natural, and entirely beyond words and thinking ... Such an exercise delivers wakefulness immediately: there is in this moment only tasting.

The calls to approach daily life with mindfulness are a central part of learning MBCT. From the first week of the course homework includes doing at least one activity with mindfulness each day. This means that the attitude with which one approaches a daily task is changed through the structured learning process of MBCT. Mindfulness is brought into seemingly banal activities of life, such as waiting for the bus, brushing one's teeth or climbing the stairs, until mindful awareness conditions the perception of the world. Anything that makes up the contingent flow of the experience of the present moment may become the focus of mindfulness: thoughts, feelings, bodily states, sounds, vision.

McMahan argues that practices and ideas of 'world-affirmation' have been a constituent aspect of modernity in the context of which Buddhist inspired mindfulness practices have flourished. He explores this through literary genres that valorise the details of daily life, the flow of consciousness, a reverence for the ordinary and the capacity for this to reflect universal forms. This echoes what Taylor has called the 'affirmation of ordinary life' in his work on modern subjectivity – a development of the idea that the good life is to be found within quotidian experience by engaging with it in a particular way (Taylor 1989: 211–304). As McMahan writes, 'In letting go of the usual concepts, attachments, aversions, and associations connected to any given object of attention, the simple wonder of things 'as they are' comes into awareness; released from egocentric appropriation, they can be seen as a "miracle"' (McMahan 2010: 216). In such a view, no matter what the circumstances of one's life, the quality of engagement that one brings to it is the locus of meaning and fulfilment. For example, the Vietnamese meditation master, Thich Nhat Hanh encourages practitioners to wash the dishes 'to wash the dishes' (Nhat Hanh 2008: 4):

> why put so much stress on a simple thing? But that's precisely the point. The fact that I am standing there and washing these bowls is a wondrous reality. I'm being completely myself, following my breath, conscious of my presence, and conscious of my thoughts and actions.

McMahan suggests that 'The contemporary adaptations of mindfulness practice become possible only because of the space opened for them by the distinctively modern valuation of ordinary life as itself the location of sacrality' (McMahan 2010: 221). He explores this through the development of the modern novel as a genre, considering the ways in which description affords a re-framing or re-creation of the familiar so that it is represented as immediate, vivid and fresh rather than 'obscured by habit and fixed conceptions' (2010: 223). In what James Joyce described as 'the sudden revelation of the whatness of a thing' (Joyce, cited in McMahan 2010: 224) the mind is able to perceive the world 'as if new', free from externally imposed perceptions or cognitive habits.

For McMahan, modernist literature illustrates and informs the ways in which Buddhism and mindfulness have been transformed in Western contexts: the interweaving of the ordinary and the extraordinary, ecstatic experiences induced through ordinary sensory perceptions in 'the cotton wool of everyday life' and 'moments of being' (Woolf 1985: 65–70; in McMahan 2010: 225) – what he nicely calls the 'interweaving of the prosaic and profound' (McMahan 2010: 233). Mindfulness here is presented as a specific technique for attending to the movements of the mind and the details of daily life. 'One withdraws from things, or from one's habitual reactions to things, but in such a withdrawal lies the possibility of apprehending a deeper mystery lying within them' (McMahan 2010: 234).

Participants on the MBCT course are being asked to be fully present to the experiences of the moment, rather than being lost in rumination or planning, the 'autopilot' that, it is suggested, people operate on most of the time. This is reflected in the use of poetry during the course, which draws on an eclectic range of sources and traditions and reflects the objectives of the course at different points. For example, taking the world 'as it is', by paying attention, is reflected in the poetry of Mary Oliver, whose poem 'The Summer Day' (1992) used during the course, concludes with the lines:

> I don't know exactly what a prayer is.
> I do know how to pay attention,
> how to fall down into the grass,
> how to kneel down in the grass,
> how to be idle and blessed,
> how to stroll through the fields,
> which is what I have been doing all day.
> Tell me, what else should I have done?
> Doesn't everything die at last, and too soon?
> Tell me, what is it you plan to do
> with your one wild and precious life?

Mindfulness here is understood as a cultivated detachment from 'automatic pilot' in order to engage more fully with the immediacy of life. It is presented as an objective capacity away from a particular belief system, and it is accessible to all, a presentation which is underscored by the stress on individual experience and practice. Mindfulness is cultivated with the intention of enabling practitioners to develop a deeper appreciation of daily activities and to cultivate a different engagement with life.

Conclusion

MBCT appears to offer a useful vantage point for thinking about Anderson's proposal with which we began: that we engage with detachment not as a certainty but as an aspiration and one that is connected with ongoing striving for various situated achievements, be they social, political or psychological. Anderson is calling for an analysis of detachment that rests on a pluralistic understanding of practices of reflection: in so doing she seeks 'to advance self-consciously pluralistic conceptions of detachment over hierarchical, exclusive, or insufficiently self-critical ones' (2001: 30). Rejecting analyses that characterise forms of detachment as either inherently exclusionary *or* progressive, Anderson engages sensitively with Victorian writers who tussle with seemingly contrastive valorisations of detachment in their work. This is clearly illustrated in her account of George Eliot's analysis of different forms of detachment. Eliot critiques cultural representations that valorise a detached relation to social life. Her concern is that distanced relations from direct experience of life lead to distortions of, and moral insensitivity to, lived experience. Eliot views a stance of detached analysis as undermining moral responsiveness, and producing essentialist, generalising or wrong forms of knowledge. At the same time, however, the disruptive conditions of modernity may themselves be addressed through 'ennobling practices of reflection' (Anderson 2001: 13) – that is, the cultivation of detachment through higher-order self-consciousness may be placed in the service of the management of modernity 'so as to curtail its excesses and fulfil its most progressive potential' (Anderson 2001: 14).

For Eliot, the self-reflexive cultivation of character that typified much of the focus of Victorian ethics and aesthetics necessitates desirable forms of detachment. This, Anderson suggests, exemplifies a more general preoccupation in Victorian cultural debate. Concern around the negative distancing effects of modernity (for example, forms of alienation, rootlessness and disenchantment) demand here the cultivation of a distanced relation towards one's self, community or object of study (Anderson 2001: 4). As such, Eliot and others understood the cultivation of specific forms of detachment to have a progressive potential – forms of life may be objectified in order to understand or transform them:

> The cultivation of detachment – which in some sense is only another name for the examined life – is always an ongoing, partial project, whose interrelated ethical and epistemological dimensions ideally promote the reflexive interrogation of its own practices and thereby further the possibility for individual and collective self-determination. (Anderson 2001: 180)

Similarly, detachment and engagement are dialectically constitutive in the practice of mindfulness. By cultivating a detached perspective on thoughts, feelings and emotions, participants on the MBCT course develop a new engagement with life. As Segal et al. write:

> attention is no longer focused narrowly on only those aspects of the present that are directly related to goal achievement; in being mode, the experience of the moment can be processed in its full depth, width, and richness. (Segal et al. 2013: 72)

By locating practices of detachment in this way, I hope to have revealed some of the significance of the cultivation of detachment for MBCT participants. The ongoing *practice* of detachment is committed to by participants who intentionally seek to change the ways in which they relate to depression and to themselves. Detachment here is important as a practice, as an intention, and as a 'stance' (Taylor 1989: 514). Mindfulness training is directed at participants' experiences of their own thought processes, emotions and bodily sensations (Allen et al. 2009).

It affects a shift in perspective on both depression and self, but one that is ongoing and requires practice. Depression becomes disassociated from the practitioner (thoughts are just thoughts rather than true reflections of reality) through the cultivation of a detached perspective in the development of mindfulness. I hope to have illustrated that participants in MBCT strive to experience things 'as they are' and that they have good reasons for wanting to do so. The focus is on 'accepting' what is, without a pressure to change it, in order to learn a mode of mind that is 'characterized by direct, immediate, intimate experience of the present' (Segal et al. 2013: 72).

Detachment, then, is necessary in order to directly engage with life; and it takes continuing and dedicated work to experience this. The cultivation of a decentred perspective through dedicated mindfulness practice in order to prevent depressive relapse may be viewed as both a response to, and a transformation within, modernity. The principle underpinning MBCT is that participants may find 'a different place to stand' in relation to ruminative and negative thought patterns. The challenges of depression, isolation and rumination, that is, aspects of negatively valued detached sociality, are addressed. This is achieved through ongoing self-reflexive work by which the immediacy of life in all of its extraordinary ordinariness may be appreciated.

Notes

1 See Yarrow and Jones (2014) for a fascinating comparative argument.
2 Disability-adjusted life years.
3 Mathers and Loncar (2006).
4 There is evidence that MBCT might help large numbers of people experiencing depressive affect and patterns of recurring depression (Baer 2003; Coelho, Canter and Ernst 2007). It was found to reduce depressive relapse in three randomised-controlled trials (Ma and Teasdale 2004; Kuyken et al. 2008; Teasdale et al. 2000). Kuyken et al. (2008) demonstrate that MBCT is equivalent to maintenance antidepressants for the prevention of depressive relapse but is superior in terms of quality of life and residual depressive symptoms. Standards for teachers were published in 2002, and MBCT teacher training programmes have been established in the UK, Netherlands and Australia (Crane and Kuyken 2012).

References

Allen, Mark, Bromley, Andrew, Kuyken, Willem and Sonnenberg, Stefanie J., 2009, Participants' Experiences of Mindfulness-Based Cognitive Therapy: 'It Changed Me in Just about Every Way Possible'. *Behavioural and Cognitive Psychotherapy* 37: 413–430.

Anderson, Amanda, 2001, *The Powers of Distance: Cosmopolitanism and the Cultivation of Detachment*. Princeton, NJ: Princeton University Press.

Baer, Ruth A., 2003, Mindfulness Training as a Clinical Intervention: A Conceptual and Empirical Review. *Clinical Psychology-Science and Practice* 10: 125–143.

Candea, Matei, 2010, 'I Fell in Love with Carlos the Meerkat': Engagement and Detachment in Human–animal Relations. *American Ethnologist* 37(2): 241–258.

Coelho, Helen F., Canter, Peter H. and Ernst, Edzard, 2007, Mindfulness-based Cognitive Therapy: Evaluating Current Evidence and Informing Future Research. *Journal of Consulting and Clinical Psychology* 75: 1000–1005.

Conze, Edward, 2003, *Buddhist Meditation*. New York: Dover Publications.

Crane, Rebecca, Kuyken, Willem, Hastings, Richard P., Rothwell, Neil, and Williams, J. Mark G., 2010, Training Teachers to Deliver Mindfulness-based Interventions: Learning from the UK Experience. *Mindfulness* 1:74–86.

Crane, Rebecca S. and Kuyken, Willem, 2012, The Implementation of Mindfulness-Based Cognitive Therapy: Learning From the UK Health Service Experience. Mindfulness. www.ncbi.nlm.nih.gov/pmc/articles/PMC3742431/

Cross, Jamie, 2011, Detachment as a Corporate Ethic: Materializing CSR in the Diamond Supply Chain. *Focaal – Journal of Global and Historical Anthropology* 60: 34–46.

Daston, Lorraine and Gallison, Peter, 2007, *Objectivity*. Brooklyn, NY: Zone Books.

Davidson, Richard J., Kabat-Zinn, Jon, Schumacher, Jessica, Rosenkranz, Melissa, Muller, Daniel, Santorelli, Saki. F. et al., 2003, Alterations in Brain and Immune Function Produced by Mindfulness Meditation. *Psychosomatic Medicine* 65: 564–570.

Foucault, Michel, 1997, *Ethics, Subjectivity and Truth: Essential Works of Foucault 1954–1980*, volume 1, edited by P. Rabinow. New York: New Press.

Fronsdal, Gil, 1998, Insight Meditation in the United States: Life, Liberty and the Pursuit of Happiness. In Charles S. Prebish and Kenneth K. Tanaka, eds, *The Faces of Buddhism in America*. Berkeley: University of California Press, pp. 163–182.

Gecas, Viktor and Burke, Peter J., 1995, Self and Identity. In Karen S. Cook, Gary A. Fine and James S. House, eds, *Sociological Perspectives on Social Psychology*. Boston: Allyn & Bacon, pp. 41–67.

Hayes, Steven C., 2004, Acceptance and Commitment Therapy, Relational Frame Theory and the Third Wave of Behavioral and Cognitive Therapies. *Behavior Therapy* 35: 639–665.

Kabat-Zinn, Jon, 1994, *Wherever you Go, There you Are: Mindfulness Meditation for Everyday Life*. London: Piatkus.

Kabat-Zinn, Jon, 2005, *Coming to Our Senses*. New York: Hyperion.

Kiss, Jemima, 2013, How Life in the Digital Fast Lane has Made us Lose Touch with our Senses, *Guardian*, 1 December 2013. www.theguardian.com/

technology/2013/dec/01/life-in-digital-fast-lane-mindfulness (accessed 20 January 2015).

Kuyken, Willem, Byford, Sarah, Taylor, Rod S., Watkins, Ed, Holden, Emily, White, Kat, Barrett, Barbara, Byng, Richard, Evans, Alison, Mullan, Eugene and Teasdale, John. D., 2008, Mindfulness-based Cognitive Therapy to Prevent Relapse in Recurrent Depression. *Journal of Consulting and Clinical Psychology* 76: 966–978.

Laidlaw, James, 2014, *The Subject of Virtue: An Anthropology of Ethics and Freedom*. Cambridge: Cambridge University Press.

Lazar, Sara W., Kerr, Catherine E., Wasserman, Rachel H., Gray, Jeremy R., Greve, Douglas N., Treadway, Michael T., McGarvey, Metta, Quinn, Brian T., Dusek, Jeffery A., Benson, Herbert, Rauch, Scott L., Moore, Christopher I., and Fischl, Bruce, 2005, Meditation Experience is Associated with Increased Cortical Thickness. *NeuroReport* 16: 1893–1897.

Linehan, Marsha M., 1993, *Cognitive-Behavioral Treatment of Borderline Personality Disorder*. New York: Guilford Press.

Ma, S. Helen and Teasdale, John D., 2004, Mindfulness-Based Cognitive Therapy for Depression: Replication and Exploration of Differential Relapse Prevention Effects. *Journal of Consulting and Clinical Psychology* 72(1): 31–40.

McMahan, David, 2008, *The Making of Buddhist Modernism*. Oxford: Oxford University Press.

Mathers, Colin D and Loncar, Dejan, 2006, Projections of Global Mortality and Burden from 2002 to 2030. *PLoS Med* 3(11): e442. Doi:10.1371/journal.pmed.0030442. Available at www.plosmedicine.org/article/fetchObject.action?representation=PDF&uri=info:doi/10.1371/journal.pmed.0030442

Mead, George H., 1934, *Mind, Self, and Society*. Chicago: The University of Chicago Press.

Mikulas, William. L., 2011, Mindfulness: Significant Common Confusions. *Mindfulness* 2: 1–7.

Nhat Hahn, Thich, 2008, *The Miracle of Mindfulness*. London: Rider.

Oliver, Mary, 1992, *New and Selected Poems*, vol. one. Boston, MA: Beacon Press

Pagis, Michal, 2009, Embodied Self-reflexivity. *Social Psychology Quarterly* 72: 265–283.

Pedersen, Morten, 2013, The Fetish of Connectivity. In Penelope Harvey, Eleanor Casella, Gillian Evans, Hannah Knox, Christine McLean, Elizabeth Silva, Nicholas Thoburn and Kath Woodward, eds, *Objects and Materials. A Routledge Companion*. London: Routledge, pp. 197–207.

Pickert, Kate, 2014, The Mindful Revolution. *Time*, 3 February 2014. http://time.com/1556/the-mindful-revolution/

Rosenberg, Morris, 1979, *Conceiving the Self*. New York: Basic Books.

Segal, Zindel V., Williams, J. Mark G. and Teasdale, J. D., 2013, *Mindfulness-Based Cognitive Therapy for Depression* (2nd edn). New York: Guilford Press.

Stasch, Rupert, 2003, Separateness as a Relation: The Iconicity, Univocality and Creativity of Korowai Mother-in-law Avoidance. *Journal of the Royal Anthropological Institute* 9: 317–337.

Taylor, Charles, 1989, *Sources of the Self: The Making of Modern Identity*. Cambridge, MA: Harvard University Press.

Teasdale, John D., 1999, Metacognition, Mindfulness and the Modification of Mood Disorders. *Clinical Psychology and Psychotherapy* 6: 146–155.

Teasdale, John D., Segal, Zindel V., Williams, J. Mark G., Ridgeway, Valerie A., Soulsby, Judith M. and Lau, Mark A., 2000, Prevention of Relapse/recurrence in Major Depression by Mindfulness-based Cognitive Therapy. *Journal of Consulting and Clinical Psychology* 68: 615–623.

Williams, Mark and Penman, Danny, 2011, *Mindfulness: A Practical Guide to Finding Peace in a Frantic World*. London: Piatkus.

Woolf, Virginia, 1985, A Sketch of the Past. In Jeanne Schulkind, ed., *Moments of Being*, 2nd edn, Orlando, FL: Harcourt Brace, pp. 61–160.

Yarrow, Thomas and Jones, Sian, 2014, 'Stone is Stone': Engagement and Detachment in the Craft of Conservation Masonry. *Journal of the Royal Anthropological Institute* 20(2): 256–275.

12

The discourse of ignorance and the ethics of detachment among Mongolian Tibetan Buddhists in Inner Mongolia, China

Jonathan Mair

Introduction

In *The Making of Buddhist Modernism*, David L. McMahan (2008) compares historical and contemporary understandings of dependent origination, a central concept in Buddhist philosophy. In the Pali canon, he argues, dependent origination describes the chain of cause and effect that produces suffering; the purpose of Buddhist teachings is to break that chain and escape from the illusory phenomenal world. In modern accounts, however, which often gloss 'dependent origination' with such terms as 'interdependence', or, 'inter-being', the interconnectedness of everything is celebrated. The causal relatedness of living beings to each other and the planet is taken as the ground of an ethical duty to care for others and the environment, a duty to be 'socially engaged' rather than reclusive. This revolutionary transformation is recognised by Buddhist modernists around the globe, many of whom call the new, reformed version of their religion 'Engaged Buddhism' or 'Socially Engaged Buddhism'.

Engaged Buddhists differ on whether their approach represents a true innovation made possible by modern advances in education and technology or a restoration of the practices of earlier generations of Buddhists whose wisdom was long forgotten. They broadly agree, however, that the key task facing Buddhists today is to replace what they see as the blind faith and empty practice characteristic of traditional forms of Asian Buddhism. In its place, they hope to develop a modern form of Buddhism based on accurate knowledge of the true message of the Buddha's teachings (the Dharma) and the will to implement the ethical message of those teachings by engaging with other living beings and the world we live in (see Queen and King 1996; King 2006). Whereas Buddhist practice has often been based on a stark division of religious labour, Buddhist modernists tend to underplay the difference between the roles of renouncer and lay devotee and encourage each follower to take responsibility for his or her own understanding of the Buddha's teachings, even adopting practices such as meditation, once reserved for elite renouncers (Cook 2010). For this reason, the religion of Buddhist modernists has been called 'Protestant Buddhism' (Gombrich and Obeyesekere 1988).

This chapter is an attempt to understand a form of Buddhism that Buddhist modernists would consider a prime target for reform: Tibetan Buddhism as practised in Inner Mongolia, northern China. These Inner Mongolian Buddhists seem at first to fit the modernist narrative, because limited opportunities for education mean that nominal Buddhists know little of the real meaning of the religion, and political restrictions on international religious exchange mean that Buddhist modernism has had little effect in the contemporary Buddhist revival. By seeing the lack of connection to the Dharma as a passive absence to be filled, however, this account misses a crucial aspect of the religious lives of many of my Inner Mongolian Buddhist informants: the cultivation of a specific awareness of ignorance and the active rejection of opportunities to acquire knowledge, elements of a detachment from knowledge underpinned by an ethics of humility.

I begin the chapter by introducing Inner Mongolian Buddhists' concerns about their own ignorance. I describe the ways in which the logic and practices associated with this concern, what I call the *discourse of ignorance*, is related to other aspects of religious life. I argue that my informants' constant assertion of their own ignorance should not be taken as evidence of an unconscious or indifferent failure to engage with the sources of the religion. On the contrary, their humility is the result of the effortful pursuit of an ethic of detachment.

Adopting a stance of humility means cultivating a relationship with Buddhism that is active and intense, but simultaneously distant and distancing. It is a relationship based on principled detachment from Buddhist teachings. For my Inner Mongolian Buddhist informants, the deep meaning of the teachings is beyond a limit, unimaginable and unapproachable, except through intermediaries. The most important of these are the living buddhas who combine the advantages of buddhas and bodhisattvas (being enlightened) with those of ordinary lamas (being in the human world), and therefore straddle the horizon of enlightenment. Trying to achieve the kind of familiarity with the teachings that would be required in order to understand them and put them to use is not only futile (because the real meaning is deep), but actually precludes the sort of humble respect required to interact with them in the only way we ordinary, unenlightened beings can, that is, by the cultivation of specific forms of sincere, faithful belief.

In the subsequent section, I argue that to make sense of Inner Mongolian Buddhist discussion about ignorance, it helps to distinguish between different forms of ignorance in terms of detachment or negation of knowledge. When we talk about knowledge, we specify a relationship: a relationship between an object of knowledge and a knowing subject. I argue that when we speak of ignorance we negate or invert that relationship, but that there are at least two distinct ways of doing that. In one form of negation, ignorance is seen as an absence of relationship or an unfulfilled potential. On this model, knowledge is indicative, ignorance is subjunctive: a missing connection between would-be knower and knowledge. Adapting a distinction from the work of Jon Elster, I describe this as an *external negation* of knowledge. It has no characteristics other than its extent, no content except a specific absence. Knowledge can take many forms, but an absence of knowledge can take only one, so if two people are ignorant of the same thing, to the same extent, their ignorance must be identical.

However, different negation of knowing becomes available if one follows the programme proposed by the editors of this volume. If one takes into account the substantiveness of modes of detachment, then there is a potentially unlimited variety of ways to establish relationships with objects of knowledge based on not knowing. These various ways of relating to knowledge are, in the terms I elaborate, alternative *internal negations* of knowing.

One may detach from something strategically, with emotion, with or without attention, in relation to others, through specific practices and in countless complex and socially embedded ways. When ignorance stems from active detachment in this way, it is has specificity, it is not simply a question of a generic gap, a passive absence. That makes it possible to differentiate between different ways of not knowing the same thing, so it is possible for anthropologists to treat ignorance, as I have argued elsewhere, as an ethnographic object (Mair et al. 2012). And if potential knowers were to distinguish between different unknowing ways of relating to a body of knowledge they might come to value certain of them above others. They might seek to cultivate specific forms of not knowing and to avoid lapsing into other forms. Under these conditions, it would be possible for them to have a meaningful debate about the right way not to know, and we would be justified in speaking of the cultivation of specific forms of ignorance through detachment from knowledge as an ethical project. In what follows I consider the extent to which these conditions do, in fact, apply for many Tibetan Buddhists in Inner Mongolia.

The problem of ignorance in contemporary Inner Mongolian Buddhism

Buddhist revival in Inner Mongolia

Inner Mongolia is a vast crescent-shaped region in northern China that stretches from the Gobi in the west to China's border with Russia in the east. Historically, the area was dominated by ethnic Mongolians, but now Mongolians are a minority of about 15 per cent, with most of the remaining population being Han Chinese. The Mongolians of Inner Mongolia were among the first Mongolians to return to Tibetan Buddhism after the fall of the Mongolian empire, and there were many large and important temples in the region. However, Tibetan Buddhist institutions and customs suffered almost a century of sustained attacks, first at the hands of Mongolian, Chinese and Japanese modernisers, then, and with much more decisive effect, in the wake of the Communist revolution.

From the early 1950s, when land reform deprived monastic establishments of their income, increasing pressure was applied to Inner Mongolian lamas to leave their monasteries until in 1958 almost all of the monks who remained were forced to leave the temples to return to lay life. Later, during the Cultural Revolution, Buddhism stood accused of association with pan-Mongolian nationalist or secessionist movements; former monks were brutally persecuted, many were killed or chose to kill themselves, and most Buddhist buildings, together with scriptures and other religious objects, were destroyed. The few buildings that survived did so mostly because they were turned to other uses – a sewing factory in the case of Ih Juu.[1]

By the time I began my research in 2003 the situation was very different.[2] Here as elsewhere across China, old temples and monasteries had been revived and new ones had been established. This revival was mandated by the Chinese government in the wake of the Cultural Revolution, but in Inner Mongolia, at least, people were for a long time very wary of being associated with religion in public. It was not until the mid-1990s that the process accelerated, as people became more confident about expressing religious enthusiasm and as local governments adopted a more positive attitude to minority and traditional culture and granted permission more frequently (they still often refuse it) for old sites to be re-established, and for lamas to be recruited to staff them.

Today's Inner Mongolian Tibetan Buddhism is therefore the result of a self-conscious revival of a tradition that has taken place against a backdrop of radical discontinuity and disconnection. Now there are more than four hundred institutions across the region, large and small, several with as many as seventy or eighty monks. Many of these monasteries hold frequent festivals that are attended by hundreds of people. The monasteries are thriving, on the back of ever greater government funding and of revenues brought in by increasing numbers of worshippers and tourists.

An interview

I had been spending my time at the main temple in the city, Ih Juu (Ch. Da Zhao), visiting my informants at home and joining them on pilgrimages to other Buddhist sites in Inner Mongolia and throughout northern and western China. Throughout that first winter I had spent days and occasionally nights in the icy, stone-floored prayer hall, sitting with the other lay participants on benches behind the chanting monks, keeping the cold at bay with the salty-milky Mongolian tea that was dispensed periodically from an enormous battered kettle. After the ceremonials were complete, I would help the younger lamas and lay volunteers serve a communal meal of boiled rice mixed with mutton. When there was no chanting to be done, the lamas would be assigned, individually or in pairs, to clean and watch over one of the many small pavilions and other buildings that made up the monastery. I would sit and chat to them, and help them with their chores – especially washing and refilling the countless bronze butter lamps they got through every day – or I would observe their interactions with disciples, pilgrims and tourists.

In this way I had made many acquaintances, and I had developed close friendships with some of the lamas and some of the small group of regular worshippers. I knew I had only just begun the work of understanding this world that I was becoming a part of, but I felt I was on the right track. In general, it had been much easier than I had anticipated to gain admission to Buddhist spaces and to get to know people. However, one important element of ethnographic research continued to elude me: the interview.

To be sure, a number of local scholars of Buddhism had agreed to let me interview them. I was grateful for that, but few of them participated in any kind of religious life, and what they told me seemed only remotely connected to the popular revival that I wanted to understand. It seemed inappropriate to use their accounts to interpret the practices of the people I met at the temple, whose concerns seemed so different.

On the other hand, hardly any of those people would allow me to record what they told me, or even to write down what they said verbatim. Polite refusal was always accompanied by a version of the same justification: 'I don't know anything about Buddhism.' Lay people told me to speak to lamas, but even the lamas would often tell me, 'I know nothing at all.' Frustratingly, it was those who spent the most time in the temple, the ones who seemed to take their religious activity most seriously, who were most insistent about their ignorance and who most firmly advised me to disregard them as sources of information.

When Tanaa, a Mongolian woman in her early forties whom I had met as she was worshipping at the temple, asked to interview me, I thought this might be a way around my problem. She was a journalist with a local newspaper and a radio station and wanted to ask me questions about my research. If I agreed to an interview, I thought, perhaps she would reciprocate. We agreed on a time to conduct the interview. Tanaa came to see me and I made her tea. She took out a tape recorder and the interview began. Afterwards, I asked her whether she considered herself a Buddhist (or more precisely, in Mongolian idiom, whether she had faith in Buddhism: *burhan-i shashin-d süjüg-tei yü?*),[3] and if so, whether she would allow me to ask her some questions for my research. At first she refused, telling me that she knew absolutely nothing (*demi yüü-ch medeh-güi*) and that I would do better to find someone else to interview. I explained that all I wanted was to hear about her own viewpoint and that it did not matter that whether she was knowledgeable or not, and she did hesitatingly agree. However she would not allow me to record her responses as she had recorded mine, and she only agreed to my taking notes on condition that I would write general summaries rather than her specific words. I accepted her conditions and asked her to tell me about her experience with Buddhism.

She began by telling me about her father. It turned out that he had been a *hubilgaan*, that is a reincarnate lama, and an important figure in Inner Mongolian Buddhism before the suppression of the religion by the Chinese government in the 1950s.[4] He had died some years before our interview. Tanaa told me that he was considered a famous Buddhist scholar before the Revolution, but despite his great learning he had always refused to teach her anything about the religion. Her father told her that if she always thought of the Buddha he would be at her side – and that that was all she needed to know. He told her not to worship (*shüteh*) because the country had changed, and religious practice had become dangerous.

In the past, Tanaa told me sadly, Mongolian culture made people very good; for example, in Shillinggool League, if a child lost its parents, it would be taken in by someone and treated as a member of the family. Those rules of behaviour (*yos*) came from Buddhist scriptures, but now no one, or almost no one, had any real knowledge of the texts, she said. Tanaa insisted again that she knew nothing at all of Buddhism herself, though she had, since her father's death, become more and more faithful. She now worshipped religious objects (*shüteen*) at a shrine at home, and attended the temple occasionally.

Having a *hubilgaan* scholar for a father, Tanaa had had much greater opportunity to learn something about Buddhism than most contemporary Inner Mongolians, but the combination of her insistence on her own ignorance and her account of the experience of ever-growing faith was something I encountered again and again. Buddhists I met through my fieldwork in Inner Mongolia were uniformly downbeat about the future of Buddhism in the region. Though temples were being allowed, gradually, to recruit more full-time monks, and though people seemed to agree that lay devotees were developing ever stronger faith, there was a widespread feeling that the real substance of the religion had not been restored; that on the contrary, it was continuing to fade and that, as Tanaa and many, many others told me, no one really understands Buddhism any more.

The Inner Mongolian Buddhist discourse of ignorance

At first I saw the protestations of ignorance as an inconvenient and frustrating obstacle to my research: if I was going to study Buddhism, I thought, I would need to find someone who knew about it and would be willing to tell me what he or she knew. After some months, however, I began to understand that there was more than the simple loss of knowledge at issue in so many of my informants' insistence on their own ignorance. What I was seeing was a cultivated sensibility or disposition, an awareness of radical separation of unenlightened beings from teachings that are said to come from the minds of the enlightened. I realised that in order to understand these people's religious lives, studying the context, form and intensity of their detachment from knowledge of the Dharma was just as important – or even more important – as understanding the content of that knowledge.

The awareness of ignorance makes itself felt in a number of ways, but the most striking (and the most frustrating for an ethnographer bent on discovering and collecting knowledge) is the ubiquitous talk about the loss or inaccessibility of knowledge about Buddhism, a *discourse of ignorance*. In Inner Mongolian Buddhism, talking about ignorance is part of a culture of faith. Through it, devotees develop an awareness of the limitless superiority of the buddhas and the lamas of the past who are the objects of their devotions. Although this is a constant topic of conversation, as few people were willing to be interviewed on the topic, the account of the discourse of ignorance that follows is necessarily an aggregation of comments made to me by many people and hastily scribbled down from memory, rather than a collection of direct quotations.

All fields of knowledge have their blind spots, of which people may be entirely unaware, but for Inner Mongolian Buddhists, the ignorance of Buddhism that arises from its mysterious 'deep meaning' is not an unnoticed blind spot but a conspicuous Bermuda Triangle. The premise of much of Inner Mongolian Buddhists' religious activity is that awareness of this ignorance needs to be nurtured, deepened and brought constantly to mind. This is the only way, my informants told me, to guard against the arrogance (*omog*) that might allow a worshipper to act as if it were possible to draw conclusions about any aspect of the teachings, or even to act on those conclusions, or worse still to think that the consequence of acting on those conclusions could ever be calculated.

The Inner Mongolian Buddhist discourse of ignorance is a set of ideas about the reasons for, and the consequences of, the separation of contemporary Buddhists from knowledge, a set of ethical principles stipulating the desirable relation of devotees to that knowledge and a set of practices through which these ideas are rehearsed, elaborated and put into practice.

The discourse is over-determined: a host of explanations for the impossibility of knowledge are in circulation. One of the most prominent is a historical narrative of decline and loss that slips between an account of the decades-long suppression of the religion in Inner Mongolia that has disrupted the transmission of traditional knowledge, and the older idea, common in Indic religions, that the world is in a period of decline, what the Buddhists call the end-of-Dharma period.

The ignorance of ordinary people in respect of Buddhist teachings is also explained in terms of depth. Even if one is fortunate enough to be able to read the scriptures or to listen to teachings from a teacher, what the unenlightened understand is only the surface meaning (*öngön utga*); the deep meaning (*gün utga*) can only be understood by the enlightened. The true meaning of all the teachings is the same deep insight and can be referred to concisely – it is emptiness, or middle-view – but it cannot be explained directly, in words, even by a buddha.

The enlightened who live among us, that is, the incarnate lamas, like Tanaa's father, do understand the whole truth of the Dharma. These beings are born with a supernatural insight, but even they are unable to teach the deep meaning to others. Their function is not to communicate knowledge, but to act as a source of supernatural power (*adis*) from which those who worship them faithfully can benefit, and as a personification of wisdom against whom their followers can cultivate their faith by sharpening their appreciation of their own ignorance.

The content of the discourse of ignorance is part of the intensely reflective experience of ignorance of the Dharma valued and cultivated as part of an ethic of faith by many of my informants. It is, of course, also a body of knowledge in its own right, though it is one that people learn and reproduce without dignifying it as knowledge. In this respect it contrasts sharply with the Dharma, which is objectified, but which is not, on my informants' interpretation, known or communicated.

Mastering the content of the discourse is crucial in one of the most important activities of contemporary Inner Mongolian Buddhists: the almost ceaseless discussion and analysis of ignorance (on the part of oneself, of contemporary humans, or of human beings in general), and the constant recapitulation of the narrative of the loss of knowledge. The narrative produces an awareness of ignorance that, as the product of specific practices, is something that must be acquired, can spread and can be studied, though it makes itself felt as a lack.

The practice of recounting the discourse of ignorance is an important activity not simply because it occupies a great proportion of the time that people spend doing Buddhism (though it does). It has significant consequences for other areas of religious activity, and because it is intimately connected with the expression and cultivation of faithfulness, the great concern of Inner Mongolian Buddhists. Faithfulness requires the development of *daruu jang*, a quiet or humble character, which entails dispositions to act (mostly in veneration or worship of, or submission to, greater beings) but also requires the acquisition of a sensibility, an intense awareness of inferiority in the presence of religious authority, and a variety of habits of speech and posture through which this awareness is expressed.

The discourse of ignorance is part of a wider set of practices through which *daruu jang* is cultivated, practised and performed; both a way of cultivating humility and a way of praising with appropriate humility the great beings who have achieved the knowledge from which we are so thoroughly cut off. Sources of power including incarnate lamas, scriptures and consecrated (*amil-san*) images provide benefits to those who come to them faithfully. The role of the faithful is to act as passive recipients, accepting and experiencing their own humility in comparison to the objects of worship.

One indication that there is more than simple loss of knowledge going on here is the critical attitude with which attempts to overcome ignorance were often greeted by my informants. The Buddhists I knew were tolerant of any form of practice, they were not interested in sectarian debates, and they generally had a positive opinion of other religious traditions, on the grounds that all religions provide a context in which to cultivate faith. The one thing they did disapprove of was a lack of humility in approaching religious topics, precisely because profound humility is, for them, a requirement of faith.

If it is impossible for the unenlightened to understand the real meaning of the teachings now, trying to do so by studying will only lead to a false impression of progress. It follows that what we need to do instead is to accept that we cannot know, and cultivate an awareness of our ignorance and a devoted faith in the power and wisdom of those enlightened beings who do understand. So it made sense that the few monks who had the opportunity to go to Beijing to study in the Tibetan Buddhist College were often viewed with suspicion by lay worshippers and other lamas. As Sain, a middle-aged and otherwise ambitious monk from one of Inner Mongolia's larger temples put it, the problem is that they tried to learn by trying to understand the theory, but now 'no one understands the theory'.

Ignorance as the external and internal negation of knowledge

Anthropologists have traditionally been hostile to any suggestion that the people they study are ignorant (Mair et al. 2012: 2). There are good reasons for this hostility, but in cases where our informants themselves assert that they do not know, we need to find a way of addressing ignorance ethnographically. To recognise discourses of ignorance as forms of knowledge and practice in their own right is a start. However, redefining ignorance as knowledge cuts out of the description any relationship between the person who is ignorant and the object of knowledge that he or she does not know. For my informants, that relationship is essential.

In her description of her own relationship to the Dharma, Tanaa encouraged me to think of her as no more knowledgeable about Buddhism than anyone else, but there is an important difference between Tanaa's intense and pervasive relationship to the Dharma, a relationship that is partly defined by ignorance, and the lack of relationship to the Dharma exhibited by an indifferent and uninformed person. Making such a distinction will be impossible so long as we continue to understand ignorance as merely a kind of absence. The solution is to pay attention to different forms of negation and, specifically, to the difference between 'external' and 'internal' negation. I derive this distinction from a discussion in Jon Elster's *Political Psychology* (1993).[5] Elster asks us to consider the following affirmative proposition:

I   A believes p.

How, he asks, do we produce the negation of this proposition? One way is to apply a negative sign to the whole proposition, to apply it, as it were, externally:

II   Not (A believes p).

This is what Elster calls external negation, and as it applies to both the subject and the predicate, it means that no relationship of belief obtains between A and p. Another form of negation results from applying the 'not' to p, like so:

III   A believes not-p.

As, in this example, the negation is applied within the original proposition, Elster calls this an internal negation. Because propositions can contain many elements, there may be several or many different internal negations, each of which can have a different meaning. So, we might add to Elster's list the following example:

IV   A not-believes p.

One way of interpreting this (there may be others) might be 'A disbelieves p'. Note that only the external negation, II, entails a complete absence of belief. The other two negations both entail the presence of a belief that is in some sense negative.

These distinctions may seem trivial in the abstract, but a concrete example makes their significance clear. Consider the following propositions:

I'   A believes God exists.
II'   Not (A believes God exists).
      [= doesn't have such a belief]
III' A believes God not-(exists).
      [= believes God does not exist]
IV'   A not-(believes) God exists.
      [= disbelieves that God exists]

This gives three distinct ways of not believing in God. III' describes the attitude of an atheist, the Psalmist's fool, who has an active belief that God does not exist. IV' could be applied to a reflective agnostic, who maintains an active disbelief in the proposition 'God exists', but does not commit to its obverse. Finally, II', the external negation, could also be described as agnosticism, but it is the passive agnosticism of someone who does not care to think about the question or has no opportunity to do so, not, perhaps, having encountered the idea of God. The number of things one is passively agnostic about is limitless, whereas the number of things one actively refrains from believing is limited.

The validity of the distinction I am suggesting has been denied in recent years by a number of people associated with what has come to be called the 'New Atheism'. For example, A. C. Grayling, asked by an interviewer if he was a 'militant' atheist, responded,

> How can you be a militant atheist? How can you be militant non-stamp collector? This is really what it comes down to. You just don't collect stamps. So how can you be a fundamentalist non-stamp collector? It's like sleeping furiously. It's just wrong. (Aitkenhead 2011)

If Grayling's statement was in earnest it is based on a mistake, a conflation of external and internal negation, or, to stick with our examples, of propositions II' and III'. One might not be able to sleep 'furiously', but it would certainly be possible to imagine the difference between someone who simply has no interest in stamps, and someone who has, say, a compulsive aversion to postage-related paraphernalia and rigorously excludes stamps from her environment. This scenario may be unlikely, but it is not 'wrong'.

The important thing about taking notice of this sort of active aversion – or detachment – is that, whereas the passivity of external negation is uniform, there may be important distinctions between different forms of active, internal negation. Everyone who died before postage stamps had been conceived of was passively not a stamp collector, and each was a non-stamp collector in the same way as all the others, and there is little meaningful sense in which they can be said to have a relationship to philately. But non-stamp collectors who have, say, actively rejected stamp collecting may have done so each for a unique reason.

Depending on our questions, we may be more interested in forms of internal rather than external negation. For instance, for all their protests to the contrary, the defining feature of the New Atheists is not a casual absence of belief in God, but their shared antipathy to theistic beliefs and institutions. In other words, they are not usefully characterised by the absence of a relationship to the idea of God, but by the intensity and negativity of their relationship to that idea.

Ignorance as external and internal negation of knowledge

The same line of reasoning is useful in thinking about ignorance, in general and in the specific case of ignorance of the Dharma on the part of Buddhists. Applying the logic of Elster's analysis of belief to knowing rather than belief, we can propose at least three distinct negations:

I" A knows p
II" Not (A knows p)
III" A knows not-p
IV" A not-knows p

The distance between ordinary Buddhists and the objectified knowledge that is seen as the essence of the religion—variously described as Dharma, 'canonical Buddhism', elite religion, or the 'Great tradition'—has long been a concern of both Buddhists and academic students of Buddhism alike. The distinctions between different negations of knowing above can help us to tease apart some important but sometimes subtly different responses to that un-knowing.

One aspect corresponds to the external negation (II") and simply indicates the absence of knowledge of the Dharma. This represents the observation that some Buddhists are cut off from all, or some, aspects of authentic Buddhist knowledge. This aspect is stressed in descriptions of the disconnection in which some Buddhists are seen as being cut off from knowledge because they are not educated, or perhaps because of the role of religious specialisation in restricting access to scriptures to clerical elites, or because of the unavailability of qualified teachers. In these narratives the nature of the disconnection is the always the same, though the extent of ignorance may be different.

As we have seen, this aspect is characteristic of the descriptions of traditional forms of Buddhism by Buddhist modernists. Although, compared to other historical and contemporary Buddhists, Buddhist modernists are unusually optimistic about overcoming problems of ignorance, the idea that there is a problem of ignorance (in the sense of I") in Buddhism is nothing new. Indeed, the Inner Mongolian Buddhist discourse of ignorance that I describe in this chapter is itself an elaborate statement in this mode. George Tanabe has concluded that, 'From at least the fifth century CE on, Buddhists have been insisting on the demise of their religion as a matter of principle and experience' (2006: 249).

Another aspect of the response to the disconnection of Buddhists from the Dharma corresponds to the first internal negation (III"), in which it is not the whole expression but the object of knowledge that is negated. An example of this is found in the populist approach of Martin Southwold in the classic ethnography, *Buddhism in Life*. The Sri Lankan village Buddhist with whom Southwold conducted his research told him, much like my informants, that they did not understand real Buddhism and that he should go to study with educated urban Buddhists who could tell him about scriptures and meditation.

The argument of the book is that the villagers did indeed not know much about canonical Buddhism, they did have knowledge of something else. Southwold calls the something else 'sapientalism', and argues that it is a more authentic expression of the true meaning of Buddhism than the urban, modernist form that even his informants believe is superior. We need not follow Southwold in describing one form of Buddhism as more authentic than another in order to agree that it is important to pay attention to what people actually know, and not only to the objectified knowledge they say is important to them, if we want to understand their lives.

My description in this chapter of the Inner Mongolian discourse of ignorance as a form of knowledge in its own right is firmly in this mould. Many of the Buddhists I got to know in Inner Mongolia have a great deal of knowledge, despite their protestations of ignorance. They know how to behave in the temple and how to worship at home, they knew many stories about the Buddha and had many theories about the effects that Buddhist rituals produce and why they are effective. They know a great deal about the ways in which, in their own view, they are cut off from real Buddhist knowledge. This is all knowledge, in the sense that it is information that these people have learned and were able to recall, but it is denied the status of knowledge in local discourse; it is only 'surface meaning'.

A final aspect of disconnection of Buddhists from Buddhist knowledge corresponds the second internal negation (IV") in which the negative sign is applied not to the statement as a whole, nor to the knowledge, p, but specifically to the act of knowing, representing an actively negative relation of knowing. In relation to knowledge of the Dharma, this might be interpreted as a relationship based on detachment such as I have described in the context of Inner Mongolian Buddhism. As we are used to thinking of relationality in terms of proximity or connection, it would be easy to miss the specific form of detachment that Inner Mongolian Buddhists develop in respect of the teaching, which is a relationship based on distance, and to see in its place only an undifferentiated knowledge gap.

As specific as the Inner Mongolian relationship no doubt is, there is certainly reason to believe that effortfully detached approaches to Buddhist knowledge are regular features of Buddhist societies. The idea of the declining world-era that means that we are now in an end-of-Dharma period – which we have already encountered in the Inner Mongolian Buddhist context – has often led Buddhists to conclude that spiritual progress by 'self power' is now impossible, and only 'other power', in the shape of various buddhas and bodhisattvas, is effective (Williams 2009: 247). Once Buddhists have concluded that religious achievement does not depend on the aspiration to know, understand and implement the teachings on one's own behalf, they are only a short step (a slip from external to internal negation) from concluding that progress does depend on the active rejection of these things.

This progression is indeed evident in the literature of Pure Land Buddhism. Paul Williams suggests, in a discussion of the thought of the Chinese patriarchs of the Pure Land School, that seeking to reach enlightenment through one's own effort came to be viewed as increasingly difficult, then, 'perhaps logically impossible', and sometimes as harmful, as 'a basis for spiritual pride' (2009: 247). In certain Japanese Pure Land texts, the exhortation to ignorance is explicit. Consider this passage, from Honen's famous 'One-Page Testament', in which those unfortunate enough to have followed the path of Self Power, even to its dead end, are told that to follow the path of Other Power, they will need to emulate the ignorant.

> Those who believe this, though they clearly understand all the teachings Shaka [Shākyamuni] taught throughout his whole life, should behave themselves like simple-minded folk, who know not a single letter, or like ignorant nuns or monks whose faith is implicitly simple. Thus without pedantic airs, they should fervently practice the repetition of the name of Amida, and that alone. (Quoted in Fitzgerald et al. 2006: xv)

Conclusions

Recent scholarship in the history of science has shown that detachment, and its opposite, engagement, are often deployed rhetorically in ways that are morally charged. Historically, detachment, associated with the scientific virtue of objectivity, has usually been accorded the greater moral value (Anderson 2001; Daston and Galison 2007). However, as Matei Candea has argued, in the context of thinking about human–animal relations, the moral scales have tipped in favour of engagement.

> In the world of intensive farming and animal-rights movements, the distancing of animals from humans has increasingly been getting a bad name; detachment (and in some discourses, 'science' itself) comes to be associated with coldness and lack of caring, a Cartesian pathology for which engagement (be it political, emotional, or just intersubjective) is presented as the cure. (Candea 2010: 243)

Candea argues that moral discourses that take for granted that relationships are either 'engaged' or 'detached' can have the effect of making these two conditions seem more solid and distinct than they are. In particular, he argues, championing a particular way of relating to something as a form of engagement can have the effect of making any alternative appear not as a different way of relating to that thing, but as an amoral, cold, disinterested absence of relation. As Candea argues, the task of social scientists in situations where such rhetoric is being deployed will be to avoid getting caught up in them, in order to understand the complex world of choices and behaviours by means of which specific degrees and kinds of detachment and engagement are actively cultivated as ethical projects in their own right.

In his paper, he discusses the Kalahari Meerkat Project, an ethological study run by research scientists and volunteers, which has become famous, thanks to a popular reality television programme, *Meerkat Manor*. The aim of the project is observation, and strict procedures are imposed to guarantee objectivity. Project scientists usually avoid intervening with the meerkats, even if that means the death of their subjects through predation or starvation. To the viewers of *Meerkat Manor*, this often seemed unthinkingly heartless, cold and amoral (Candea 2010: 242).

However, Candea's ethnography shows that the scientists see their behaviour quite differently. Instead of casual disinterest, they see a hard-won relationship that Candea calls 'inter-patience', a reciprocal relationship between observer and meerkat achieved over a long period of mutual habituation and effort. This relationship is the result of an explicitly ethical project of self-formation whose goal is the cultivation of objectivity, and ultimately the production of scientifically valid knowledge.

Candea's study shows that, once ethnographic attention is focused on scientific objectivity, it is not entirely a matter of detachment. The scientists' detachment, 'emerges as the constant counterpart and complement of engagement, not as its radical alternative' (2010: 244). In other words, despite the widespread tendency to attach moral value either to engagement or detachment, and then to describe relationships in terms of one or the other, real relationships are made up of complex combinations of attempts to establish proximity in some dimensions and distance in others.

Like the human–animal literature that Candea reviews (2010), Engaged Buddhism (like Buddhist modernism in general), is based on a critique of cold detachment, including 'scientific, "Cartesian" ways of understanding and acting in the world' (McMahan 2008: 151).

According to this critique, some traditional forms of Buddhism are in need of reform because they are considered passive, indifferent to suffering and egotistical, disconnected from the true meaning of the Dharma, from society and from the environment.

Though the attitude of Inner Mongolian Buddhists seems to exemplify this traditional, unreformed religion, passivity is not the whole story. Inner Mongolian Buddhists' relationship to the teachings is the result, on the one hand, of a self-conscious abstention from learning, and on the other, of an active cultivation of the awareness of ignorance. The general disconnection of Buddhist lives from Buddhist teachings – in terms of study, self-cultivation and socially oriented good deeds – that Engaged Buddhists deplore follows from this actively cultivated detachment. This is not a failure to pursue a life in the light of ethical reflection, but an aspect of a particular complex of values centred on the virtue of humility.

From an ethnographic, rather than a religious point of view, it would be as inadequate to describe my informants' ignorance as a lack of knowledge as it would be to describe Candea's scientists' professional objectivity as a lack of involvement (Candea 2010: 250). The flavour of the detachment at the heart of the relationship in each case is very different; whereas the relationship between the scientists and the meerkats is one of acquired indifference, in the Buddhist case, it is an intense relationship of faithful devotion that demands a carefully cultivated distance. And whereas the scientists cultivate detachment as a condition of scientifically valid knowledge, my informants cultivate humility as a condition of faith. The result is objectified and legitimate ignorance (rather than objectified and legitimate knowledge) both in the sense of a positive awareness of not knowing (an internal negation of knowledge), and in the sense that humility undermines the acquisition of knowledge of the Dharma (so resulting in an absence of knowledge, an external negation of knowledge).

Buddhism and domestication

The failure of Buddhists to live up to the ideals expressed in Buddhist scriptures has been a source of puzzlement and consternation for generations of anthropologists and other scholars of religion. The standard explanation for this is a Weberian one: Buddhism teaches otherworldly values, but the perpetuation and dissemination of those values depends on successful institutionalisation, and all the worldliness that entails. This means not only that there is a separate way of doing things for ordinary people who cannot follow the elite path (see, e.g. Terwiel 1976), but also that the values of both the elite and ordinary paths are compromised as the high ideals of the 'Great Tradition' are sacrificed to provide what sociologically successful religions always must: life-cycle rituals and magical rites aimed at securing success and wealth in this life and in future lives (Spiro 1971: 13f; Carrithers 1979; Strenski 1983). The 'discrepancy between precept and practice', as Charles Ramble puts it, alluding to the title of Gombrich's classic monograph on the paradox of Buddhist ethics (Gombrich 1971), 'most often manifests itself as a compromise between the effort to live according to the rule and the exigencies of living in the world at all' (Ramble 1990: 186).

However, the attitudes of Inner Mongolian Buddhists I have been discussing in this chapter show that the distance between Buddhist lives and Buddhist ideals is not, in this case at least, the result of a passive compromise. It is clear that devotees have a strong view about the ways in which a proper relationship of faith and respect ought to be based on proximity (enthusiasm, emotion, sincerity, faith), and the ways it ought to be built on distance (ignorance, humility). Establishing this very specific relationship requires active and continuous efforts of detachment.

Acknowledgement

I am grateful for the editors and participants in the Detachment Project, Naor Ben-Yehoyada, Caroline Humphrey and Alice Wilson for their comments on earlier drafts of this chapter.

Notes

1 The history of a nearby temple that was turned into an army base is described in Humphrey and Ujeed's book on the Mongolian-liturgy tradition, which is parallel to, but somewhat distinct from, the much more widespread Tibetan liturgy tradition which was the primary object of my fieldwork (2013).
2 The fieldwork on which this chapter is based was carried out in 2003–5. I made follow-up visits in 2007, 2008 and 2010. Names used in this chapter are pseudonyms.
3 Foreign language terms are in Mongolian unless marked 'Ch.', in which case they are in Chinese (*pinyin* transliteration). There is no agreed form of transliteration for Mongolian, and here I have tried to give as accurate as possible an impression of the pronunciation of my informants rather than trying to represent Mongolian spellings, which are sometimes quite distant from the spoken language.
4 For more on reincarnations in contemporary Inner Mongolia, see Mair (2013).
5 Similar distinctions have been made by Lars Højer (2009), who writes about 'present absence', drawing on Hegel, whose philosophy is also cited by Elster.

References

Aitkenhead, Decca, 2011, AC Grayling: How can you be a Militant Atheist? It's Like Sleeping Furiously. *The Guardian* (available online: www.guardian.co.uk/books/2011/apr/03/grayling-good-book-atheism-philosophy (accessed 3 April 2011).

Anderson, Amanda, 2001, *The Powers of Distance: Cosmopolitanism and the Cultivation of Detachment*. Princeton, NJ: Princeton University Press.

Candea, Matei, 2010, 'I Fell in Love with Carlos the Meerkat': Engagement and Detachment in Human–Animal Relations. *American Ethnologist* 3: 241–258.

Carrithers, Michael, 1979, The Modern Ascetics of Lanka and the Pattern of Change in Buddhism. *Man* 14: 294–310.

Cook, Joanna, 2010, *Meditation in Modern Buddhism: Renunciation and Change in Thai Monastic Life*. Cambridge: Cambridge University Press.

Daston, Lorraine, and Galison, Peter, 2007, *Objectivity*. Brooklyn, NY: Zone Books.

Elster, Jon, 1993, *Political Psychology*. Cambridge: Cambridge University Press.

Fitzgerald, J. A., Strand, C., Bloom, A., Coates, H. H., and Ishizuka, R., 2006, *Honen The Buddhist Saint: Essential Writings and Official Biography*. Bloomington, IN: World Wisdom, Inc.

Gombrich, Richard and Obeyesekere, Gananath, 1988, *Buddhism Transformed: Religious Change in Sri Lanka*. Princeton, NJ: Princeton University Press.

Højer, Lars, 2009, Absent Powers: Magic and Loss in Post-socialist Mongolia. *Journal of the Royal Anthropological Institute* 15: 575–591.

Humphrey, Caroline and Ujeed, Hurelbaatar, 2013, *A Monastery in Time: The Making of Mongolian Buddhism*. Chicago: University of Chicago Press.

King, Sallie B., 2006, *Being Benevolence: The Social Ethics of Engaged Buddhism*. Honolulu: University of Hawaii Press.

Mair, J., 2013, Rebirth Control: Inner Mongolian Buddhism and the Religious Authority of the Chinese State. In J. Whalen-Bridge and P. Kitiarsa, eds, *Buddhism, Modernity, and the State in Asia: Forms of Engagement*. New York: Palgrave Macmillan, pp. 209–228.

Mair, J., Kelly, A. and High, C., 2012, Introduction: Making Ignorance an Ethnographic Object. In C. High, A. Kelly and J. Mair, eds, *The Anthropology of Ignorance: An Ethnographic Approach*. Palgrave Macmillan, pp. 1–17.

McMahan, D. L., 2008, *The Making of Buddhist Modernism*, vol. 1. Oxford: Oxford University Press.

Queen, Christopher S. and King, Sallie B., 1996, *Engaged Buddhism: Buddhist liberation movements in Asia*. Albany, NY: SUNY Press.

Ramble, C., 1990, How Buddhist are Buddhist Communities: The Construction of Tradition in Two Lamaist Villages. *Journal of the Anthropological Society of Oxford* 2: 254–274.

Spiro, Melford E., 1971, *Buddhism and Society: A Great Tradition and its Burmese Vicissitudes*. London: Allen & Unwin.

Strenski, Ivan, 1983, On Generalized Exchange and the Domestication of the Sangha. *Man* 18: 463–477.
Tanabe, G., Jr, 2006, The Death and Rebirth of Buddhism in Contemporary Japan. *Buddhist Studies Review* 23(2): 249–258.
Terwiel, B. J., 1976, A Model for the Study of Thai Buddhism. *The Journal of Asian Studies* 35:391–403.
Williams, Paul, 2009, *Mahāyāna Buddhism: The Doctrinal Foundations*. London and New York: Routledge.

13

Detaching and situating knowledge: comment
Marilyn Strathern

What is there about the concept of 'detachment' that it has such an arresting quality? For a book conceived in reaction to the widespread apprehension that especially in anthropology 'relationality' has run away with too much, the antidote seems to take immediate effect. Is that an effect of 'detachment' appearing to be doing its work largely unelaborated, yet almost invariably in an oppositional context? And of the way its opposites, its counterparts, proliferate – relations, desire, society, engagement, situatedness, involvement, worldliness and so on? People may detach themselves, or those who write about them may evoke that move, from many such locations. The striking power of the concept in English is that it invites one to think of any of these locations as instantiations of 'attachment'. (The same goes for disconnection and connection.) These four chapters, with their focus on knowledge, demand reflection on this.

I propose to steer this reflection from a couple of vantage points. The first describes a situation familiar to anthropological knowledge-making in its generalities if not particulars and offers a background to the chapters by Corsín Jiménez, and Jensen and Winthereik. The second briefly looks back from the kind of world out of which anthropological theorising sprang and which itself accords values to some of the issues analysed by Cook and Mair.

Vantage point I

The first vantage point concerns explicit practices of combining and separating in the transformation of kin relations over time in Muyuw (Woodlark Island, part of the Kula ring; Damon 1983). Children are regarded as formed and nurtured by their father's work, and precisely in so far as they are products of his work (Damon's deployment of Marxist categories need not detain us here) are separate from him in their distinct identity as members of their mother's matrilineal subclan. Whereas a married woman's subclan exercises the right to reclaim from the husband her (detached) labour in the transformed state of a Kula valuable, a father's labour, its transformation evident in the bodily form of his wife's offspring (thereby attached to her subclan), initiates a much longer cycle of eventual detachments. Otherwise put, if marriage combines the work of the mother (wife) and father (husband), it establishes, from the perspective of the obligations that fall on their children, divergent futures for that combination.

The conjugal relation that brings together persons of distinct origins has to move through time, from being one of separation to one of combination, signalled at the outset in a switch from a couple exchanging tokens each indicative of the other's separate gender to a substitution of labour in which each undertakes work that would have been done by an opposite sex (subclan) relative of the other. The joining of husband and wife turns on the un-joining of brother and sister. This is an explicit performative. Brother and sister, initially identified in so far as their labour is combined in the flourishing of the subclan, must each be divided off from any procreative outcome of their (opposite sex) sibling's labour in order to combine their efforts with that of their initially 'unrelated' spouse. Disconnection, it follows, can only be *realised* through another connection, here the conjugal relationship. That relationship becomes crucial in turn to what men and women can achieve as brothers and sisters, namely with respect to their natal subclan; they cannot normally be active subclan members without marrying. Separation produces new persons and transforms relationships – including that of siblings to one another.

Such an account may be of events and times removed from Baroque Europe or Asian ecotourism, but shares with the authors of these two chapters one of the axioms on which this book is based, that as far as human sociality is concerned detachment (like separation or other terms these passages introduce) is as much a relational construct as its counterparts. I put it like this to draw attention to its routine work in anthropological knowledge-making. The Muyuw example is useful in that were one to read 'detachment' into various moves people make, it is clear that for them there is no sense that the separations involve separation from social life, or from relationships understood as interpersonal connections or collectivities, or cosmologies for that matter. The cutting – as in the literal cutting that elsewhere accompanies male and female preparation for marriage, with moral and social consequence as Boddy (2007: 112) has recently put it for the Sudan – separates out ('purifies') aspects of relationships. For Muyuw kinsfolk, 'different identities [are] perpetually being metamorphosed into other identities' (Damon 1983: 324).

Corsín Jiménez performs something of a transformation in describing the possibilities of Velázquez's achieving a kind of detachment within the constraints of contemporary representations of court life. If a Baroque epistemology enabled observers to hold 'forms and effects in mutual suspension', then those presenting canvases for observation were able to invite observers to know they were observing. This is the trick that Corsín Jiménez calls 'the detachment of detachment'. It is a detachment that at increasing distances from the retreating subject matter of Velázquez's painting draws the observer in as an ever more alert participant. Can we not talk of the observer as transformed thereby, through his or her exquisite consciousness of detachment, and thus of description as re-description? And when we put it in epistemological terms the apprehension of such detachment, the objectification of the act of observing, simultaneously enrols the perceiver (and conceiver) of such an object in the effects that the artefact has.

At the same time Corsín Jiménez suggests that, through the trick of at once deploying and inventing upon courtly conventions of representation, the painter was enacting a stance of 'resistance', a strand to which we return later. The implication in this case is that he painted his awareness of the conventions precisely by innovating upon them. The chapter itself then takes a transformative turn. If the reader thought we were in the seventeenth century, we are shown (by the author-observer) that we are as well in our own. Baroque society was the first media society, he observes, with a dramaturgical conception of social life, forever embracing new connections or 'articulating novel annexations' in its enthusiasm for enhancement. This gives Corsín Jiménez a platform of sorts from which to outline a kind of resistance at work in today's regime of informational obsession, where the demand for information replicates 'beings that aim for the replication of themselves in and through information', as though attachment were an infinite possibility. There is no need to repeat how he so evocatively describes it, so I offer a homely analogue. 'Feedback', the apparently innocuous familiar of 'impact', these days demanded at almost every delivery of a service, is rampant in higher education. Yet it remains as true as it did when the audit culture was getting under way that students do not thrive exclusively on materials that are instantly communicable. Where is knowledge without its puzzles? Or without some apprehension of its tricks too?

Now Jensen and Winthereik set the reader a puzzle, putting forward a supposition about the kind of knowledge anthropologists make for themselves: let us suppose that what is meant by detachment is in fact severance from relations. They swiftly demonstrate the impossibility of such a situation, epistemically speaking, and in the specific instance of actor-network theory point out that, anyway, it hardly needs saving from accusations of too much relationality. The accusations both misinterpret the founding assumption that we can never know what might be related and misplace the locus of infinity. For what is 'potentially infinite' is rather all the ways in which sufficient equivalence is established to bring relations into being, and thus all the ways in which actors (regardless of the kinds of actors they are) are made commensurate (regardless of whether this entails perceptions of similarity or difference).

Through the unfolding stages of an ecotourism project in Vietnam, they offer an intricate description of numerous moments at which now attachment to and now detachment from this or that set of aspirations, assumptions, policies, interests, and so forth, seem to be the best way to this or that outcome. Attachment and detachment are the authors' terms for what they discern as diverse and sometimes divergent commensurations initiated by various human actors. It is a story of globalisation, among other things, with the epistemological puzzle everyone works so hard at, in so many venues and not only this one, namely conserving/maintaining/bringing into being 'community life'. Although finessed through very different categories, the intentions of the overseas aid professionals and Vietnamese villagers have to be transformed, like the labour of Muyuw siblings and spouses, into a project that is recognisably the outcome of combined work, which all parties recognise as both theirs and not theirs. Thus the ubiquitous language of 'traditional culture' carries attachment and detachment with it, whether pointing to what brings authenticity or distinguishing 'celebration' from 'work', indicating thereby when now a relationship is to be valued, now not valued. Above all, the community needs to exist as an immutable mobile, a sign of the project's – local, regional, international – success, while also being, as Jensen and Winthereik make so clear, crucially, autonomously, apart from the process that brings success. Whether you are standing next to the building or looking at a glossy print(out), the imagery of the completed long house serves as everyone's evidence that something has happened. It has become a graspable piece of knowledge.

Vantage point 2

The initial fragment of Melanesian ethnography was extracted from a dense Muyuw narrative of people's connections to, and disconnections from, one another being formed and reformed through circulations of 'things'. Apropos diverse exchanges, Damon (1983: 310) observes, 'things are used to produce some transformation in the relationship between the exchanging persons ... But once the process is completed ... this relationship is inverted, and the social relationships emanating from the persons define the relationship between things'. Yet if to the observer there is a seeming infinity to these permutations, it does not have the same echoes as the infinitude of (moments of) commensuration that Jensen and Winthereik elucidate. Commensuration is not an issue where people's formulae take relations – whatever the entities involved – as (already, integrally) the measure of one another. It *is* an issue in a world that imagines relations having to be constructed; they thereby become instruments of comparison, with people aware, we have learnt, that some comparisons are be evaded. Here the maker of relations can make comparisons with, add relations to, anything. Thus, in this folk thinking, pre-existing entities come into being at the same time. We might wish to recall, from Corsín Jiménez's chapter, one such 'pre-existing entity', the kind of person that itself grows on attachments, and by person understand any actor, human or non-human, conceived individually with relations attached.

This introduces the second vantage point, a brief composite, drawn from the presence of Victorian colonials in the Sudan and more generally from nineteenth-century British/English articulations of attachment and detachment in the pursuit of empire. Here the two conditions of being acquire specific values, openly acknowledged in expatriate understandings of how to keep British culture British, in foreign locales. Sustaining aloofness from too much personal engagement with the locals, the British struggling to civilise the Sudan attached to themselves (in)numerable commodities to keep up morale, 'a host of commercially produced "things"', not least in regimental baggage trains, as was wickedly satirised in the literature of the time (Boddy 2007: 35–36). This replays the omnipresence of portable property so significant in the settling of India, in ways that make it possible for a specialist in Victorian literature to settle different values on the crucial terms here. Talking of household goods that are also mementos, of journals and letters eagerly penned, Plotz (2008: 60) describes people's oft-times achingly sentimentalised ruminations on home elsewhere; this served, in turn, a commitment to remain 'detached from India, lest its culture come to life as powerfully as English objects do'. Advocating an emergent field of 'thing theory', Plotz also removes himself from anthropological argumentation. So he knowingly writes about the 'cultural value attached [by the expatriates] to markedly English portable property' as separating these things off from fungible commodities: they are meaningful 'precisely because they *do not civilize* [others]; instead [for the expatriates], they embody

English culture' (Plotz 2008: 20, original emphasis). It is hard not to read into the impassiveness of the rulers and the treasured possessions of the homesick a deliberate cultivation of a culture-carrying self-hood.

Just such an invitation comes from Cook's argument-by-ethnography into different ways in which a notion of self-cultivation, under conditions of modernity, enrol pluralistic understandings of detachment. According to one version, unhealthy rumination (and I borrowed Cook's term for the dialogues the Victorians had with themselves) implies people too much embodied in some world or other, at least in so far as their thoughts attach them to it. Their thoughts have to be detached in order for people to observe them without the need for unthinking reaction or a need to 'fix' them. That is, they have to cut themselves off from their thoughts in the prevention of depressive relapse. Therapeutic possibilities thus emerge from interpreting what perpetuates misery or depression as a matter of 'attachment'. For that opens up the potential for treating individuals as though their relationships were external – attached – to them, even and especially to the extent of including a relationship to the self. In the author's words, in mindfulness-based cognitive therapy 'participants cultivate a detached perspective in relation to thoughts, feelings and bodily sensations in order to engage more fully in the immediacy of life'.

Cook attends to Buddhist-inspired mindfulness practices in their medical application and thus with the circulations of knowledge involved. Commensurations abound. A wilful practice to increase distanced perspective may reappear as a therapeutic practice to decrease it; self-knowledge can involve changing one's relationship to one's thoughts (as above) or conversely delving more deeply into hidden levels of existence; above all, the connotations of detachment flow in and out of people's discourses to disconcertingly contrasting effects. There is no one understanding or implementation. What remains is the practice of detachment as a work of cultivation that mindfulness training can bring the self. Such practice may be articulated, and the reader may hear it with Baroque sensibilities in mind, in terms of the knowing observer being aware of observing that self. In so far as the effect of achieving detachment is a re-engagement with the world, Cook's conclusion is to ponder the implications of understanding what is seen as detachment and engagement, mutually constitutive in the cultivation of particular forms of perspective, as a *practice* of detachment.

When we consider the kind of knowledge people must cultivate in the cultivation of themselves, Mair turns by contrast to detachment in the context of practices of engagement. Less an issue of sociality, it would seem, than sociability: what, over the course of the four chapters, is to be learnt from thinking about personhood has morphed into questioning subject positions and subjectivities. That is, we find we are dealing with people's different orientations to relationships (with selves, with others, with the world) as embodying various types of knowledge for how to act. Such an orientation has been present all along, beginning at the outset with the concept of resistance. However, the things of academic 'exchange' across the chapters – the different fields of knowledge – for which 'detachment' seems such an apposite concept have transformed its identity, have made it at this juncture ('over time') into a different kind of starting point for discussion. Taking up the modernist Buddhist call to 'engagement' Mair reflects on what is lost when detachment is understood only from this, the perspective of engagement. He demonstrates that the active detachment of present-day Buddhists outside the purview of such modernism (specifically monks in Inner Mongolia) requires no antonym, complementary or otherwise, and certainly not one that equates engagement with attachment.

Much of what has been said about knowledge up to this point evaporates. These particular monks practice resistance to knowledge, actively refraining from knowing; their detachment is the humility of ignorance in the face of a known forever inaccessible to them. While English speakers can always call their awareness of ignorance a kind of knowledge, that would miss the point of the monks' faithful devotions, which is the example they set to lay persons in their studied distance from, and respect of, the wisdom of the enlightened. Theirs is an 'actively negative relation' to such wisdom. It is the ('socially') engaged Buddhists who press an actively acquired (positive) knowledge into the service of the relations they wish to engender, and make it a point of moral judgement, of comparison, thereby illustrating once again all the affect that ideas of attachment carry. This might be an ethically inspired engagement, but it is conceptually blind, as all enthusiasms are, to what it displaces. Their (the engaged Buddhists') lamentations about ignorance of symbolic meaning are lamentations about lack of information and communication. One wonders, then, about the charge made against the 'partial and studiously ignorant Indian travel books' coming out of the British occupation (Plotz 2008: 55), or of the veil of ignorance drawn over body-changing practices that in the Sudan compelled – and still compel – campaigns against them. What sorts of ignorance are these?

If the many types of ignorance that Mair unravels confound any simple notion of knowledge, the chapters in this section have adroitly teased out diverse points at which anthropologists might recognise elements of their own practices.

References

Boddy, Janice, 2007, *Civilizing Women: British Crusades in Colonial Sudan.* Princeton, NJ: Princeton University Press.

Damon, Fred, 1983, Muyuw Kinship and the Metamorphosis of Gender Labour. *Man* (NS) 18(2): 305–326.

Plotz, John, 2008, *Portable Property: Victorian Culture on the Move.* Princeton, NJ: Princeton University Press.

Index

Note: 'n.' after a page reference indicates the number of a footnote on that page

academia 7, 51
　academic writing 4–5, 7, 11, 13, 22, 169–170, 173, 193
　ethnographic fieldwork 86, 172–173, 202
　humanities 2, 12, 193
accountability 11, 16, 202
　and food 81
action, theories of 150
　inaction 220
activism 202
　and animals 86
　engaged Buddhism 237
　NGOs 237
　social movements 237
Actor-Network Theory 16, 22, 24, 106–107, 201, 259
Adams, Vincanne 106
Adorno, Theodor 172
affect *see* emotion
alterity 14
anatomy 35, 38–40
　classes on 19, 39
Anderson, Amanda 4–5, 13–14, 38, 50, 151, 163, 198–199, 219, 230–231, 250
animals
　animal-rights movements 250
　as commodities 84
　and de-animalisation 89, 98n.18
　as gifts 154
　human–animal literature 252
　human–animal relations 10, 23, 76n.4, 80, 82, 85, 88, 95, 131, 169, 206, 250
　husbandry 82, 85, 89
　laboratory animals 109
　livestock 79–101, 106
　meerkats 1, 251
　and welfare 81, 94, 108
　and well-being 85
　as workers 87
anthropological fieldwork 123, 125, 127, 131
　and agency, limits of 14
Arnold, Matthew 5
attachment 58, 64, 74–75, 86, 95–97, 123, 126–127, 134, 144–149, 186, 198–202

Barth, Fredrick 143
Bentham, Jeremy 36, 46
biology 1, 102, 172
　biological rhythms 108
　and inheritance 161
　molecular biology 104
　and pigs 84, 107
body, the
　anatomy 38–47
　bodily discipline 84
　bodily sensation 220, 222, 224, 228, 231, 261
　body-changing practices 262
　body parts 20, 47, 49, 182
　dead persons 8, 38, 109
　and disease 48

body, the (cont.)
    and dissection 24
    and donation 36–37, 43, 48–49
    embodiment 1–2, 42, 69–70, 75, 82, 102, 106, 140, 160, 171, 224, 260–261, 262
    gendered 7–8, 42
    and mind 10
    and multiplicity 107
    organs 24, 35–53, 105–109
    redefinition of 35
    representations of 45
    and sacrifice 53n.2
    the social body 35, 52, 108
    as social relation 127
    and spirit-possession 117, 124
    and technology 52, 224–225
boundaries 2, 42–44, 60, 115, 147, 189
    between bodies and cadavers 43
    between dissection room and social worlds 43
    between pure science and engineering 104
    between subjects and objects 108
    boundary maintenance 94, 143
    boundary making practices 76n.4
    and cognition 40
    and community 207
    and emotions 91, 93
    of faith 126
Bronte, Charlotte 5
bureaucracy 1, 9, 11, 24, 59, 82, 131, 171, 185–187
    and mindfulness 221
    Weber on 6
Buddhism
    engaged 252, 262
    and ethics 253
    and mindfulness 228–229, 261
    Mongolian 21, 25, 242–252
    Thai 2, 145
Buriadism 147–167

Candea, Matei 1–3, 10, 16, 22, 25n.1, 54n.18, 59, 128n.2, 131, 133, 139, 198–199, 220, 250–252
capitalism 8–9, 11, 94, 189, 210
    commodification 89
        of animals 82, 86
    illegal markets 105
    and tourism 211

care 51, 54n.14, 86–87, 91–95, 170, 186, 223, 236
    Intensive Care Units (ICU) 36
Cartesianism 10, 194n.4, 250, 252
China 148, 151–152, 236–237, 239–240
Christianity 20, 24, 115, 117–118, 120–121, 123, 125–127, 128n.3, 171
    anthropology of 122
    charismatic 24, 117–119
    and ethnography 172
    Pentecostal 24, 117–121, 169, 217, 234
    Protestant 43, 116, 120
    rituals 20, 24, 118–119, 121, 124–125, 128n.3
colonialism 260
    post-colonialism 7
Communism 164n.6, 239
complexity, 7, 59–60, 65, 74, 80
connections
    affective 23
    between humans and animals 19
    between practices of detachment 109
    broken connections 24
    and complexity 60
    and empathy 2
    fetish of connectivity 199–200, 215n.2
    kinship 15, 260
    links to disconnection 14, 16, 141, 256
    managing 64
    and negation 143–154
    relational 35–51, 72, 139, 257
    severed 201
    social scientists approaches to 115, 126, 198–199
    and sociality 130
    valorisation of 12
Cook, Joanna 2, 19, 22–24, 141, 145, 237, 256, 261
corporate social responsibility 73, 106
cosmopolitanism 38, 52, 58, 161, 163
    art 151
culture
    audit 19, 258
    British 260–261
    Chinese Cultural Revolution 239
    cultural change 120

cultural other 123
cultural representations 230
cultural theory 189
the cultural turn 12
and development 212–213
invention 191
and nature 4, 15
political 105
'traditional' 259

Das, Veena 8, 24
Daston, Lorraine 4, 13–14, 39, 43, 45, 60, 199, 220, 250
De Castro, Viveiros 14
death
  animal slaughter 82–84, 87–89, 98n.10, 106
  cadavers 38–47, 106–109
  and detachment 18
  and fasting 18, 21, 140, 144–145
  human 82, 87
    in combat 8
    see also the body, and donation
  killing 8, 58, 82–94, 106, 118, 212
  and rebirth 134
  relationship to life 43–44, 49, 52, 88, 106, 110, 161
  and spirits 118
  and suicide 18, 21, 140–145
  and violence 137
  and vulnerability 24, 109
Deleuze, Gilles 59, 168
democracy 1, 8, 11, 186
depression see medicine
detachment passim
Dickens, Charles 5
discipline 39, 45, 84, 92, 137, 169, 173
  see also the body
  detachment as 18, 51
  and meditation 2
  and renunciation 134, 174
  and work 226
Durkheim, Émile 6, 37, 59, 116

Eco, Umberto 2
ecology 9
  of meaning 180
education 8, 12, 38, 43, 51, 54n.15, 158, 174, 181, 236–237, 248–249, 258
Elias, Nobert 116–117, 198, 201
Eliot, George 5, 230–231

Elster, Jon 21, 141, 238, 245–246, 248, 253n.5
emotion
  affect-free 80
  and care 94
  see also connections, affective
  emotional attachment 86, 148
  emotional detachment 4, 51, 95, 238
  emotional engagement 250
  emotional labour 85, 87–93, 108
  emotional proximity 253
  emotional stance 24
  happiness 148
  and intimacy 163
  see also mindfulness-based cognitive therapy
  and reason 45–46, 52, 54n.15
  and well-being 221
  in workplace 93
empathy 1–2, 52, 54n.15, 87, 89, 94–96, 98n.16, 171, 186, 192
empowerment 1, 9, 185, 197, 206–207
engagement passim
entanglement
  and academic discourse 11
  between social domains 186
  of detachment and engagement 2, 97, 130, 201, 213
  of people and things 60
  relational entanglement 7
  of scholars with their studies 108
  of subjects and objects 107
entrapment 179–180, 185
environmentalism 9, 62, 85, 180, 197, 202, 206, 213–214, 215n.3
epistemology 3, 11, 24, 45, 58–59, 64, 74, 194n.1, 231, 258, 259
ethics
  academic ethics 172–173
  anthropology of 13, 16, 20
  bioethics 43, 46, 52
  Buddhist (paradox of) 253
  care ethics 93–94
  see also corporate social responsibility
  detachment as ethical stance 24–25, 82, 130–146, 220, 237
  of engagement 236, 262
  ethical choices 85, 96
  ethical neutrality 9
  of faith 244

ethics (*cont.*)
  and Foucault 226
  and ignorance 236–255
  and knowledge production 12, 23
  see also Levinas, Emmanuel
  and non-relations 21
  and objectivity 14, 251
  organisational ethics 185–186
  professional ethics 85, 95
  Victorian ethics 231
  virtue 3, 5, 39, 94, 105, 131–132, 142–144, 160
    epistemological 45
    of humility 252
    of objectivity 250
  virtuous detachment 64–65, 69, 71, 75, 76n.2, 103–104
  and Weber 193
experimentation 8, 11, 25n.1, 60, 69–71, 187, 203, 207–209, 211, 213–215, 216n.5
experts 23, 61, 157
  engineers 58–78
  medical 9, 36
    students 23–24, 38–41, 43, 46, 51, 108
    transplant surgeons 23–24, 35, 38, 48–52, 103–106, 108
  scientists 4, 8, 60–62, 67, 69, 103, 198, 251–252

feminism 7, 9, 51, 79, 94
  criticism of 198
Ferguson, James 10
food 81, 85, 106, 135, 137–139, 165n.22, 208
  animals as 110
  fasting 18, 21, 24, 133–135, 140–141, 144–145
  feasting 135, 151, 153, 158–161, 164n.4, 165n.22, 216n.4
Foucault, Michel 6, 20, 84, 225–226
French Revolution, the 40
Furedi, Frank 12
future
  of Buddhism 242
  and development 214
  future-oriented knowledge 66, 68
  futures trading 68
  and imagination 211
  and past 221
  and responsibility 71, 162
  and scientific advancement 8
  and time 211
  undetermined 61

Galison, Peter 4, 13–14, 39, 43–45, 60, 191–192, 250
gender 92, 94, 257
  bodies 7, 42
gift, the 36–37, 46, 53n.3, 105, 117, 139, 151, 153, 160
  and food 137
Goffman, Erving 93–94, 137, 139, 144, 150
government *see* state, the

Hacking, Ian 60
Haraway, Donna 9–10, 76n.4
Heidegger, Martin 102
hierarchy 1, 151, 154–155, 230
  of gods 122
  moral 221
  organisational 63
Hobbes, Thomas 187–189, 194n.5
humanism 22
  post-humanism 10
humility 25, 237, 244–245, 252–253, 262
humour 46, 164n.4
Humphrey, Caroline 13, 20, 23–24, 253n.1
Husserl, Edmund 122

identity 94, 110, 143–144, 147, 186, 201, 257, 262
ignorance 25, 74, 142, 174, 237–238, 241–245, 247–250, 252–253, 262
imagination 2, 85, 116, 145, 169, 188, 214, 228
  Pentecostal 119
  postmodern 7
India 24, 105, 131–133, 136, 144, 212, 260, 262
indifference 2, 79, 93, 131–133, 139, 144, 149, 201, 207, 237, 245, 252
  civil indifference 173
  to pigs 89
individualism 37, 119, 168, 193
Ingold, Tim 10, 59, 168, 215n.2
Inner Mongolia 151–158, 236–255
inter-patience 139, 220, 251

Index

intimacy 71, 88, 94, 163, 232
  see also emotion
Islam 122

Jainism 21, 24, 133-145 173–175
Judaism 122

Kant, Immanuel 13
kinship 6, 14, 59, 85, 103, 109, 153, 256
  see also connections
knowledge
  academic knowledge 185, 257–258
  and belief 143
  Buddhist knowledge 236–255
  circulation of 261
  detached knowledge 2, 4, 13, 20, 231
  embodied knowledge 69
  engaged knowledge 12
  engineering 64
  experiential 69
  expert 102–103, 105, 109
  and feminism 9
  and ignorance 236–255
  knowledge claims 143
  knowledge production 1, 7–9, 11–12, 43, 125, 193, 262
  knowledge stabilisation 75
  meta category 43
  modern forms of 59–60
  and participation 11
  and politics 188
  professional knowledge 85, 97, 102–109
  and rationality 9–10
  and ritual 158
  and self-distancing 220
  self-knowledge 220, 261
  sociology of knowledge 116
  and subjectivity 4, 39, 45

labour 8, 82–83, 85, 94, 105, 183–184, 187, 220, 236–237, 257, 259
  apprenticeship 80, 92
  artisanal work 82, 89, 97, 106
  craft 10, 97, 183
  production 80, 82–83, 85, 95, 98n.8, 105
  workers see work
    animal 81, 87
Laidlaw, James 13, 14, 20-21, 24, 52

Latour, Bruno 4, 6, 15–16, 25n.3, 37, 58, 59–60, 67, 74, 168, 199–201, 209, 215n.2
Leach, Edmund 148, 153
learning
  active learning 12
  apprenticeship 80
  see also Buddhism
  detachment as learned skill 108, 219–232
  learning environments 38–41
  and the senses 43, 45
  technologies of learning 52
Lévi-Strauss, Claude 148–149, 153–154, 156, 159, 163–164
Levinas, Emmanuel 131–132
Lillehammer, Hallvard 17–18, 132

Marx, Karl 6
  Marxism 257
materiality 35, 61, 68, 105
Mauss, Marcel 53n.3
medicine 35, 38–39, 44, 51–52
  Ayurvedic 207
  depression 219–223, 225–226, 231–232, 232n.4, 261
  medical curriculum 38
  medical legislation 44
  medical students 23–24, 38–41, 43, 46, 51–52, 108
  medical technology 39, 47
  patient 35–36, 47–49, 51, 105, 223
meditation 2, 18, 131, 134–135, 140, 221, 225, 229, 237, 249
Merleau-Ponty, Maurice 102
Mill, John Stuart 5
mindfulness-based cognitive therapy (MBCT) 19, 24, 219–221, 226, 228, 231–232, 261
Mitchell, Timothy 67–68
modernity 5–6, 16, 50, 159, 192, 194n.4, 219–220, 228, 231–232, 261
  modernist detachment 3–7, 9–10, 15–16
  Buddhist 262
Mol, Annemarie 7, 25n.2, 54n.14, 59
monotheism see religion
morality
  amoral indifference 133, 251
  see also ethics
  and identity 132

morality (*cont.*)
  moral aesthetic 172
  moral agency 85
  moral character 163
  moral economy 185
  moral failing 142
  moral hierarchies 221
  moral judgements 262
  moral materiality 35, 105
  moral positionality 45
  moral responsiveness 231

nature 4, 7, 15, 23, 39, 43, 45, 58, 72, 74, 108, 188, 197, 206
  see also culture; culture, and nature
nature spirits 118–119, 127n.1
Needham, Rodney 148
negation 2, 10, 21, 24, 122, 141–145, 238, 245–252
networks
  see also Actor-Network Theory
  cutting of 15, 109, 199–201, 209
  see also Strathern, Marilyn
  and Ingold, Tim 10, 59, 215n.2

objectification 44, 79, 249, 258
objectivity
  critiques of 9
  see also Elias, Nobert
  as ethical goal 14, 96
  scientific 4, 22, 60–61, 103, 250–252
  and subjectivity 39, 45, 54n.15
ontology
  ontological choreography 51
  ontological multiplicity 46, 107
  ontological orders 48
  ontological shifts 35
  relational ontologies 71
  and science 45
  spiritual ontologies 117, 120
otherness 14, 161

participation 1, 11, 17, 65, 80, 125, 128n.3, 137, 144, 169, 206, 208
pathology 17, 40, 50–51, 250
Pedersen, Morten 15, 25n.4, 115, 198–200, 215n.2, 220
'The Fetish of Connectivity' 199
perspectives
  distanced perspective 3, 148–149
  duality of perspectives 45
  situated perspective 24

Peru 19, 23, 58–75, 103
politics
  of academia 11
  and anticipation 68
  anti-politics 10, 69
  and bureaucracy 186–187
  and corruption 105
  courtly politics 179, 258
  detachment from 75, 104–105, 180
  of information 181, 190
  liberalism 187
  policy-making 173, 198, 204
  political culture 105
  political engagement 193, 199, 250
  politicisation 132
  relations to science 4, 8–9, 15
  of responsibility 23, 61, 65
  see also state, the
polytheism 121–122
post-Second World War 46
post-structuralism 7, 20, 198–199
power 5, 9, 12, 66, 74–75, 132, 199–201, 244–245, 250
  biopower 84
  colonial 5
  shamanic 161
  supernatural 243

Rabinow, Paul 4
reason 103, 105–106, 132, 142, 174, 247
  see also emotion, and reason
reflection 2, 19, 22, 43, 122, 189–190, 220, 225–226, 230–231, 244, 252
  introspection 220
  reflexivity 22, 190, 223–224, 226
relationality
  asserting and denying relational connections 141, 253
  between persons and things 61–62, 70–71, 260–261
  detached relationality 2, 23, 25, 60, 130, 249
  see also inter-patience
  as engagement 12, 18
  see also human–animal relations; kinship
  in opposition to engagement 18, 256
  post-relationality 15, 25n.4
  relations with knowledge 238–249
  scholarly relations 169, 193

Index

with the self 220, 223, 227, 261
see also sociality; Strathern, Marilyn
relativism 12, 59, 140
religion
   alms-giving 24, 134, 137–139, 143
   and belief 115–127
   see also Buddhism; Christianity
   counter-religion 122
   disbelief 120, 122, 126, 246
   enlightenment 133–134, 226, 237, 250
   see also Islam; Jainism; Judaism
   martyrdom 140
   monasticism 2, 134, 239
   monotheism 117–122, 127
   New Atheism 247
   renunciation 18, 134, 158
response 161, 220, 223–224, 248
responsibility 58–75, 83, 93–94, 104–106, 171, 183, 237
   see also corporate social responsibility
Riles, Annelise 11, 68
ritual 24, 109–110, 118–125, 128n.3, 150–153, 157–158, 212, 216n.4, 249, 253
romanticism 4–5, 7, 23, 168

scale 17, 20, 62, 65, 82, 91, 107, 119, 182, 210, 213, 250
science 3–5, 8–9, 15, 36, 39, 44, 51–52, 59–61, 103–104, 109, 131, 198, 216n.4, 222
   engineering 91
   history of 250
   laboratories 58, 69–72, 103–104, 109
   regulation 67, 76n.2, 104
   reproduction 91
science and technology studies (STS) 59, 103, 198–200
Sennett, Richard 10
separation
   the art of 186, 193
   as broken connection 149
   detachment as 17–18, 22, 24–25
   versus detachment 148–149
   of emotions from data 4
   engaged 220
   and kinship 148, 257
   from knowledge 243
   of persons from office 187
   physical 36, 82

   radical 242
   resistance to 155
   of self from body 43–44
   from social life 143, 257
   staged 83–84
Serres, Michael 107, 201
Simmel, Georg 6, 14, 115, 150, 198
Sloterdijk, Peter 6, 13, 122–123
social movements 8–9
   NGOs 123, 197, 201–204, 207, 210–212, 214, 215n.3
sociality 12, 18, 59, 109, 130, 132–133, 214, 220, 232, 257, 262
space
   conceptual 15, 18, 191
   distance and distancing practices 1, 4, 14, 63, 79–95, 106, 116–117, 124, 139, 150, 153, 198, 201, 214–215, 249, 251–252, 262
   interstitial spaces 96
   and ritual 159
   and time 84
spirits *see* nature; death
stabilisation 61, 66, 69
Stasch, Rupert 14, 147, 220
state, the 68, 73–74, 106, 186, 206, 212
   government 11, 62, 66, 84, 123, 152, 186, 206, 223, 239–241
subjectivity 4, 25, 39, 45, 54n.15, 228, 262
Sudan 257, 260, 262
surgery 35, 38, 40–41, 47–48, 51–52, 104–105
   organ transplantation 35–38, 48, 51–52, 105, 108

Taylor, Charles 11, 102–103, 106, 226–229, 231
technology 10, 36, 72, 74, 109, 187, 189
time 41, 45, 49–50, 54n.13, 84, 91–92, 107–108, 140, 147, 157, 165n.20, 211, 225, 257, 262
   temporality 2, 13, 84, 98n.12, 108, 184, 193, 201, 214
Tönnies, Ferdinand 6
transparency 86–87, 192–193
Trundle, Catherine 2, 8, 53, 201
typologies, detachment 3, 18, 20–21, 95

universality 5, 10, 39, 51, 131, 226, 228

value 1
  of animals 85
  market worth 85, 90
Velázquez, Diego 24, 179–185, 187, 190–192, 194n.1, 194n.2, 258
Vietnam 19, 24, 197, 203–207, 210, 212–215, 216n.5, 229, 259
volunteers 2, 48–49, 240, 251
vulnerability 24, 60, 76n.2, 88, 109–110, 119, 168, 171

Weber, Max 6, 170, 186, 193, 253
Wilde, Oscar 5
Wilkie, Rhoda 80, 85–87, 91–92, 95
Wittgenstein, Ludwig 102, 107
Wolin, Sheldon 194
work
  dirty work 90
  and discipline 226
  gendered work 94
  intellectual work 122
  see also labour
  professionalism 23, 35–36, 38, 60, 76n.2, 76n.4, 80, 86–88, 93, 161–162, 186–187, 193, 252, 259
  skilled and unskilled 81
  workers 58, 63–64, 75, 85, 87, 95–97, 161, 207–208, 210, 221
  workplace 93
  work ethic 95

Yarrow, Thomas 1, 3, 22, 202, 232

EU authorised representative for GPSR:
Easy Access System Europe, Mustamäe tee 50,
10621 Tallinn, Estonia
gpsr.requests@easproject.com

www.ingramcontent.com/pod-product-compliance
Lightning Source LLC
Chambersburg PA
CBHW071404300426
44114CB00016B/2179